University Language

# Studies in Corpus Linguistics

SCL focuses on the use of corpora throughout language study, the development of a quantitative approach to linguistics, the design and use of new tools for processing language texts, and the theoretical implications of a data-rich discipline.

**General Editor**

Elena Tognini-Bonelli

**Consulting Editor**

Wolfgang Teubert

**Advisory Board**

Michael Barlow
University of Auckland

Robert de Beaugrande

Douglas Biber
Northern Arizona University

Chris Butler
University of Wales, Swansea

Sylviane Granger
University of Louvain

M. A. K. Halliday
University of Sydney

Susan Hunston
University of Birmingham

Stig Johansson
Oslo University

Graeme Kennedy
Victoria University of Wellington

Geoffrey Leech
University of Lancaster

Anna Mauranen
University of Helsinki

John Sinclair
The Tuscan Word Centre

Piet van Sterkenburg
Institute for Dutch Lexicology, Leiden

Jan Svartvik
University of Lund

John Swales
University of Michigan

H-Z. Yang
Jiao Tong University, Shanghai

**Volume 23**

University Language: A corpus-based study of spoken and written registers
by Douglas Biber

# University Language

A corpus-based study
of spoken and written registers

Douglas Biber

Northern Arizona University

John Benjamins Publishing Company

Amsterdam / Philadelphia

™ The paper used in this publication meets the minimum requirements
of American National Standard for Information Sciences – Permanence
of Paper for Printed Library Materials, ANSI z39.48-1984.

Cover illustration from original painting *Random Order*
by Lorenzo Pezzatini, Florence, 1996.

**Library of Congress Cataloging-in-Publication Data**

Douglas Biber
　　University Language : A corpus-based study of spoken and written registers
　　　/ Douglas Biber.
　　　p.　cm. (Studies in Corpus Linguistics, ISSN 1388–0373 ; v. 23)
　　Includes bibliographical references and indexes.
　　　1. Academic language--Data processing. 2. Register (Linguistics)--
　　Data processing.

　　P120.A24 B53　2006
　　401/.41--dc22　　　　　　　　　　　　　　　　　　2006045871
　　ISBN 90 272 2295 9 (Hb; alk. paper)
　　ISBN 90 272 2296 7 (Pb; alk. paper)

© 2006 – John Benjamins B.V.

John Benjamins Publishing Co. · P.O. Box 36224 · 1020 ME Amsterdam · The Netherlands
John Benjamins North America · P.O. Box 27519 · Philadelphia PA 19118-0519 · USA

# Table of contents

# Acknowledgements

The research presented in this book grew out of the efforts of a large research team. The research occurred as part of two consecutive grant projects sponsored by the Educational Testing Service (ETS). Without the generous financial support of ETS, I could not have imagined carrying out a project of this magnitude and scope.

The first project focused on the construction and grammatical tagging of the T2K-SWAL Corpus; Susan Conrad, Randi Reppen, Pat Byrd, and Marie Helt worked with me as Co-Principal Investigators on that project. In the second project, we focused on analysis of the patterns of linguistic variation, plus construction of computational tools for automatic linguistic analysis of texts used in the TOEFL; Susan Conrad worked with me as Co-Principal Investigator on the second project.

Several research assistants worked on one or both of these projects, including Victoria Clark, Viviana Cortes, Eniko Csomay, Alfredo Urzua, and Jenia Walter. In addition, many other student workers were involved in the project at various stages. The research assistants and student workers carried out most of the day-to-day tasks for both projects, including collection of the corpus texts, transcriptions, tag-editing, helping to develop software tools, etc. The project would not have been possible without the combined efforts of the entire research team.

In addition, several chapters in the present book have been made possible through specific contributions from other researchers: Kimberly Becker who prepared an extensive annotated bibliography of previous research on academic language; Eniko Csomay, who developed the computer programs to analyze vocabulary patterns in the corpus; Alfredo Urzua, who carried out descriptive research into the distribution of stance features; Casey Keck, who contributed to the analysis of modal verbs in the expression of stance; and Viviana Cortes, who contributed to the study of lexical bundles in university registers. I owe a special thanks to Susan Conrad, who read and commented on drafts of most chapters in the book. Thanks also to John Swales for reviewing the book manuscript and offering numerous helpful comments and suggestions.

Several publications coming out of the T2K-SWAL projects have appeared previously:

Biber, D., Randi Reppen, Victoria Clark, & Jenia Walter (2001). Representing spoken language in university settings: The design and construction of the spoken component of the T2K-SWAL Corpus. In R. Simpson & J. Swales (Eds.), *Corpus linguistics in North America* (pp. 48–57). University of Michigan Press.

Biber, D., S. Conrad, R. Reppen, P. Byrd, & M. Helt (2002). Speaking and writing in the university: A multi-dimensional comparison. *TESOL Quarterly, 36*, 9–48.

Biber, D. (2003). Variation among university spoken and written registers: A new multi-dimensional analysis. In Charles Meyer & Pepi Leistyna (Eds.), *Corpus analysis: Language structure and language use* (pp. 47–70). Amsterdam: Rodopi.

Biber, D., S. Conrad, R. Reppen, P. Byrd, M. Helt, V. Clark, V. Cortes, E. Csomay, & A. Urzua (2004). *Representing Language Use in the University: Analysis of the TOEFL 2000 Spoken and Written Academic Language Corpus* (ETS TOEFL Monograph Series, MS-25). Princeton, NJ: Educational Testing Service.

Biber, D., S. Conrad, & V. Cortes (2004). *If you look at...* : Lexical bundles in university teaching and textbooks. *Applied Linguistics, 25*, 371–405.

Keck, C. M. & D. Biber (2004). Modal use in spoken and written university registers: A corpus-based study. In Roberta Facchinetti & Frank Palmer (Eds.), *English modality in perspective: Genre analysis and contrastive studies* (pp. 3–25). Frankfurt am Main: Peter Lang Verlag.

The material included in the present book is mostly new, extending the descriptions contained in these earlier publications.

# CHAPTER 1

# Introduction

## 1.1 The student perspective: Language in the university

Students who are beginning university studies face a bewildering range of obstacles and adjustments, and many of these difficulties involve learning to use language in new ways. The high school experiences of English-educated students help to facilitate these adjustments to some extent, especially through exposure to classroom teaching and textbooks. However, all students – whether native speakers of English or non-native speakers – need to adjust to a wide range of tasks in the university accomplished through language.

The most obvious of these tasks is the ability to understand complex academic discourse, especially academic research articles and books, as well as course lectures. However, there are also a slew of requirements and other expectations that students must figure out, including: university catalogs, program descriptions and requirements, instructions for registration, advising recommendations, and course requirements as specified in syllabi or described in class sessions. Clearly, students must understand the language used for these purposes to succeed in the university.

At present, universities do relatively little to prepare students to cope with this wide range of 'registers'. In fact, most universities do not even introduce students to the linguistic demands of written academic prose. Instead, the only required English language course at most American universities is English Composition, which often emphasizes personal narrative and personal opinion writing, with little exposure to the kinds of language typically required in university courses.

ESL/EFL programs have been more innovative in matching language instruction to the actual language tasks required in university courses. Many programs adopt an ESP/EAP approach (English for Specific Purposes / English for Academic Purposes). ESP programs emphasize the different linguistic patterns used for different registers (e.g., conversation vs. writing), while EAP programs emphasize the different vocabulary and linguistic patterns associated with specific academic disciplines.

To provide the basis for ESP/EAP instruction, we need full linguistic descriptions of the registers that students encounter, and as a result, there have been numerous research studies that document the important linguistic characteristics of academic registers (see Section 1.2 below). For the most part, these studies have focused on written academic registers, especially the academic research article. Surprisingly, there have been only a few studies of textbooks or classroom teaching. Other university registers have been virtually ignored; these include registers like study groups, office hours, and course packs. The 'institutional' registers might be the most important of these for students. These include written registers like handbooks, catalogs, program web pages, and course syllabi. There are also important spoken institutional registers, like service encounters with departmental staff, or the classroom management talk provided by instructors at the beginning of class sessions. To better understand the tasks that in-coming students encounter in the university, and ultimately to help students develop the language skills required for those tasks, we need a comprehensive linguistic description of the range of university spoken and written registers. The present book is a first attempt to provide such a description.

## 1.2   A short case study: Textbooks versus classroom teaching

ESP/EAP instructional approaches are motivated by the assumption that there are important linguistic differences across language tasks and academic disciplines, and that language instruction should prepare students to deal with those differences. In fact, empirical research shows that the differences across academic registers are even more important than most of us would expect.

For example, it might be expected that academic lectures and textbooks on the same topic would be similar in their linguistic characteristics. However, it turns out that this is usually not the case. If you are reading the present book, you are already well familiar with the language of university textbooks. Text Excerpt 1.1, from an accounting textbook, illustrates many of the typical linguistic characteristics of this register.

> Text Excerpt 1.1: Introductory accounting textbook: 'Auditing Concepts and Applications'
> **Components of Internal Control.**
> In this section, the five internal control components, as identified in the COSO report, are defined and described. They are as follows:
> 1.   Control environment;
> 2.   Risk assessment;
> 3.   Control activities;
> 4.   Information and communication; and
> 5.   Monitoring.
>
> The first component, the control environment, forms the foundation for the others (see Fig. 6.2 [Components of Internal Control]). The absence of one or more

significant elements of this component will cause the system to be ineffective, notwithstanding the strength of the remaining four components.

### Control Environment.

The control environment is defined by the attitudes of the persons in charge of the internal control system. Management's attitude toward control can have a significant impact on control effectiveness. To this end, management must be strongly supportive of internal control and must communicate that support throughout the organization.

Conversely, management that does not possess a control-conscious attitude will serve to undermine the system. Internal control is only as strong as the ethics and competence of the persons who are responsible for it. Achievement of sound internal control, therefore, requires a commitment to high integrity and strong ethical values. If internal controls are to be properly designed and implemented, these values must start at the top with the chief executive officer and permeate the organization. Many companies have established written codes of corporate conduct as means of communicating the entities' ethical values to their employees. A written code of conduct typically defines conflicts of interest, illegal acts, improper payments, and other behavior considered unacceptable to the entity. Penalties for violations of code provisions also may be specified in the written document.

The language of this textbook excerpt seems 'normal' to us: what we expect academic language to be like. The excerpt relies on technical vocabulary to express specific shades of meaning; the sentences are all complete and employ complex syntax; the text has obviously been carefully crafted and edited, resulting in a formal, 'academic' style.

Surprisingly, the language of classroom lectures in American universities differs in almost every respect. In fact, classroom lectures tend to use many linguistic characteristics that are more typical of conversation than academic writing. The following excerpt, from a business lecture on accounting, deals with the same general topic as the textbook excerpt above. However, despite the topical similarity, the lecture illustrates strikingly different linguistic characteristics:

Text Excerpt 1.2: Lower Division Accounting Lecture
**Instructor:**
OK, now, um, I handed out, something that looks like this, did everybody get one of these? did you get one of those? chapter eight is gonna seem um, a little tough, unless you keep some things in mind. it really isn't all that hard. and so, and as I was thinking about what I was going to talk to you about, about how to approach this chapter, I thought well, I'll type them out, and that might help. in chapter eight they introduce, um, a way of thinking about costs that's called variable costing. now, it's something you really know a lot about already, because

you've done the contribution margin income statement. you know that that's sales minus variable costs is contribution margin minus fixed costs is net income. well now we're going to use that with a company making product. um, you know that, when in our former chapters, when we were talking about product costs, we talked about direct materials, direct labor, and overhead, as being product costs. [...] fixed overhead, in one piece, is considered a variable cost. OK? so, if you look at this piece of paper that I gave you, the first thing to remember, is that variable costing is not generally accepted accounting principles, it's not G.A.A.P., and because it's not G.A.A.P., we can't use it for external disclosures. OK? um, and for variable costing we use the contribution margin for that income statement, sometimes variable costs contribution margin minus fixed cost is net income.

Excerpt 1.2 illustrates many of the typical colloquial characteristics of university classroom teaching. These include features that directly acknowledge and engage the audience, including questions (*did everybody get one of these?*), comprehension checks like *ok?*, and the pronouns *I*, *we*, and *you*. In contrast to the informational focus of textbooks, the instructor in this lecture describes his own attitudes and thought processes using mental verbs like *think* and *know*; stance adverbials like *really* and *a lot*; and modal and semi-modal verbs like *can* and *be going to*. In fact, the language produced is in some ways a direct reflection of the instructor's thought processes. That is, the instructor is thinking and producing language at the same time, resulting in repetitions, 'false starts', pauses (e.g., *um*), and the frequent use of 'discourse markers' like *well*, *so*, and *ok*. The discourse often consists of a loosely connected sequence of ideas, with many utterances functioning to provide personal background for the main ideas, as in the following sequence of utterances:

and so,
and
    as I was thinking about what I was going to talk to you about,
      about how to approach this chapter,
I thought
    well,
I'll type them out, and that might help

The basic grammar of class lectures tends to be clausal: the text is made up of a series of relatively short clauses. Some of these are main clauses, and some are dependent clauses, but the net effect is a text composed of many clauses in a series. For example, the following excerpt repeats the opening utterances of this lecture with the verbs highlighted:

OK, now, um, I **handed** out, something that **looks** like this, **did** everybody **get** one of these? **did** you **get** one of those? chapter eight **is gonna seem** um, a little tough, unless you **keep** some things in mind. it really **isn't** all that hard. and so, and as I **was thinking** about what I **was going to talk** to you about, about how to **approach** this chapter, I **thought** well, I**'ll type** them out, and that **might help**. in chapter eight they **introduce**, um, a way of **thinking** about costs that**'s called** variable costing. now, it**'s** something you really **know** a lot about already, because you**'ve done** the contribution margin income statement.

In contrast, university textbooks rarely refer directly to the author or the student; authors rarely express their own attitudes or feelings explicitly, and they almost never use language that indicates their actual thought processes. Authors think and plan their language before they write it down, and the final version that we read in a textbook has been subsequently revised and edited. Thus, textbook language never includes the production features or dysfluencies that are common in classroom teaching (like repetitions, 'false starts', pauses, or 'discourse markers' like *well, so, ok*).

The language of textbooks differs from classroom teaching in other ways that are less obvious. In terms of their typical sentence structures, textbooks rely heavily on complex phrasal syntax rather than clausal syntax. The following excerpt is repeated twice; once highlighting the verbs, showing that there are only four clauses, and once highlighting the nouns and prepositions, showing the heavy reliance on phrasal syntax:

> Textbook excerpt with **verb phrases marked in bold**:
> The control environment **is defined** by the attitudes of the persons in charge of the internal control system. Management's attitude toward control **can have** a significant impact on control effectiveness. To this end, management **must be** strongly supportive of internal control and **must communicate** that support throughout the organization.

> Textbook excerpt with **noun phrases marked in bold**; prepositions are underlined:
> **The control environment** is defined <u>by</u> **the attitudes** <u>of</u> **the persons** <u>in</u> **charge** <u>of</u> **the internal control system**. **Management's attitude** <u>toward</u> **control** can have **a significant impact** <u>on</u> **control effectiveness**. <u>To</u> **this end, management** must be strongly supportive <u>of</u> **internal control** and must communicate **that support** <u>throughout</u> **the organization**.

The verbs used in textbooks are often 'weak' verbs with minimal lexical meaning (e.g., *have, be*), but they connect long and complex noun phrases with embedded prepositional phrases (e.g., *the attitudes of the persons in charge of the internal control system*).

The primary goal of the present book is to identify and describe linguistic differences of this type. The discussion above merely provides an indication of the scope of these differences. The following chapters show that university lectures and textbooks differ in many additional ways, ranging from vocabulary to complex syntactic constructions.

## 1.3  Previous research on academic language

Over the past 20 years, we have witnessed an explosion of research on academic discourse. Much of this research has been motivated by applied concerns: as linguists have come to recognize that language characteristics differ dramatically from one register to the next, they have also argued that we should teach the specific kinds of language that a learner will need. For learners with educational goals, the most important target registers are the various kinds of speech and writing found in schools and universities. Obviously, the linguistic characteristics of these target registers must be fully described before we can develop adequate teaching materials and methods. Towards this goal, there have been numerous descriptive studies focusing on the linguistic characteristics of particular academic registers (see, e.g., the extensive survey of research in Grabe & Kaplan 1996). The journal *English for Specific Purposes* has been one of the major forums for descriptive research of this type over the past two decades, while more recently, the *Journal of English for Academic Purposes* has focused more on the pedagogical implications of these descriptive studies.

Most studies of academic language have focused on written academic registers (see, e.g., the papers in J. Flowerdew 2002; Hewings 2001; Markkanen & Schroder 1997; see also the survey of research in L. Flowerdew 2002). These studies have described the distinctive use of linguistic features at many different levels. For example, Halliday (1988) provides a useful survey of features that are characteristic of physical science writing. Biber et al. (1999) describe the range of grammatical features in academic prose, in comparison to conversation, fiction, and newspaper reportage (as part of a corpus-based reference grammar; see 1.3 below). Multi-Dimensional studies describe the characteristics of academic written registers with respect to a large number of co-occurring linguistic features (e.g., Biber 1988; Atkinson 1992, 1996, 1999, 2001; see 1.2.1 below).

The expression of evaluation and stance in academic research writing has been an especially popular area of research (e.g., Charles 2003; Crompton 1997; Grabe & Kaplan 1997; Holmes 1986; Hyland 1994, 1996a, b; Meyer 1997; Myers 1989, 1990; Salager-Meyer 1994; Silver 2003; Varttala 2003; see also Biber et al. 1999, especially Chapter 12). Many of these studies have focused on the use of hedging devices. Hyland (1996a, b, 1998) is one of the most important studies in this area of research, documenting the range of functions and grammatical devices used to express tentativeness and possibility in academic research articles. For example, content-oriented hedges have two major functions: indicating the accuracy of a proposition (e.g., adverbials like *generally, approximately, partially, possibly*), or limiting the writer's commitment to a proposition (e.g., *the present work indicates..., the model implies...*). Hyland (2002a) extends this line of research by investigating the ways in which authors refer to themselves (and when they do not refer to themselves) in academic prose. One of the themes that Hyland has developed over recent years is that academic research articles are interactive, in that authors actively try to involve the reader in the communication process. Specific studies in this line of research have investigated the use of addressee features (Hyland 2001), questions (Hyland 2002d), and directives (Hyland 2002c).

Several other studies of academic research articles have focused on special classes of verbs (e.g., Hunston 1995; Williams 1996). These verbs often function to express evaluation or stance; for example Thompson and Ye Yiyun (1991) and Hyland (2002b) describe the use of reporting verbs (like *state, consider, find*) and the different kinds of stance meanings expressed by those verbs (e.g., 'factive': *acknowledge, identify, prove*; 'counter-factive': *confuse, disregard*; and 'non-factive': *claim, propose*).

A second line of research has focused on the complex types of noun phrase structures typical of academic prose (e.g., Halliday 1988; Varantola 1984; Biber & Clark 2002; Biber et al. 1999: Chapter 8). The use of inanimate (abstract) noun phrases as subjects with dynamic verbs is also prevalent in academic prose (e.g., *the development of capitalism* [*produces*] *a larger reserve army*; see Master 2001; Biber et al. 1999: 378–380). At the other extreme, Chih-Hua (1999) describes the use of personal pronouns to mark role relations in academic prose.

Other studies have focused on the use of more specialized linguistic features. Many of these features are used for information packaging functions, signaling topic, focus, or overall discourse organization. Studies of this type include: Swales et al. (1998) on imperatives; Ferguson (2001) on conditionals; Huckin and Pesante (1988) on existential *there*; and Hewings and Hewings (2001) on constructions with anticipatory *it*. Citation patterns (Salager-Meyer 1999) are used for a different kind of discourse framing, situating a study relative to the body of previous research. Procedural vocabulary and the structure of definitions (Marco 1999; Williams 1998) is similarly important for providing required background knowledge.

The study of academic vocabulary is also a rapidly expanding area of research, with considerable interest in the development of word lists based on corpora of academic texts that might reasonably be encountered by students (e.g., Coxhead 2000). Additionally, much attention is now focused on the act of learning specialized vocabulary (including academic vocabulary; see Huckin, Haynes, & Coady 1995; Nation 1990, 2001; Schmitt 2000; Schmitt & McCarthy 1997). Several studies have approached academic vocabulary from the perspective of collocations: the matic ways in which words tend to occur together in texts (Williams 1998; Gledhill 2000; Marco 2000; Oakey 2002; Biber et al. 1999: Chapter 13).

Finally, many studies of written academic prose have adopted a rhetorical or social/historical perspective, describing the rhetorical structure of academic texts and how the conventions of academic genres are shaped by the practices of researchers in particular discourse communities. Most of these focus on written scientific or medical prose (see, e.g., the book-length studies by Atkinson 1999; Bazerman 1988; Berkenkotter & Huckin 1995; Gilbert & Mulkay 1984; Halliday & Martin 1993; Swales 1990; Valle 1999).

Most of the above studies have focused on scholar-to-scholar written communication, rather than on the types of discourse encountered by and used by students in colleges and universities. More recently, though, applied researchers have become interested in task-based syllabi and in needs-based analyses of the communication required of students in their college study (e.g., Carson 2001; Crookes & Gass 1993; Long & Crookes 1992). Task-based syllabi and realistic assessment of language proficiency cannot be achieved without identification and analysis of the language demands of the college-university setting. Studies of this type have investigated a variety of topics: the nature of the teacher-lecture, communication patterns in the college classroom, academic vocabulary, academic writing, and the linguistic and/or rhetorical characteristics of published textbooks and other written materials assigned by teachers for student use.

The literacy demands of academic writing have also been studied, especially considering the growth of student control over academic writing conventions (e.g., Braine 2002; Carson et al. 1992; Johns 1997; Parkinson 2000; Silva & Matsuda 2001). Hale et al. (1996) study academic writing from a task-based point of view. One result of these studies has been a growing awareness of the limited and specialized writing required of undergraduates in most U.S. universities, especially during entry-level courses (Carson, Chase, & Gibson 1993). Studies of academic reading are often connected to academic writing (e.g., Belcher & Hirvela 2001).

University textbooks are the focus of an expanding number of studies. Conrad (1996, 2001) uses a multidimensional approach to analyze biology and history textbooks, while Carkin (2001) focuses on lower division textbooks and lectures in economics and biology. Other studies investigate specialized aspects of textbook language in college and university settings. For example, Byrd (1997) describes the use of naming practices in textbooks. Love (1993) shows how the use of selected subject noun phrases and verbs are used to mark different rhetorical sections of geology textbooks. For example, nominalizations and general nouns are common as clause subjects in process sections, while more specific nouns tend to occur as subjects in product or circumstance sections of the text. Hyland (1999) contrasts the use of metadiscourse in textbooks vs. academic research articles. Finally, studies like Love (2001) investigate the overall discourse organization of textbooks.

Although earlier ESP/EAP studies usually focused on written academic discourse, more recently researchers have begun to turn their attention to university classroom discourse. Several of these studies describe how specific linguistic features are used to signal the overall organization and coherence of a lecture, providing a discourse frame for the content and therefore aiding comprehension. For example, Chaudron and Richards (1986) and Flowerdew and Tauroza (1995) describe the use of discourse markers for these purposes, while Strodt-Lopez (1991) shows how 'asides' are used for similar functions. A related line of research describes how longer lexical phrases and chunks serve to signal discourse organization and coherence in classroom teaching (e.g., DeCarrico & Nattinger 1988; Nattinger & DeCarrico 1992; Khuwaileh 1999). Camiciottoli (2004) similarly describes the use of discourse structuring expressions, while Thompson (2003) describes the interaction of metadiscourse and intonation in relation to the overall organization of lectures. Flowerdew (1992) describes the structure and use of definitions in lectures. Other studies describe the overall discourse organization of university lectures, including the papers by Benson, Dudley-Evans, Young, and Hansen in a book edited by Flowerdew (1994).

The MICASE project (Michigan Corpus of Academic Spoken English; see Powell & Simpson 2001) has been one of the most productive efforts to describe spoken university registers (including lectures). This project has already resulted in a series of published studies describing the functions of specific linguistic characteristics in 'academic speech'. For example, Poos and Simpson (2002) describe the uses of *kind of* and *sort of* as hedges. Lindemann and Mauranen (2001) describe the functions of *just* for metadiscourse and hedging, while Mauranen (2004) compares the functions of a number of hedging devices in spoken academic discourse. Swales (2001) analyzes the collocations of the general purpose nouns *point* and *thing*, describing how they are used for information packaging and emphasis. Swales and Malczewski (2001) document the structure and function of 'new episode flags' for discourse management purposes, while Swales and Burke (2003) focus on the functions of evaluative adjectives and intensifiers. Fortanet (2004) investigates the functions of the pronoun *we* in university lectures. Mauranen (2001) looks at the use of reflexive language in academic speech, while Mauranen (2003a, b) describes the expression of evaluation and other kinds of metadiscourse (see also Mauranen & Bondi 2003). Finally, Simpson and Mendis (2003) and Simpson (2004) discuss the use of idioms and other formulaic expressions in academic discourse.

While most MICASE studies describe the general characteristics of 'academic speech', a few other studies focus on specific spoken registers that are common in university life (apart from lectures). For example, Cutting (1999) analyzes the conversations of a group of post-graduate students, and Basturkmen (2003) studies the conversational exchange structure of study groups, with and without a tutor.

Farr (2003) describes the linguistic signals of 'engaged listnership' in student-tutor meetings.

Rather than considering how a single language skill is used in college and university classes, some studies consider academic communication patterns that require the integration of speaking and writing. Carson et al. (1992) discuss how undergraduates are required to integrate written and spoken registers, specifically reading textbooks to prepare to listen to lectures, while Carrell et al. (2002) demonstrate the effectiveness of note-taking during lectures, as students combine writing with listening (see also Benson 1994).

Academic language poses special problems for language learners, and there have been several studies focused on those issues. For example, several of the papers in Granger (1998a) systematically investigate and compare English language learners' academic language to that of native speakers. DeCock (1998) and Granger (1998b) describe the use of formulaic language for academic purposes by learners of English. Leki and Carson (1997) describe observations by non-native speakers of English about the differences between ESL and "regular" academic courses. In addition, some studies have focused on the spoken communication of international teaching assistants as well as the cultural issues involved in interactions between ITAs and U.S. undergraduates (e.g., Madden & Myers 1994).

Taken together, these studies provide important insights into the use of particular linguistic characteristics in particular spoken and written university registers. However, no previous study sets out to describe and compare the patterns of language use across the range of spoken and written university registers: the registers that students regularly encounter as part of a university education. The present book is a first step towards filling this gap.

### 1.3.1 "Register" and "genre" perspectives on academic language

The terms 'register' and 'genre' have been central to previous investigations of academic language. Both terms have been used to refer to varieties associated with particular situations of use and particular communicative purposes. Most studies simply adopt one of these terms and disregard the other. In some cases, these authors might be assuming a theoretical distinction between the two terms, but that distinction is usually not explicitly noted. For example, studies like Bhatia (2002), Samraj (2002), Bunton (2002), Love (2002), and Swales (2004) exclusively use the term 'genre'. In contrast, studies like Ure (1982), Ferguson (1983), Hymes (1984), Heath and Langman (1994), Bruthiaux (1994, 1996), Conrad (2001), and Biber et al. (1999) exclusively use the term 'register'.

A few studies attempt to define a theoretical distinction between the constructs underlying these two terms. For example, Ventola (1984) and Martin (1985) refer to register and genre as different 'semiotic planes': genre is the 'content-plane' of register, and register is the 'expression-plane' of genre; register is in turn the 'content-plane' of language. Lee (2001) surveys the use of these terms, providing one of the most comprehensive discussions of how they have been used in previous research (as well as terms like *text type and style*).

When research studies have attempted to distinguish between *register* and *genre* (such as Ventola 1984; Martin 1985; Couture 1986; Swales 1990; Ferguson 1994), the distinction has been applied at two different levels of analysis:

1.  to the object of study;
2.  to the characteristics of language and culture that are investigated.

With regard to the first – the object of study – the term *register* (when it is distinguished from *genre*) has been used to refer to a general kind of language associated with a domain of use, such as a 'legal register', 'scientific register', or 'bureaucratic register'. In contrast, the term *genre* has been used to refer to a culturally recognized 'message type' with a conventional internal structure, such as an affidavit, a biology research article, or a business memo. However, it is difficult to pin down specific differences in the object of study referred to by the two terms; both are used in reference to linguistic varieties associated with particular situations of use and particular communicative purposes. For example, Ferguson (1994) notes that 'cookbook recipes' can be studied both as a register and as a genre.

With regard to the second – the characteristics of language and culture that are described – *register* studies have focused on lexico-grammatical features, showing how the use of particular words, word types, and grammatical features vary systematically in accord with the situation of use (factors such as interactivity, personal involvement, mode, production circumstances, and communicative purpose). In contrast, *genre* studies have usually focused on socio-cultural actions; for example, genres are "how things get done, when language is used to accomplish them" (Martin 1985:250), and "frames for social action" (Bazerman 1997:19). As a result, genre studies have often been concerned with issues of ideology and social power.

The analytical approach in the present book incorporates elements from previous conceptions of both 'register' and 'genre': The objects of study in the present book are culturally-recognized varieties with conventional internal structure, like office hours, service encounters, textbooks, and course syllabi. However, the level of analysis focuses on characteristic lexico-grammatical linguistic features, rather than discussions of discourse communities and issues of ideology and power.

I use the term *register* in the present study, as in my previous recent studies (e.g., Biber 1995; Biber, Conrad, & Reppen 1998; Biber et al. 1999; Conrad & Biber 2001), to refer to situationally-defined varieties described for their characteristic lexico-grammatical features. Thus, *register* is a general cover term, with no implied theoretical distinction to 'genre' as it has been used in some other studies:

*Register* is used as a cover term for any language variety defined in terms of a particular constellation of situational characteristics. That is, register distinctions are defined in non-linguistic terms, including the speaker's purpose in communication, the topic, the relationship between speaker and hearer, and the production circumstances. However, as illustrated by the papers in this book, there are usually important linguistic differences across registers that correspond to the differences in situational characteristics.

In many cases, registers are named varieties within a culture, such as novels, biographies, letters, memos, book reviews, editorials, sermons, lectures, and debates. However, registers can be defined at any level of generality, and more specialized registers may not have widely used names. For example, 'academic prose' is a very general register, while 'methodology sections in experimental psychology articles' is a much more highly specified register.

Because registers vary in the extent to which they are specified situationally, the texts within registers also vary in the extent to which their linguistic characteristics are similar. At one extreme, texts from a specialized register (such as methodology sections of experimental psychology articles or air-traffic-controller talk) tend to be very similar in their linguistic characteristics, corresponding to the extent to which the register is specified situationally. In contrast, the texts in a general register, such as academic prose or fiction, tend to exhibit a wide range of linguistic variation.                                        (Biber & Conrad 2001: 3)

### 1.3.2  Previous Multi-Dimensional studies of academic registers

Multi-Dimensional studies have attempted to provide comprehensive linguistic descriptions of academic registers in comparison to other registers. Multi-Dimensional (MD) analysis identifies the salient linguistic co-occurrence patterns in a language – the 'dimensions' – and then spoken and written registers are compared in the linguistic space defined by those dimensions. The analysis is comprehensive in that a wide range of linguistic features is analyzed in each text (see Biber et al. 2003). Those features are reduced to a few underlying dimensions, where each dimension represents a set of individual features that tend to co-occur in texts. Registers are then described and compared with respect to the underlying dimensions, rather than with respect to individual features. A fuller description of the methodology is given in Chapter 8 below.

MD analysis was originally developed to study the overall patterns of variation among spoken and written registers in English (Biber 1985, 1986, 1988). Academic prose was one of the registers included in those analyses, described in comparison to 24 other spoken and written registers. Biber (1988: 180–195) additionally provides more detailed MD descriptions of the variation among selected subdisciplines within academic prose (e.g., Natural Science, Medicine, Social Science, etc.). Grabe (1987) also uses MD analysis to study the overall patterns of variation among academic disciplines, in comparison to other written registers.

Building on those early studies, a number of subsequent MD investigations have focused on the characteristics of particular academic registers. For example, Atkinson (1992) and Biber and Finegan (1994c) focus on the MD characteristics of medical research articles in relation to other registers. Atkinson (1996, 1999) provides a detailed description of scientific research articles, using MD analysis to trace the historical evolution of this register, and interpreting the linguistic patterns relative to changes in rhetorical structure and function.

Conrad (1996, 2001) provides a detailed MD comparison of research articles and textbooks from two major academic disciplines: ecology and American history. Carkin (2001) also analyzes the MD characteristics of textbooks in comparison to classroom teaching, focusing on introductory undergraduate courses in biology and macroeconomics. Csomay (2000) surveys the MD characteristics of classroom lectures. Finally, Biber, Conrad, Reppen, Byrd, and Helt (2002, 2003) apply MD analysis to compare a wide range of spoken and written university registers, using the same corpus as in the present study (see Chapter 2 below). Chapter 8 in the present book extends this line of research, considering the MD characteristics of academic prose in relation to the range of other spoken and written university registers.

### 1.3.3 The grammatical description of written academic prose in The *Longman Grammar of Spoken and Written English*

Most previous studies of academic language have described the functions of a particular linguistic feature in a particular register. The research goal has been to document the distinctive uses of the target linguistic feature in that register, rather than to provide a comprehensive linguistic description of the register.

One major exception to this trend is the *Longman Grammar of Spoken and Written English* (LGSWE; Biber, Johansson, Leech, Conrad, & Finegan 1999), which provides a comprehensive linguistic description of academic prose. The LGSWE is a corpus-based reference grammar of English; it describes the range of grammatical features in English and compares the use of these features in four major registers: conversation, fiction, newspapers, and academic prose. The register comparisons are based on analysis of a representative corpus of texts (the Longman Spoken and Written English Corpus) containing approximately 5 million words from each register (see LGSWE, pp. 24–35). The LGSWE describes the structural characteristics of grammatical features in English, but at the same time, it describes the patterns of use for those features: register differences and other contextual factors that influence the patterns of variation. For this reason, the

LGSWE provides relatively comprehensive descriptions of the four registers. The description of academic prose is especially relevant for our purposes here.

The academic prose subcorpus used for the LGSWE consists of both academic books (2.65 million words) and academic research articles (2.68 million words; see LGSWE, pp. 32–34). Texts from both books and research articles were collected from a number of academic disciplines, including biology, chemistry, medicine, sociology, education, and law/history/politics. The corpus thus represents academic prose as a general register.

The LGSWE presents many frequency findings that describe the patterns of use for particular grammatical features. Table 1.1 lists the major 'academic features' identified in the LGSWE: features that occur much more frequently in academic prose than in the other registers. For example, corpus analysis in the LGSWE shows that there are about 300,000 nouns per million words in academic prose, compared to only around 150,000 per million words in conversation (p. 235). Similarly, there are about 80,000 adjectives per million words in academic prose versus only 20,000 per million words in conversation (and around 60,000 per million words in fiction and newspapers; p. 506). Thus, these grammatical features can be considered characteristic of academic prose by virtue of their distribution: although they can be used in all registers, they turn out to be much more common in academic prose.

Taken together, the findings reported in the LGSWE show that 'academic' grammatical features come from most structural categories. Three word classes are especially prevalent: nouns, adjectives, and prepositions. Overall, these grammatical classes are more frequent in academic prose than in other registers, and there are many related specific features that are especially characteristic of academic prose (e.g., nominalizations, noun phrases with multiple modifiers, stance noun + of-phrase). In contrast, verbs overall are much less common in academic prose than in other registers, although there are specific verb categories that are typical of academic prose (e.g., copula be, existence verbs, derived verbs, and passive voice verbs). Similarly, there are specific categories of adverbs and adverbials (e.g., linking adverbials) that are especially common in academic prose, even though adverbs overall are more common in spoken registers.

It is difficult to make any global generalizations for dependent clauses. Rather, specific clause types have their own distributions. For example, finite relative clauses are much more common in writing than in conversation, but they are most common in newspaper writing and fiction rather than academic prose. However, relative clauses with the relative pronoun *which* are most frequent in academic prose. Non-finite relative clauses (*-ing* clauses and *-ed* clauses) are also especially common in academic prose (and newspaper writing). Many complement clause types are actually much more common in conversation than academic prose, especially *that*-clauses controlled by verbs (e.g., *I know that he did it*). Only one

**Table 1.1** Grammatical features that are especially common in academic prose (based on a survey of the *Longman Grammar of Spoken and Written English*)

| Feature | Pattern of use |
| --- | --- |
| **Nouns and noun phrases:** | |
| Nouns: overall <br> p. 65 | Approximately 60% of all content words in academic prose are nouns |
| Nouns vs. pronouns <br> pp. 235–236 | Nouns are much more common than pronouns in academic prose, especially in object positions |
| Absence of pronouns <br> pp. 235–236 | Pronouns are generally rare in academic prose |
| Specific pronouns: *this* and generic *one* <br> pp. 349–350, 354–355 | Much more common in academic prose; *this* is used for immediate textual reference; *one* is used for generic rather than specific reference |
| Plural nouns <br> pp. 291–292 | Much more common in writing than in conversation; most common in academic prose |
| Nominalizations <br> pp. 322–323 | Much more common in academic prose, especially nouns formed with -*tion* and -*ity* (e.g. *distribution, similarity*) |
| Anaphoric expressions <br> pp. 237–238 | Anaphoric reference is usually expressed with a determiner + noun (rather than a pronoun) |
| Definite article *the* <br> pp. 267–269 | Much more common in writing than in conversation; most common in academic prose |
| Demonstrative determiners <br> pp. 270, 274–275 | Most common in academic prose; especially *this* and *these* |
| Noun phrases with modifiers <br> p. 578 | 60% of all noun phrases in academic prose have a modifier |
| Noun phrases with pre-modifiers <br> pp. 589, 597 | Very common in academic prose (and newspapers) |
| Nouns as pre-modifiers <br> pp. 589–596 | Very common in academic prose (and newspapers) (e.g., *government agencies*) |
| Noun phrases with post-modifiers <br> pp. 606–608 | Very common in academic prose (and newspapers) |
| Noun phrases with multiple post-modifiers <br> pp. 640–644 | Most common in academic prose (e.g., *the utilization of such devices for social purposes*) |
| Noun *and/or* noun binomial phrases <br> pp. 1033–1034 | Most common in academic prose (e.g., *size and shape*) |
| **Adjectives and adjective phrases:** | |
| Adjectives: overall <br> pp. 65, 506 | Adjectives are much more common in academic prose than in conversation or fiction |
| Attributive adjectives <br> pp. 506, 589 | Much more common in academic prose (e.g., *the basic logical content*) |

**Table 1.1** (*continued*)

| Feature | Pattern of use |
|---|---|
| Specific predicative adjectives p. 440 | Several predicative adjectives are notably more common in academic prose than in other registers: *different, important, difficult, possible, necessary, available, useful* |
| Derived adjectives pp. 531–533 | Much more common in academic prose, especially adjectives formed with *-al* (e.g. *functional, regional*) |

**Verbs and verb phrases:**

| Feature | Pattern of use |
|---|---|
| Copula *be* and copular verb *become* pp. 359–360, 437–439 | Most common in academic prose |
| "Existence" verbs pp. 366, 369, 419 | Much more common in writing than in conversation; Most common in academic prose (e.g., *include, involve, indicate*) |
| Specific lexical verbs pp. 367–372 | Several verbs are notably more common in academic prose than in other registers: Activity verbs: *use, produce, provide, apply, form, obtain, reduce* Communication verbs: *describe, suggest* Mental verbs: *consider, assume, determine* Causative / Occurrence / Existence verbs: *follow, allow, require, include, involve, contain, exist, indicate, represent* |
| Specific prepositional verbs pp. 416–418 | Several prepositional verbs are notably more common in academic prose than in other registers: Activity verbs: *deal with, BE applied to, BE used in, BE derived from* Communication verbs: *refer to* Mental verbs: *BE known as* Causative / Occurrence / Existence verbs: *lead to, result in, occur in, depend on, consist of, BE based on, BE associated with, BE related to* |
| Verbs with inanimate subjects pp. 378–380 | Common only in academic prose (e.g., *such comparisons suggest...*) |
| Derived verbs pp. 400–403 | Most common in academic prose, especially verbs formed with *re-* and *-ize* (e.g. *redefine, computerize*) |
| Tense and aspect pp. 456–462 | Academic prose relies primarily on simple aspect, present tense verb phrases |
| Passive voice pp. 476–480, 937–940 | Much more common in academic prose, especially the 'short' passive (with no *by*-phrase) |
| Specific passive verbs pp. 478–480 | Several verbs are especially common with passive voice in academic prose; for example: *BE + made, given, taken, used, found, seen, considered, shown* |

**Adverbs and adverbials:**

| Feature | Pattern of use |
|---|---|
| Specific adverbs . pp. 560–563 | Several adverbs are notably more common in academic prose than in conversation: *often, usually, significantly, more, relatively, especially, particularly, generally, indeed* |
| Specific amplifiers pp. 560–563 | A few amplifiers are notably more common in academic prose than in conversation: *extremely, highly* |

**Table 1.1** (*continued*)

| Feature | Pattern of use |
| --- | --- |
| Specific degree adverbs pp. 566–569 | A few degree adverbs are notably more common in academic prose than in conversation: *relatively, fairly, slightly* |
| Linking adverbials pp. 766, 880–882 | Most common in academic prose; especially *however, thus, therefore, for example (e.g.)* |
| Purpose and concessive adverbials pp. 784, 786, 820–826 | Most common in academic prose (e.g., *in order to, although*) |
| **Dependent clause features:** | |
| Relative clauses with the relative pronoun *which* pp. 609–612 | Most common in academic prose |
| Participle clauses as post-modifiers in noun phrases pp. 606, 630–632 | Very common in academic prose (and newspapers) (e.g., *the assumptions <u>given above</u>*) |
| Noun complement clauses as post-modifiers in noun phrases pp. 645–655 | Very common in academic prose (and newspapers) (e.g., *the fact that...; the attempt to...*) |
| Abstract noun + *of* + *ing*-clause pp. 653–655 | Most common in academic prose, especially with the head nouns *way, cost, means, method, possibility, effect, problem, process, risk* (e.g., *methods <u>of assessing error</u>*) |
| Extraposed *that*-clauses pp. 672–675 | Most common in academic prose, especially controlled by the adjectives *clear, (un)likely,* and *(im)possible* |
| Extraposed *to*-clauses pp. 672–675 | Most common in academic prose, especially controlled by adjectives (e.g., *(im)possible, difficult, hard, important, necessary*) |
| Subject predicative *to*-clause pp. 714–715, 723 | Common only in academic prose (and newspapers) (e.g., *The first step is <u>to evaluate the expression</u>*) |
| *ing*-clauses controlled by adjective predicates p. 749 | Most common in academic prose; (e.g., *capable of, important for/in, useful for/in: formalist strategies are <u>useful for analyzing drama</u>*) |
| Concessive adverbial clauses pp. 820–825 | Most common in academic prose (and newspapers) (*though, although*) |
| **Other features** | |
| Prepositions p. 92 | Most common in academic prose |
| *Of*-phrases pp. 301–302 | Much more common in writing than in conversation; Most common in academic prose |
| Prepositional phrases as post-modifiers in noun phrases p. 606–608, 634–638 | Very common in academic prose (and newspapers) (e.g., *the effect on the final state*) |

**Table 1.1** (*continued*)

| Feature | Pattern of use |
|---|---|
| Stance noun + *of*-phrase pp. 984–986 | Most common in academic prose, especially *possibility of, value of, importance of, problem of, understanding of* |
| *that/those* + *of*-phrase pp. 307–308 | Common only in academic prose |
| Preposition + *which* in relative clauses with adverbial gaps pp. 624–626 | Common only in academic prose, especially *in which* and *to which* |
| Selected coordination tags: *and so on, etc.* pp. 116–117 | Common only in academic prose |
| Quantifier *each* | Most common in academic prose |
| Semi-determiners *same, other, certain,* and *such* pp. 282–283 | Much more common in academic prose |
| Dual gender reference: *he or she, his or her, he/she* pp. 316–317 | Common only in academic prose |
| Lexical bundles with noun phrases and/or prepositional phrases pp. 997, 1015–1019 | Very common in academic prose; e.g., *the end of the, the nature of the, one of the most, the way in which, the extent to which, the fact that the, as a result of, at the time of, in the case/absence/form/presence of on the basis of, on the other hand* |

major type of complement clause is especially characteristic of academic prose: extraposed clauses controlled by adjectives (e.g., *It is possible that...*, *It is important to...*). (Subject predicative *to*-clauses are also found primarily in academic prose, although they are not especially frequent overall.) Finally, adverbial clauses are most common overall in fiction. Even conversation uses adverbial clauses to a slightly greater extent than academic prose. Only one sub-type of adverbial clause is especially frequent in academic prose: concessive clauses.

In summary, there are few general linguistic features that are uniquely characteristic of academic prose. The most distinctive features of academic prose are specific grammatical features associated with a particular set of words, such as extraposed complement clauses controlled by stance adjectives. However, a much larger set of features – such as nouns and prepositional phrases – occur to some extent in every register; these features can be considered 'academic' because they are especially common in academic prose.

## 1.4 Strengths and weaknesses of previous research

As the survey in the preceding sections show, there have been numerous studies on academic language over the past two decades. Most of these studies focus on the use of a particular word or linguistic feature in a particular academic register, such as the hedge *kind of* in geology lectures. Taken together, these studies provide a useful foundation for the study of linguistic similarities and differences among university registers.

From a structural perspective, previous studies have described features at many different linguistic levels: words (e.g., *thing*), extended collocations and formulaic language (e.g., *come into play*), part-of-speech classes (e.g., modals), grammatical/functional classes (e.g., hedges), syntactic constructions (e.g., noun phrase modifiers, conditional adverbial clauses), and overall discourse organization. In most studies, linguistic features are described relative to their discourse functions, such as: conveying informational content; expressing hedging, evaluation, and stance; and signaling the discourse organization (topics, background context, informational focus or packaging, etc.). In addition, most studies focus on a particular register and academic discipline, such as biology textbooks or medical research articles.

Despite the large number of previous studies, there are still some obvious gaps in what we currently know about university language. First, we lack comprehensive linguistic descriptions of most university registers. While written academic prose has been thoroughly investigated, we do not have comprehensive linguistic descriptions for other academic/university registers. Textbooks and academic speech are probably the best studied of these other registers, with several studies describing the functions of particular linguistic features. Taken together, these studies identify some of the salient features of those registers, but they do not amount to a comprehensive linguistic description of either textbooks or academic speech. And we know even less about registers like office hours, study groups, and institutional writing (e.g., university catalogs), because there have been few studies of any kind based on texts from those registers. In addition, apart from previous Multi-Dimensional studies, we know little about the overall patterns of variation among university registers. The T2K-SWAL Project, introduced in the following section, was designed to help fill these gaps.

## 1.5 Background of the present book: Introduction to the T2K-SWAL Project

The present book grew out of the TOEFL 2000 Spoken and Written Academic Language (T2K-SWAL) Project, sponsored by the Educational Testing Service (see Biber et al. 2004). The project included three major components:

- the construction of a large corpus of spoken and written university registers (the T2K-SWAL Corpus);
- the description of language use in the university based on extensive linguistic analysis of that corpus;
- the development of analytical tools to describe the linguistic characteristics of exam prompts relative to the corpus.

The initial motivation for the project grew out of the need for an external standard to evaluate the representativeness of ESL/EFL materials. That is, given the lack of a comprehensive description of university language, it has been nearly impossible to evaluate the extent to which textual materials for ESL/EFL instruction and assessment actually represent the language of the target registers. Specifically in the context of the TOEFL 2000 effort undertaken by ETS (see Jamieson et al. 2000), we lacked the tools to determine whether the texts used in listening and reading portions of the TOEFL exam accurately represent the linguistic characteristics of spoken and written academic registers (see Enright et al. 2000; Bejar et al. 2000).

One reason for this gap is that there have been no readily available text corpora of university language that could be used for research studies. The T2K-SWAL Corpus was compiled to meet this need. Then, based on analysis of that corpus, the T2K-SWAL project focused on two primary goals:

- to identify the salient patterns of language use found in each university register (and across disciplines, levels, etc.);
- to develop diagnostic tools and procedures for assuring that the language used in TOEFL Listening Comprehension and Reading Comprehension tasks were representative of actual language use in the university.

Biber et al. (2004) is a technical report describing the T2K-SWAL Project and the design, construction, and linguistic analysis of the T2K-SWAL Corpus.

The T2K-SWAL Project was a large-scale study, involving the collaborative efforts of multiple researchers. Although the project was coordinated at Northern Arizona University, and most linguistic analyses were carried out there, the collection of texts for the corpus was supervised by four co-principal investigators at different universities: Susan Conrad at Iowa State University; Randi Reppen at NAU; Pat Byrd at Georgia State University; and Marie Helt at California State University, Sacramento. In addition, there were numerous research assistants and student workers from all four universities who helped collect, transcribe, scan, tag, tag-edit, and analyze the corpus.

Work on the T2K-SWAL Project proceeded in three major stages: (1) design, construction, and grammatical "tagging" of the T2K-SWAL Corpus; (2) linguistic analysis of the patterns of register variation in the corpus; and (3) development of diagnostic tools for the evaluation of exam prompts, using the corpus analyses as a baseline.

In the first stage of the project, we constructed the T2K-SWAL Corpus, which was designed to represent both spoken and written university registers, as well as the major academic disciplines (e.g., humanities, natural sciences, social sciences) and academic levels (lower division, upper division, graduate). The corpus included both academic registers, such as lectures, textbooks, and course reading packets, and institutional registers, such as university catalogs, course syllabi, and service encounters on campus. The corpus is described in detail in Chapter 2.

In the second stage of the project, we analyzed the linguistic patterns of variation in the corpus, considering differences associated with register, discipline, and level. All linguistic features included in Biber (1988) were analyzed, as well as many additional grammatical features from the LGSWE (Biber et al. 1999). In addition, we carried out extensive analyses of vocabulary distribution and lexical bundles. The procedures for these analyses are described in Chapters 2 and 3, while the results of the analyses are covered in Chapters 4–8.

In the final stage of the project we shifted our attention to the development of diagnostic tools. These tools analyze the linguistic characteristics of a particular text and assess the extent to which that text is representative of a target register. For example, an exam author might want to evaluate the representativeness of a new text constructed as an upper division science lecture, or assess whether a certain textbook passage is representative of the textbook category overall. The tools present the linguistic characteristics of the target register as the baseline for comparison, and then they analyze the linguistic characteristics of the selected text in relation to that baseline. These diagnostic tools are described in Biber et al. (2004).

## 1.6  Overview of the present book

The present book builds on the research efforts in the T2K-SWAL Project to provide a broad linguistic description of university language. Rather than focus on academic research articles and other stereotypically academic registers, the book analyzes a wide range of registers encountered by students in university life. These registers fall into two general categories: (1) educational language, and (2) task management language.

Educational language includes all spoken and written registers that relate to teaching or learning. Educational language can be primarily teacher-centered (e.g., classroom lectures and textbooks) or co-constructed by teachers and students (e.g., lab sessions, office hours, and study groups). The focus of the present investigation is on the language that students encounter in the university, rather than the language that students actually produce. As a result, the study excludes registers like student term papers or student class presentations.

Task management language occurs in situations where students are told how to successfully complete a university education: registers like course syllabi, university catalogs, program brochures, and classroom management talk (e.g., discussions of course requirements). Some registers, like office hours, will normally include both educational language and task management language.

The central goal of the book is simple: to provide a relatively comprehensive linguistic description of the range of university registers, surveying the distinctive linguistic characteristics of each register. These linguistic descriptions include vocabulary distributions, semantic categories of words, extended lexical expressions ('lexical bundles'), grammatical features, and more complex syntactic constructions. The linguistic patterns are interpreted in functional terms, resulting in an overall characterization of the typical kinds of language that students encounter in university registers: academic and non-academic; spoken and written.

The following chapter provides a detailed description of the T2K-SWAL Corpus and introduces the methods used for the linguistic analyses. The remainder of the book, then, is organized according to different types of linguistic research questions. These descriptions begin with the study of vocabulary distributions (Chapter 3) and grammatical characteristics (Chapter 4). The following two chapters then focus on more specific aspects of language use: the linguistic expression of stance (Chapter 5) and the use of lexical bundles in university registers (Chapter 6). Chapter 7 takes a different perspective, presenting the results of a Multi-Dimensional analysis that describes the overall patterns of linguistic variation among university registers and academic disciplines. Finally, Chapter 8 synthesizes these linguistic descriptions, providing an overall description of the distinctive characteristics of each register.

## Note

1. In earlier Multi-Dimensional studies (e.g., Biber 1988), I use the term *genre* instead of *register* as a general cover term for situationally-defined varieties.

# CHAPTER 2

# The Spoken and Written Academic Language (T2K-SWAL) Corpus

Chapter co-authors: Susan Conrad, Randi Reppen, Pat Byrd, Marie Helt

The descriptions of university language in this book grew out of the TOEFL 2000 Spoken and Written Academic Language (T2K-SWAL) Project (see Biber et al. 2004). As explained in the last chapter, that project was sponsored by Educational Testing Service to carry out a comprehensive linguistic analysis of university registers, with the ultimate goal of determining whether the language used in the TOEFL exam tasks is representative of actual language use in universities.

The first stage of the project was to construct the TOEFL 2000 Spoken and Written Academic Language Corpus (T2K-SWAL Corpus). We designed the T2K-SWAL Corpus to be relatively large (2.7 million words) as well as representative of the range of spoken and written registers that students encounter in U.S. universities and of the major academic disciplines (e.g., humanities, natural sciences) and academic levels (lower division, upper division, and graduate). The corpus included both academic registers, such as lectures, textbooks, and course reading packets, and institutional registers, such as university catalogs, course syllabi, and service encounters. We did not include more general registers – such as fiction, newspapers, or casual conversation. Although these registers are used on campus, they are not university-specific registers. We also did not include e-mail correspondence between instructors and students or electronic postings by students as part of course work. Although these registers deserve study in the future, they were not part of the focus for the T2K-SWAL project.

A detailed description of the T2K-SWAL Corpus is given in Biber et al. (2004; also available on-line at www.ets.org/ell/research/toeflmonograph.html). The following sections summarize the major aspects of design and construction.

**Table 2.1** Composition of the T2K-SWAL Corpus

| Register | # of texts | # of words |
|---|---|---|
| **Spoken:** | | |
| Class sessions | 176 | 1,248,800 |
| Classroom management* | (40) | 39,300 |
| Labs/In-class groups | 17 | 88,200 |
| Office hours | 11 | 50,400 |
| Study groups | 25 | 141,100 |
| Service encounters | 22 | 97,700 |
| **Total speech** | **251 (+40)** | **1,665,500** |
| **Written:** | | |
| Textbooks | 87 | 760,600 |
| Course packs | 27 | 107,200 |
| Course management | 21 | 52,400 |
| Institutional writing | 37 | 151,500 |
| **Total writing** | **172** | **1,071,700** |
| **TOTAL CORPUS** | **423** | **2,737,200** |

* Classroom management texts are extracted from the "class session" tapes so they are not included in the total tape counts.

## 2.1  Design and construction of the T2K-SWAL Corpus

The register categories chosen for the T2K-SWAL corpus were sampled from across the range of spoken and written activities associated with academic life, including classroom teaching, office hours, study groups, on-campus service encounters, textbooks, course packs, and institutional written materials (e.g., university catalogs, brochures). The depth of sampling for each register category reflects our assessment of its relative availability and importance; for example, there are many more different texts and total words for class sessions and textbooks than for office hours and course packs. Table 2.1 shows the overall composition of the corpus by register category.

Data collection focused on capturing naturally-occurring discourse. One major concern that we needed to address was that the presence of researchers in spoken settings was likely to be intrusive and therefore result in somewhat artificial discourse. As a result, we employed participants who already worked or studied in the settings where we wanted to collect data. They carried tape recorders and recorded speech as it occurred spontaneously. We obtained high quality, natural interactions using this approach; the major disadvantage was that we did not observe the interactions first-hand and thus were not able to obtain detailed information about the setting and participants.

For the spoken corpus, we used students as our primary participants, recruiting them to record classroom teaching, study groups, and other academic conversations. Student participants recorded the class sessions and study groups that they were involved in during a two week period, keeping a log of speech events and participants to the extent that it was practical. We also recruited faculty members to help with the recording of office hours, and university staff for service encounters.

The collection of texts from class sessions was designed to include a range of teaching styles, as measured by the extent of interactiveness. Three levels of interactiveness are distinguished for classroom teaching:

> **Low interactiveness:** fewer than 10 turns per 1,000 words (i.e., average length of turn longer than 100 words per turn): 54 class sessions; 337,800 words
>
> **Medium interactiveness:** between 10 and 25 turns per 1,000 words (i.e., average length of turn between 40–100 words per turn): 64 class sessions; 448,400 words
>
> **High interactiveness:** more than 25 turns per 1,000 words (i.e., average length of turn shorter than 40 words per turn): 75 class sessions; 550,900 words

Service encounters were recorded in locations where students regularly interact with university staff conducting the business of the university. We distinguished two major types of service encounters: for regular commerce (coffee shop, university book store, copy shop) and for other university services (student business services, academic department offices, the library reference desk, the front desk in a dormitory, the media center). We collected 22 tapes at these locations; these represent 97,700 words and hundreds of individual service encounters.[1]

For classroom teaching and textbooks, we sampled texts from six major disciplines (Business, Education, Engineering, Humanities, Natural Science, Social Science) and three levels of education (lower division undergraduate, upper division undergraduate, graduate). Table 2.2 shows the breakdown of texts by discipline.

Recognizing the existence of systematic variation within each of these high-level disciplines, the corpus design targeted specific sub-disciplines (e.g., accounting, anthropology, astronomy; see Biber et al. 2004, Tables 6 and 7). Rather than aiming for an exhaustive sampling of sub-disciplines, we collected texts from specific sub-disciplines within each major discipline (represented by at least 3 text samples). While these distinctions will enable register comparisons at a more specific level in future research, the analyses in the present book are restricted to the major disciplinary categories.

Course packs include written texts of several types: lecture notes, study guides, and detailed descriptions of assignments or experimental procedures written by the instructor, in addition to photocopies of published journal articles and book

**Table 2.2** Breakdown of classroom teaching and textbooks by discipline

| Discipline | # of texts | # of words |
|---|---|---|
| Classroom teaching | | |
| Business | 36 | 236,400 |
| Education | 16 | 137,200 |
| Engineering | 30 | 171,300 |
| Humanities | 31 | 248,600 |
| Natural Science | 25 | 160,800 |
| Social Science | 38 | 294,400 |
| Textbooks | | |
| Business | 15 | 116,200 |
| Education | 6 | 50,100 |
| Engineering | 9 | 72,000 |
| Humanities | 18 | 164,100 |
| Natural Science | 18 | 145,200 |
| Social Science | 21 | 213,000 |

**Table 2.3** Breakdown of texts within institutional writing

| Category | # of computer files | # of words |
|---|---|---|
| Academic program brochures | 7 | 22,500 |
| University catalogs: academic program descriptions | 10 | 27,400 |
| University catalogs: admissions, requirements, etc. | 9 | 52,500 |
| Student handbooks | 9 | 43,800 |
| University magazine articles | 2 | 2,700 |

chapters. Similar to the sampling procedures used for textbooks, course packs were collected from all the major disciplines and a range of the sub-disciplines.[2]

Finally, the category of 'institutional written material' attempted to represent the range of miscellaneous campus-related written texts that students encounter. Many of these texts are among the first material that a prospective student receives from a university, either through paper copy or on the Web: informational brochures about student services and academic programs, university catalogs (including both discussion of general requirements and specific programs), etc. Although not often considered 'academic discourse', written material of this type is ubiquitous on campus and required reading for the prospective student attempting to navigate the maze of university requirements and services. Many of these texts are very short (e.g., from academic program brochures), so in some cases we include multiple texts in a single computer file. Table 2.3 displays the breakdown of texts within institutional writing.

**Table 2.4** Breakdown of spoken texts by university

| University | # of texts | # of words |
|---|---|---|
| Northern Arizona University | 140 | 787,700 |
| Georgia State University | 56 | 369,200 |
| Iowa State University | 49 | 275,400 |
| Cal State University, Sacramento | 34 | 222,800 |

We collected spoken texts at four academic sites (Northern Arizona University, Iowa State University, California State University at Sacramento, Georgia State University). Table 2.4 shows the breakdown of transcribed texts by university. (Many additional texts were tape recorded but not able to be transcribed in the scope of the project.) Written materials were collected from all four universities, with the exception of course packs. Because there was little variation in the types of texts included in course packs at the four universities, we collected these texts only at Iowa State University.

Although we did not achieve full demographic/institutional representativeness, we aimed to avoid obvious skewing for these factors. Thus, the corpus materials were collected from four major regions in the U.S.: west coast, rocky mountain west, mid-west, and the deep south. Further, we collected materials from four different types of academic institutions: a teacher's college (California State, Sacramento), a mid-size regional university (Northern Arizona University), an urban research university (Georgia State), and a Research 1 university with a national reputation in agriculture and engineering (Iowa State). The collection procedures were approved by the Human Subjects Review Boards at all the universities. The amount collected from each written text conformed to copyright laws as interpreted by legal advisors at Educational Testing Service.

## 2.2 Transcription, scanning, and editing of texts in the T2K-SWAL Corpus

All texts in the corpus are coded with a header to identify content area and register. Spoken texts were transcribed using a consistent transcription convention (see Edwards & Lampert 1993), and to the extent possible speakers were distinguished and some demographic information supplied in the header for each speaker (e.g. their status as instructor vs student). Conventional spellings were used for all words except the following: *OK, cuz, yup, nope, mm, mhm, um, uh.* Grammatical dysfluencies were transcribed exactly as they occurred.

Written texts were scanned to disk or copied from websites. All texts were edited to insure accuracy in scanning.

## 2.3  Grammatical tagging and tag-editing

All texts in the T2K-SWAL Corpus were grammatically annotated using an automatic grammatical "tagger" (a computer program developed and revised over a 10 year period by Biber). The tagger is designed to identify a large number of linguistic features in written and spoken (transcribed) texts. It has various rules built in for the tokenization of words (e.g., contractions are separated and treated as two words, multi-word prepositions or subordinators are marked with ditto tags, phrasal verbs are identified as such, etc.). However, it does not have rules to disambiguate punctuation marks (especially '.' – which can be used as sentence-final punctuation and for a wide range of abbreviations).

The tagset incorporates an extended version of the CLAWS tagset (see Garside, Leech, & Sampson 1987). For example, the CLAWS VBN tag (past participle) is extended by several tags that identify grammatical function, such as perfect aspect verb, passive voice verb (further distinguishing among finite BY-passives, finite agentless passives, and non-finite post-nominal modifiers), and participial adjectives.

The tagger has four major components: a simple 'look-up' component for closed classes and multi-word fixed phrases (e.g., identifying sequences of words as fixed multi-word prepositions); a probabilistic component for individual words (e.g., considering the probabilities for the word *abstract* occurring as a noun, verb, or adjective); a probabilistic component to compare the likelihood of each possible tag sequence (working on a four-word window); and a rule-based component.

The tagger uses a number of on-line dictionaries. For example, one dictionary lists common content words, identifies their possible part-of-speech categories (e.g., the word *run* would be listed as a verb and a noun), and records the probability for each of those part-of-speech categories. Other dictionaries store multi-word grammatical units (e.g., *such as, that is, for example*) or other lists of words with a specific grammatical function (e.g., all verbs that can control a *that*-clause).

The probabilities used by the tagger were originally computed from a distributional analysis of the LOB (Lancaster-Oslo-Bergen) Corpus. For example, *book* and *runs* are both noun-verb ambiguities, but *book* has a very high likelihood of being a noun (99% in the LOB expository genres), while *runs* has a high likelihood of being a verb (74%). Separate dictionaries were compiled for expository/informational discourse versus non-expository discourse, to reflect the differing lexical and grammatical preferences of the two. For example, many past participial forms (e.g., *admitted, expected*) are much more likely to function as past tense or perfect aspect verbs in fiction and other kinds of non-informational discourse, while they are much more likely to function as passive constructions in exposition. Many noun/verb ambiguities (e.g., *trust, rule*) are much more likely to occur as verbs in non-informational discourse and as nouns in exposition. Among

**Table 2.5**  Sentences from tagged texts

| university textbook | class session |
|---|---|
| The ^ati++++ | I ^pp1a+pp1+++ |
| dissolved ^jj+atrb++xvbn+ | want ^vb++++ |
| components ^nns++++ | you ^pp2+pp2+++ |
| that ^tht+rel+subj++ | to ^to++++ |
| precipitate ^vb++++ | have ^vbi+hv+vrb++ |
| to ^to++++ | two ^cd++++ |
| form ^vbi++++ | books ^nns++++ |
| these ^dt+dem+++ | for ^in++++ |
| rocks ^nns++++ | the ^ati++++ |
| are ^vb+ber+aux++ | class ^nn++++ |
| decomposed ^vpsv++agls+xvbnx | . ^.+clp+++ |
| from ^in++++ | |
| pre-existing ^jj+atrb++xvbg+ | |
| rocks ^nns++++ | |
| and ^cc++++ | |
| minerals ^nns++++ | |
| . ^.+clp+++ | |

the function words, some preposition/subordinator ambiguities (e.g., *before, as*) are more likely to occur as subordinators in non-informational discourse, but more likely to function as prepositions in exposition.

Tagged texts are produced in a vertical format: the running text appears in the left-hand column, and the tags associated with each word are given to the right (beginning with the delimiter '^'). Table 2.5 shows examples of tagged sentences from a university textbook and a classroom session. The first tag field identifies the major part of speech for each word; for example, **jj** marks an adjective, and **nn** marks a noun. The remaining tag fields identify particular grammatical functions or larger syntactic structures. For example, **atrb** in Field 2 marks an adjective as 'attributive'. The tag sequence **tht+rel+subj**++ is used to characterize the function word *that* functioning as a 'relative pronoun', where the gap in the following relative clause is in 'subject' position.

After the texts in the corpus were grammatically coded by the automatic tagger, the codes (or 'tags') were edited using an interactive tag-checker. While this step is labor-intensive and extremely time consuming, it assured a high degree of accuracy for the final annotated corpus (see Biber, Conrad, & Reppen 1998; Methodology Boxes 4 & 5). We paid special attention to words that are multifunctional and hard to disambiguate automatically, including *that*, WH words, the form *'s*, and past participles when they are not in main clauses (e.g., passive verbs as postnominal modifiers). We also checked the tagging of words that were not in the dictionaries.

Tagging the corpus made it possible to conduct a series of more sophisticated analyses than would have been possible with an untagged corpus. Using the grammatical tags, further coding and categorizing of words and structures was undertaken in order to facilitate the linguistic analyses of the corpus (see Appendix A).

## 2.4 Overview of linguistic analyses

The primary goal of the present book is to provide a relatively comprehensive linguistic description of university registers. Thus, the descriptions are based on as wide a range of linguistic characteristics as possible, including any linguistic features that have obvious functional associations (since these should be important indicators of the differences among registers).

In selecting linguistic features for analysis, I relied on several previous corpus-based studies. The descriptions incorporate many of the analytical distinctions used in the *Longman Grammar of Spoken and Written English* (Biber et al. 1999; referred to as LGSWE below). These were especially important for the semantic categories, lexico-grammatical associations, and the analysis of lexical bundles. The descriptions also include all linguistic features used in previous Multi-Dimensional register studies (see especially Biber 1988: Appendix II): 67 different linguistic features identified from a survey of previous research on speech and writing. Finally, the descriptions include several analyses of vocabulary features, motivated by a survey of previous research on vocabulary use in academic language.

Computer programs were developed for each type of linguistic analysis, using the tagged version of the T2K-SWAL Corpus (see Section 2.3 above). The tagged corpus was useful even for the vocabulary analyses, because the grammatical tags made it possible to distinguish among the different uses of a single word form when it occurs with different parts of speech (e.g., *measure* used as a noun vs. verb). However, the tagged corpus was more important for the grammatical/syntactic analyses, since the distribution of those features could not have been accurately analyzed in an untagged corpus.

Some computer programs performed straightforward counts of features that had been identified in the tagging procedures (e.g., simple counts of nouns or adjectives). Other programs were developed for more specific analyses of linguistic features, such as the distribution of specific syntactic constructions in particular lexico-grammatical contexts. For example, *that*-complement clauses were analyzed for each of the major syntactic types (e.g., controlled by a verb, adjective, or noun) and for the major semantic classes of the controlling word (e.g., mental verbs or likelihood adjectives). Lexico-grammatical analyses at these more specific levels allow much more insightful descriptions of register differences than general analyses.

Appendix A provides a more detailed description of the procedures used for some of the linguistic feature categories. The following chapters show how university registers employ different constellations of features to achieve their particular communicative goals.

## Notes

**1.** Classroom management talk occurs at the beginning and end of class sessions, to discuss course requirements, expectations, and past student performance. Office hours are individual meetings between a student and faculty member, for advising purposes or for tutoring/mentoring on academic content. Study groups are meetings with two or more students who are discussing course assignments and content.

**2.** Written course management includes syllabi (196 syllabi totaling ca. 34,000 words) and course assignments (162 texts totaling ca. 18,500 words). The main communicative purpose of these texts is similar to classroom management, namely communicating requirements and expectations about a course or particular assignment.

# CHAPTER 3

# Vocabulary use in classroom teaching and textbooks

## 3.1 Introduction

The description of vocabulary use in university contexts is an essential prerequisite to the development of effective teaching materials and approaches. There are many important research questions about word use in university language. For example, how many words would a student need to know to read a typical university textbook? How many to understand a typical university lecture? Do different academic disciplines use the same words? If not, how much overlap is there across disciplines? Do some disciplines use a greater range of different words? Are some words common in everyday use and also common in academic language? What proportion of a typical academic text is made up of those common words?

Several studies in the past have investigated such questions. Nation and Waring (1997) provide a thorough survey of previous research on vocabulary size and text coverage. For example, they cite a study by Goulden, Nation, and Read (1990), who found that a university graduate will understand about 20,000 'word families'. Learners with a much smaller vocabulary size can be fairly successful reading many texts. For example, Hirsh and Nation (1992) found that the 2,000 most common word families would provide 90% coverage of a corpus of teenage novels.

Studies like these are based on word lists that identify the most important words in different domains. The most famous of these is the General Service List (GSL; West 1953), which contains 2,000 common words, identified from analysis of a 5-million-word general written corpus. The GSL also includes detailed information not found in most other word lists, such as percentage figures for different meanings and different part-of-speech uses of each headword.

Two other word lists have been developed specifically for academic applications. The University Word List (UWL; Xue & Nation 1984) includes 836 word families generally common in written academic texts but not included in the GSL. The Academic Word List (AWL; Coxhead 2000) is similar to the UWL, but it is derived from a more comprehensive corpus analysis considering the frequency of academic words, their 'range' (distribution across texts from several different subdisciplines), and their restriction to academic rather than general texts. The

AWL, with only 570 word families, achieves comparable (or even better) coverage of most academic texts than the UWL.

Resources like these have been employed to investigate the number of words required to understand written texts from different registers and different academic disciplines. Similar approaches have been applied to spoken texts. For example, McCarthy and Carter (1997) describe how vocabulary use in spoken texts is quite different from what a learner will normally encounter in writing, while Adolphs and Schmitt (2003) show that normal conversations employ a much wider set of vocabulary than previously expected.

The present chapter adopts a similar approach to the Adolphs and Schmitt study, comparing the word use patterns among spoken and written university registers and academic disciplines (rather than identifying lists of the most important words). Thus, the following descriptions focus on the distribution of all words in the T2K-SWAL corpus, comparing the patterns of use for words with different distributional profiles (with respect to frequency and range) and for words functioning in different part-of-speech categories.

Specifically, the chapter describes vocabulary use in classroom teaching and textbooks from three major perspectives:

- The breakdown of words by frequency level for each register: How many different words are used in each register? How many of these are high-frequency words and how many are low-frequency, specialized words?
- The breakdown of words by part of speech. For example, how many different words are nouns, verbs, adjectives, etc.?
- The use of vocabulary in different disciplines. For example, do disciplines differ in their reliance on specialized vocabulary and how many words are restricted to a single discipline?

Exhaustive word lists are not included in the present book. However, interested readers are referred to Biber et al. (2004, Appendix B) for a list of all words in the T2K-SWAL Corpus. (The monograph can also be accessed on-line, at www.ets. org/ell/research/toeflmonograph.html.) The sub-lists in that report are organized by frequency level, and they also distinguish among the words that are found primarily in speech versus those found primarily in writing versus words that are common in both modes.

## 3.2 A note on methodology

One key research issue for vocabulary analyses is to decide what to count as a word. In the present case, the analyses were based on 'lemmas': the base form for each word, disregarding inflectional morphemes. For example, *eat, eats, ate, eating,* and *eaten* are all realizations of a single lemma: *EAT*. These inflected word forms all express the same core meaning associated with the verb lemma *EAT*. These inflected variants are thus all treated as realizations of a single vocabulary item in the word counts. (See Appendix A for a fuller discussion of the methods used to identify lemmas.)

For the vocabulary analyses, the frequency of each lemma was counted in each register of the T2K-SWAL Corpus. However, registers are not equally well represented in the corpus. For example, the sub-corpus for classroom teaching contains 1.248 million words, while the sub-corpus for textbooks includes only .76 million words (see Table 2.1 in Chapter 2). To compensate for these differences, it is necessary to 'normalize' all raw frequency counts to a rate of occurrence per 1 million words. These normalized rates of occurrence can then be compared directly across registers.

For example, the lemma *work* as a noun occurs 1095 times in the spoken texts of the T2K-SWAL corpus, and the total word count for the spoken part of the corpus is c. 1,665,000 words. Thus, the normed rate of occurrence for *work/n* in the spoken mode is:

$$1,095 / 1,665,000 * 1,000,000 = 657.15 \text{ times per million words}$$

There are two other major methodological considerations that should be borne in mind for any quantitative study of vocabulary: the representativeness of the corpora (including the actual topics covered in the corpus), and the problems encountered in comparing vocabulary distributions across corpora of different sizes (because word type distributions are not linear relationships). Because these are both relatively complex methodological issues, I deal with them in some detail in Appendix B. That appendix includes the results of a series of methodological experiments, testing the effects of corpus size on the apparent vocabulary diversity. In sum, those experiments show that a small corpus will (misleadingly) seem to use a larger stock of different words than a large corpus, because words tend to be repeated in a larger corpus. The appendix introduces a formula to 'normalize' word type counts to a common basis (per one million words), together with experiments that illustrate how this formula enables comparisons across corpora of different size.

This normalization procedure is used for the findings presented in Section 3.3 below, which compares the patterns of word use for two registers: classroom teaching and textbooks. That section also discusses differences in word use across the academic disciplines within each register. These results should be considered preliminary, because they are based on a corpus that is small for the purposes of vocabulary investigations, and because the norming of word type counts provides only an estimate of the non-linear relationship between word types and corpus size (see Appendix B). It would be inappropriate under these circumstances to

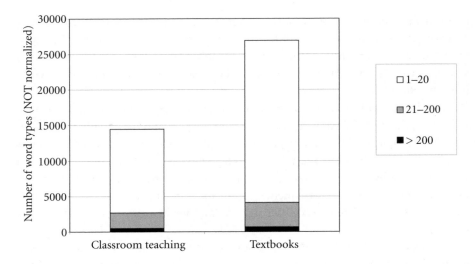

**Figure 3.1** Number of word types at three frequency levels (rates per million words)

do detailed analysis of individual words. However, Section 3.3 shows that there are large differences in the general patterns of vocabulary use across university registers and disciplines, and the methods applied here are more than adequate for describing those major trends.

### 3.3  Vocabulary use in university registers

### 3.3.1  Vocabulary in classroom teaching and textbooks

Classroom teaching and textbooks are similar in their overall purposes and topics. The primary situational difference between the two is that classroom teaching is spoken and produced in real time, while textbooks are written and therefore carefully planned, revised, and edited. However, it turns out that this situational difference has a strong influence on word choice: classroom teaching in the T2K-SWAL Corpus uses c. 14,500 different words, while textbooks use c. 27,000 different words.[1]

Further analysis shows that the greater diversity in word choice in textbooks is due mostly to the use of specialized vocabulary. Figure 3.1 plots the breakdown of word types by frequency level: very common words (occurring more than 200 times per million words; e.g., *become, make, great*); moderately common words (occurring between 21 and 200 times per million words; e.g., *afraid, compare, confidence*), and rare words (occurring fewer than 20 times per million words; e.g., *affiliation, buoyancy, commensurate*).

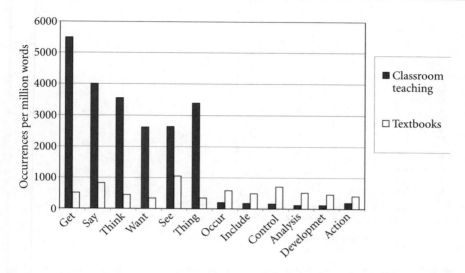

**Figure 3.2** Selected words with especially high frequencies in classroom teaching or textbooks

Both registers are similar in using relatively few high-frequency word types. But the registers differ dramatically in their reliance on rare word types, with textbooks using a much larger set of these specialized words than classroom teaching. In contrast, many common words occur with extremely high frequencies in classroom teaching. Figure 3.2 plots the normed rate of occurrence for some of these words. For example, verbs such as *get, say, think, want,* and *see* all occur well over 2,000 times per million words in classroom teaching, while the noun *thing* occurs over 3,000 times per million words in teaching. There are also many words that occur especially in textbooks, but none of these words occur with extremely high frequencies. For example, Figure 3.2 shows that some relatively common verbs (e.g. *occur, include*) and several relatively common nouns (e.g., *control, analysis, development, action*) occur more often in textbooks, but even the most frequent of these words occur less than 1,000 times per million words.

Thus, the general picture emerging from Figures 3.1–3.2 is the following:

– Textbooks use a much greater range of different word types than classroom teaching.
– Textbooks and classroom teaching both use a relatively small set of common words.
– Many of these common words occur with extremely high frequencies in classroom teaching.
– In contrast, textbooks use a wide range of word types that occur with low frequencies.

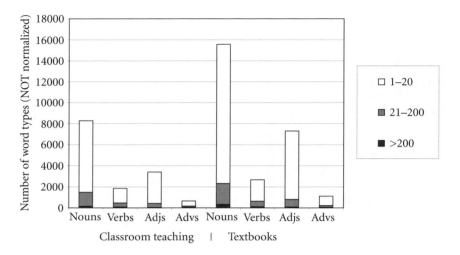

**Figure 3.3** Number of word types at three frequency levels, by grammatical word class (rates per million words)

Figure 3.3 shows that the majority of the different word types in the T2K-SWAL Corpus are nouns. This is especially the case for rare word types, although moderately common word types (with frequencies between 21–200 per million words) show the same pattern. These nouns include some everyday words that generally are not the normal topic of discussion in teaching or textbooks, such as *chalkboard, cigarette, doorway*. However, most of these nouns have more specialized meanings, like *disillusionment, enhancement, globalization, hominid, locus*. Textbooks use an especially large number of different word types functioning as nouns. There are also a large range of different adjectives used in textbooks (and to a lesser extent classroom teaching); these are words such as *occupational, pediatric, representational,* and *sensory*. There are a smaller number of different verbs in either register, and adverbs show the least diversity of the four content word classes.

The following two text excerpts, from a classroom lecture and a textbook in engineering, illustrate these basic patterns. Both excerpts describe engineering problems, one concerning flow rate and the other road surfaces. The two excerpts are also similar in showing a mix of high-frequency and less common words. The major difference between the two excerpts is in the extent to which they rely on the different kinds of words.

In the classroom teaching text (Excerpt 3.1) there are several less common words conveying specialized information (e.g. *reaction, molar, reactant, concentration, differential*). However, there is an even greater reliance on common content words, and many of these are extremely high frequency words, such as: *again, look, see, make, here, gonna, guess, now, mean, have, need, use*. It is interesting to note how these extremely common words are interspersed with technical vocabulary in the spoken discourse. This seems to reflect the instructor's awareness of the classroom audience, using everyday terms to explain what he is doing as he develops a complex mathematical equation on the blackboard.

In contrast, the excerpt from the engineering textbook (3.2) is noteworthy for its use of rare words; for example: *profilometers, wavenumber, wavelength, amplitude, deviations, deteriorating, bituminous, cycle.*

**Text Excerpt 3.1:** Engineering Classroom Teaching (engceleudli100.txt), chemical engineering
Relatively frequent content words (occurring more than 400 times per million words) are in **bold**; Less frequent content words (occurring fewer than 200 times per million words) are *in italics*

**So**, **again taking** a **look** at a specific **example**, of this, we **look** at a **first** order *reaction*, the *mole balance*, for, *plug* flow *reactor* **is remember**, D.F.A.B.V. **is equal** to, uh, the **rate** of *reaction*. Instead of **writing** it in terms of *molar* flow **rate**, I'm **gonna put everything** in **terms** of *concentration*. And **so**, since the *molar* flow **rate**, **is** the **same** as, uh *concentration* **times**, the *volume* (that your) flow **rate**, I **write** it this **way**. And, you **see**, I've **sort** of **made another** *assumption* **here** and that is that the *volume* and the flow **rate is** not a function of position in a *plug* flow *reactor*. So this equation, in addition, **another** *restriction* to this one **is gonna be**, **note**, the *volume* **changes** … and the, the negative sign **is here** because, A **is** *disappearing*. It's a *reactant*. And, *plugging* **now** into the energy *balance* the **rate** [2 sylls]. I **mean** they don't **have** these two *boxed* equations to *solve simultaneously*. And they're, *ordinary differential* equations **so** we'll **need** to **use**, **need** to **use** the *homework*.

**Text Excerpt 3.2:** Engineering Textbook (TBMCE3.GVD), mechanical engineering
Relatively frequent content words (occurring more than 400 times per million words) are in **bold**; Less frequent content words (occurring fewer than 200 times per million words) are *in italics*

Road *elevation profiles* can be *measured* either by *performing* close *interval rod* and level *surveys* or by **high** *speed profilometers*. When the *PSDs* are determined, *plots* such as those **shown** in Figure 5.2 are *typically obtained*. Although the *PSD* of every road section **is** *unique*, all roads **show** the *characteristic* drop in *amplitude* with *wavenumber*. This simply *reflects* the **fact** that *deviations* in the road surface on the order of **hundreds** of feet in *length* may **have** *amplitudes* of inches, whereas those only a **few** feet in *length* **are** *normally* only *fractions* of an inch in *amplitude*. The general *amplitude* level of the *plot* **is** *indicative* of the *roughness* level with **higher** *amplitudes implying rougher* roads. The *wavenumber range* in the figure *corresponds* to *wavelengths* of 200 feet (61 m) on the left at 0.005 *cycle*/foot (0.016 *cycle/meter*), to about 2 feet (0.6 m) on the **right** at 0.5 *cycle*/foot (1.6 *cycles/meter*).

Another perspective on vocabulary use is to consider the specialized word types that are restricted to either speech or writing. Figure 3.4 shows that there are very few word types used in classroom teaching that are not also used in textbooks. That is, most of the word types that a student encounters in classroom teaching are also used in textbooks. In contrast, textbooks rely on many specialized word types that are not found in the corresponding classroom teaching sessions.[2] Here again we see the greatest degree of specialization for nouns: almost half of the different nouns in the T2K-SWAL Corpus are found only in textbooks. These include some relatively common words like *self, agent,* and *combination*. However, many of these nouns are rare words with highly specialized meanings, like *agglomeration, chromatography, dialectic, electrode, felony.*

Surprisingly, Figure 3.4 shows there are some nouns found exclusively in classroom teaching. Many of these nouns are everyday words with meanings that are not normally discussed in a written textbook, e.g.: *bagel, bakery, banana, nail, tourist, parking*. There are also colloquial nouns (and other words) used in classroom teaching that would usually not be considered appropriate in a textbook; for example: *bug, buzz, cop, chump, dude, fluff.*[3] However, the existence of this small set of words found exclusively in classroom teaching does not obscure the overall

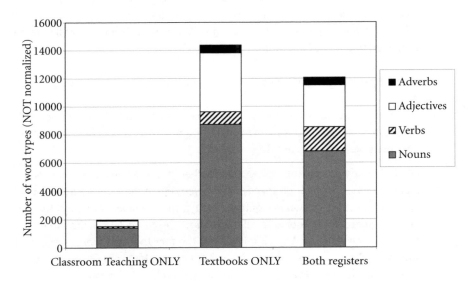

**Figure 3.4** Distribution of specialized word types – restricted to either classroom teaching or textbooks (by grammatical class)

pattern: that there is a much greater range of word types used in textbooks than in classroom teaching, and most of these different words are nouns.

These patterns are mostly a reflection of the different production circumstances of classroom teaching versus textbooks. Textbook authors have extensive time for producing their texts, including the initial writing as well as revision and editing. In contrast, instructors in classroom teaching usually pre-plan their discourse, but the actual spoken text is created as it is produced in the classroom. As a result, instructors in classroom teaching rely on a relatively small set of words, but they use a few words with extremely high frequencies. (Their speech also tends to rely on clauses rather than elaborated noun phrases; see Chapter 4.) In contrast, the extended production opportunities for textbook authors allow the use of a much larger stock of words, including the selection of words with specific rather than general meanings. Textbook authors are also motivated by a stylistic preference for varied vocabulary, rather than using the same word repeatedly (at least in some academic disciplines – see Section 3.3.2 below). Finally, textbook authors employ elaborated noun phrase constructions, relying to a large extent on phrases rather than clauses to convey information (see the discussion of grammatical features in Chapter 4). As a result, textbooks show much greater vocabulary diversity than classroom teaching, with most of that diversity being realized as an extremely large set of different nouns.

### 3.3.2 Vocabulary across academic disciplines

In addition to the overall differences between classroom teaching and textbooks, there are also important differences in word use across academic disciplines. Figure 3.5 plots the number of word types (normalized per 1-million words) in each discipline. Classroom teaching and textbooks both show the same overall patterns: Business and engineering have much less diversity in word choice than natural science, social science, and humanities. These differences are much more pronounced in textbooks than in classroom teaching. Humanities textbooks are especially noteworthy, with an extremely large set of word types. However, social science and natural science textbooks also use a very large set of different word types. Figure 3.6 shows the breakdown of specialized word types across academic disciplines, plotting the number of word types found in only a single discipline (i.e., 'specialized' words) versus word types that are used in several disciplines. Similar to Figure 3.5, Figure 3.6 shows a major difference between Business and Engineering, on the one hand, and the more general Sciences and Humanities (Natural Science, Social Science, and Humanities) on the other.

In part, these differences seem to reflect the range of subject areas included under each of these academic disciplines. Business and engineering are professional disciplines, training students in specific skills and methods. As a result, the set of

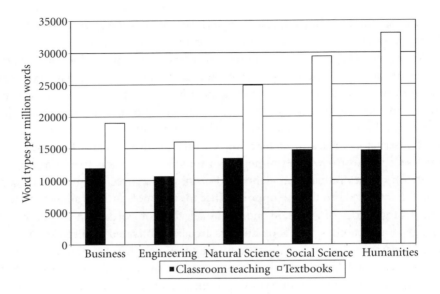

**Figure 3.5** Number of word types across academic disciplines

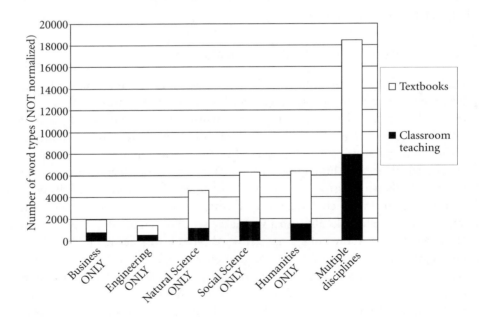

**Figure 3.6** Distribution of specialized word types – restricted to a single academic discipline (vs. general word types found in multiple disciplines)

topics covered in these general disciplines is somewhat more constrained than in the sciences and humanities. Natural science might be characterized as a discipline of discovery, identifying and describing entities that had not been previously considered. As a result, natural science employs a large set of highly technical words, like *dextrinoid, electrophoresis,* and *phallotoxins.* Most of these words do not have commonplace synonyms, because they refer to entities, characteristics, or concepts that are not normally discussed in everyday conversation. In contrast, humanities and social science textbooks are more likely to deal with aspects of everyday life, discussing people, events, and social behavior from new perspectives. Humanities and social sciences employ a very large set of specialized words, but many of these terms provide a single word for an entity or concept that can easily be discussed in everyday conversation with a fuller phrase. For example:

> *ingrate* = someone who doesn't appreciate something
> *misconception* = a really strange idea
> *pedagogy* = a style of teaching
> *sanctimonious* = he thinks he's "holier-than-thou"

To illustrate the kinds of words preferred in each academic discipline, I carried out a case study considering all specialized vocabulary beginning with the letter 'A' in the T2K-SWAL Corpus. Table 3.1 shows the breakdown of these specialized words across disciplines.

Business and Engineering are similar in having only a few technical terms that are restricted to that single discipline. These are words like *accrual, annuity,* and *audit* in Business, and *absorber, aerodynamics,* and *attenuate* in Engineering. More commonly, these two disciplines use everyday terms with a specific technical meaning, resulting in an extremely frequent use of the term; these are words like *account, act,* and *adjust* in Business, and *address, arm,* and *assembly* in Engineering.

The pattern of word use in Natural Science is quite different. Table 3.1 lists a large number of specialized terms found exclusively in this discipline; most of these words are highly technical in meaning and have no counterpart in everyday usage. These are words like *abscission, acastia, acetylation, achene, acyanogenic,* etc.

Humanities and social sciences also have a large number of specialized words that are restricted to these disciplines. However, as noted above, these words tend to refer to concepts or entities that could easily be described in normal conversation with a fuller expression. For example:

> *altruism* = caring about other people
> *ambivalence* = having mixed feelings about something
> *amoral* = doesn't care about right or wrong

Detailed consideration of these specialized words shows that there are strikingly different patterns of use across disciplines. Figures 3.5 and 3.6 show a general

**Table 3.1** Specialized vocabulary beginning with the letter 'A', broken down by academic discipline

**Business**
Words found only (or primarily) in Business:
*accredited, accrual, adjusted/ing, adversarial, affective/ity, amend, annualized, annuity, apprentice, arbitration, audit, auditor, averse/ion*

Words that are much more common in Business than in other disciplines:
*accommodation, account, accounting, accumulated, accuracy, achievement, act* (noun), *action, activate, activity, ad, adjust, administer, adopt, advantage, adverse, advertise, advertiser, affect, affiliation, affirmative, agency, agent, agreement, allege, allocation, allowance, alternative, amend, amendment, analysis, annual, approach, ask, aspect, assertion, assess/ment, asset, assurance, attention, attractive/ness*

**Engineering**
Words found only (or primarily) in Engineering:
*absorber, adiabatic, aerodynamics, aerospace, algorithm, alloy, analyzer, annular, artifactual, attenuate/ion, automated, axle*

Words found only in Engineering and Science:
*absorb, acetone, advection, airflow, algebraic, ammonia, ammonium, analog, angular, anisotropic, annulus, anthracite, approximately, aqueous, aquifer, asbestos, aspherical, axis*

Words that are much more common in Engineering than in other disciplines:
*absolute, acceleration, access, accordingly, actual, address, alpha, ambiguous, amplify, amplitude, analogous, applicability, application, apply, approximate/ion, arbitrary, architecture, arithmetic, arm, array, arrow, assembly, assignment, associate*

**Natural Science**
Words found only (or primarily) in Natural Science:
*abscission, acastia, accretion, acetate, acetylation, achene, actin, acyanogenic, adnation, adsorb, adsorption, advection, aeration, agaric, albumin, alder, algae, aliele, aliphatic, alkaline, alleghaniensis, allotropic, allozyme, alluvial, alphape, aluminosilicates, amanita, amatoxin, amphibole, anaerobic, andesite, anemophilous, anhydrite, anionic, anisotropic, anode, anoxic, antiparallel, antiquark, antiviral, aperiodic, apetalous, aphyllophorale, apophysis, appendage, arbuscules, archaebacteria, archean, ardente, arkose, armillaria, ascomycete, asepalous, asteroid, asthenosphere, autochory, autoclastic, autodeliquescence, axil, axillary*

**Humanities and Social Science**
Words found only (or primarily) in Humanities and/or Social Science:
*altruism, ambivalence, amoral, anachronistic, anarchy, ancillary, anecdotal, angel, anger, anguish, animosity, annexation, antagonism, anthology, antiquity, antithesis, antiwar, anxiety, apathy, apostle, apostrophe, apprehend, apprehension, archaic, archetype, aristocracy, arousal, arrest, arrogant, artifice, artisan, artistic, ascetic, ascribe, asocial, aspiration, assailant, assassin, assault, assimilate, astonishment, astrology, astronomical, asylum, atheism, atonement, atrocity, attendant, attentive, attribution, atypical, auspicious, austere, authenticity, authoritative, autobiography, autocratic, autonomy, autopsy, avenge, avert, avid, awful*

similarity between Natural Science, Social Science, and Humanities: all three disciplines have a large number of different word types, including many words restricted to a single discipline. However, this quantitative similarity corresponds to very different patterns of word use in the disciplines. Natural Science uses a large stock of technical terms for highly specialized reference: words that refer to entities, characteristics, and concepts that are not readily discussed in everyday conversation. In contrast, Humanities and Social Sciences often offer new perspectives on concepts and entities that are taken from our everyday experience. As a result, the extensive stock of specialized words in these disciplines are often technical terms to refer to these everyday experiences.

## 3.4 Conclusion

This chapter has taken a different approach to vocabulary study than most previous studies of academic discourse, focusing on the diversity of vocabulary and the frequency distributions of common and rare words across registers (rather than the use of specific words or the identification of lists of the most common words). This perspective exposed interesting contrasts between spoken and written registers and across disciplines. Overall, classroom teaching was found to use a relatively small set of different word types, but to rely heavily on a few of those words, which therefore occur with extremely high frequencies. Textbooks, in contrast, were found to use a larger set of different word types (especially different nouns), but none of those individual word types occur with extremely high frequencies. Such distributions are consistent with the differences between the two registers with respect to their planning and revising time, as well as the presence of a face-to-face audience.

The comparison of vocabulary patterns across disciplines highlighted the relationship between word use and subject matter. Business and engineering were found to have less diversity in word choice, using words that are adapted from everyday use but have specific technical meanings. Natural science has more diversity in vocabulary, reflecting the diversity of its sub-disciplines, and it has more rarely occurring technical terms that have no everyday counterparts. The humanities and social sciences also evidence diverse word choice, consistent with their diverse subject matter; many words in these disciplines could be summarized with longer phrases in everyday language, as the disciplines address matters that are more often part of our everyday experience.

Other perspectives on vocabulary use in academic language are of course needed. For example, it would be useful to investigate the use of multi-word terms, such as "hard income measure" in business or "truth value" in philosophy. Nevertheless, even the limited analyses possible with the relatively small sub-corpora in the T2K-SWAL corpus have revealed important patterns in vocabulary use across university registers and disciplines.

## Notes

**1.** Remember that 'word type' is defined as a lemma occurring with a particular part-of-speech function. Thus, *use* as a verb and *use* as a noun are two separate word types in the analysis. See Section 3.2.

**2.** This pattern is found despite the fact that the classroom teaching sub-corpus is 50% larger than the textbook sub-corpus (see Section 2.1). If the textbook sub-corpus were as large as the classroom teaching sub-corpus, we would predict an even larger number of word types found exclusively in the written textbook category.

**3.** There are also a few technical terms unique to classroom teaching, such as *affidavit, annuity, compressor, dramatization, existentialism*. These words relate to particular academic topics that happened to be discussed in the classroom teaching texts but not textbook texts included in the T2K-SWAL Corpus. The fact that these words were not found in textbooks reflects the relatively small size of the T2K-SWAL Corpus for vocabulary studies, rather than a genuine difference between classroom teaching and textbooks.

# CHAPTER 4

# Grammatical variation among university registers

## 4.1 Introduction

Many studies of academic registers document the use of individual grammatical features. As described in Chapter 1, most previous studies have focused on written academic prose, especially research articles. As a result, we know relatively little about the grammatical characteristics of the wider range of university registers that students encounter: are there systematic patterns of linguistic variation among university registers, associated with differences in mode, purpose, situation, and academic discipline/level?

The last chapter began to answer this question by considering patterns of vocabulary use across university registers; the present chapter describes the patterns of use for grammatical and syntactic features, including the general distribution of content word classes (nouns, verbs, adjectives, and adverbs), as well as the semantic categories of nouns and verbs. The chapter ends with a discussion of variation within the verb phrase (tense, aspect, and voice) and the distribution of dependent clause types across registers.

## 4.2 Content word classes

One of the most striking linguistic contrasts among university registers is the differential reliance on the four content word classes (nouns, verbs, adjectives, adverbs). Chapter 3 included some discussion of these differences by considering the breakdown of word types across word classes (see especially Figures 3.4 and 3.5). Figure 4.1 shows that there is also a fundamental difference in the overall frequencies of these word classes. Written registers use nouns to a much greater extent than any other word class. In contrast, spoken registers use nouns and verbs to about the same extent. As a result, verbs are much more common in the spoken registers than in the written registers. Adjectives and adverbs are distributed in a similar way: adjectives are used more commonly in the written registers, while adverbs are favored in the spoken registers.

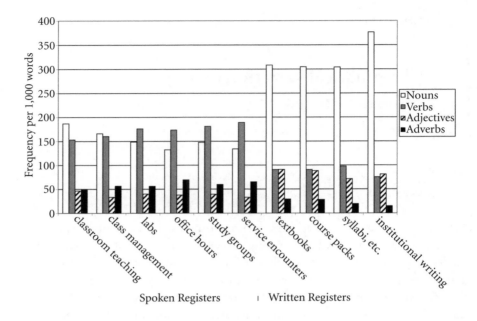

**Figure 4.1**  Content word classes across registers

Text Sample 4.1, from an ecology textbook, illustrates the heavy reliance on nouns in written university registers; Text Sample 4.2, from a service encounter in a copy shop, illustrates the dense use of verbs in spoken registers. (Nouns are underlined, and *verbs* are given in bold italics.)

**Text Sample 4.1:** Ecology Textbook, lower division (tbeco1.own)

Wildlife photography *represents* the nonconsumptive use of wildlife, which *is* the use, without removal or alteration, of natural resources. For much of this century, the management of wildlife for the hunter has been *emphasized* by wildlife managers. In recent years, however, management for nonconsumptive uses such as wildlife photography and bird-watching has *received* more attention.

**Text Sample 4.2:** Service Encounter, copy shop (servencs_n115)

clerk:       Hey there.
customer:  Hi.
clerk:       How's it *going*?
customer:  OK. I *want* these, uh, *copied*, just as they *are*.
clerk:       Mhm.
customer:  [2 sylls] and the holes *punched* and the whole bit.
clerk:       OK. How many copies?

| customer: | Tabs, you don't have to **worry** about the <u>tabs</u> I'll **worry** about the <u>tabs</u>. **Wait** you **need** to **mark** where the <u>tabs</u> **go** though. I'd **put** a pink <u>sheet</u> or something where every <u>tab</u> **is**. |
|---|---|
| clerk: | OK. |
| customer: | Or something. So I **know** where the <u>tabs</u> **go**. |
| clerk: | All right. |

The basic grammatical characteristics of these two text samples are extremely different. The textbook sample has only three main clauses (*Wildlife photography represents...; management has been emphasized...; wildlife photography has received...*) and one dependent clause (a relative clause: *use of wildlife, which is...*). The four main verbs in the textbook sample – *represents, is, emphasized, received* – convey little information. Instead, their primary function is to connect long and complex noun phrases, which convey most of the new information in the passage (e.g., *the management of wildlife for the hunter; management for nonconsumptive uses such as wildlife photography ...*).

In contrast, the service encounter relies heavily on verbs and short clauses, a total of 8 main clauses and 7 dependent clauses in this short interaction. In this interaction, the verbs communicate much of the essential information: the required actions (*copied, punched, mark, put*) and the speakers attitudes and desires (*want, worry, need, know*). In contrast, nouns are rare and add relatively little new information to the exchange. Note, for example, how the single noun *tab(s)* is used repeatedly in the sample.

Classroom teaching is more similar to the written registers than most other spoken registers, in that it relies on nouns to a slightly greater extent than verbs (see Figure 4.1). Text Sample 4.3 illustrates the mixed use of nouns (<u>underlined</u>) and verbs (in **bold**) in classroom teaching.

**Text Sample 4.3:** Business Classroom Teaching, upper division (busbaleudln049)

Uh, one of the <u>U.S.</u> <u>Court</u> <u>District</u> <u>Judges</u>, I **think** it **was** <u>W. C.</u>, in the <u>CITY</u> <u>U.S.</u> <u>District</u> <u>Court</u>, **made** a <u>statement</u> one <u>time</u> that in his <u>opinion</u>, one half of the <u>lawyers</u> who were, uh **presenting** <u>cases</u> before him were incompetent. And he wasn't **saying** mentally incompetent, he was just **saying** they weren't **practicing** <u>law</u> with a <u>skill</u> that **was** professional. Now, now, I'm not **trying** to **scare** you, you **know** what I'm **trying** to **do**? I'm **trying** to **let** you **know** that you, you better **pay** <u>attention</u> to who your <u>lawyer</u> **is**, and **get** someone who **has** respect. Uh, or it could **affect** the <u>outcome</u> of your <u>case</u>. You **know**, and uh again, that's not what the <u>system</u> was **designed** to **do** and I don't **think** it should **be** <u>part</u> of the <u>system</u>, I'm just **saying**, in <u>fact</u>, it **is**.

At the other extreme, institutional writing represents the densest use of nouns (underlined), at the expense of verbs (in **bold**). Text Sample 4.4, from a brochure for a graduate program, illustrates these patterns:

> **Text Sample 4.4:** Institutional Writing, brochure for forestry graduate programs (Otbroa.pha)
>
> Graduate education and research opportunities in the School of Forestry **provide** motivated individuals with the knowledge and expertise necessary to successfully **pursue** their career objectives in forest land management or research. The School of Forestry and the Department of Geography and Public Planning are **located** in the College of Ecosystem Science and Management.

We might expect the linguistic style of institutional writing to be highly accessible, since these are probably the first university texts that a student encounters, with the primary goal of informing (and sometimes recruiting) incoming students. Despite these goals, the style of discourse in this register is at the opposite end of the spectrum from everyday conversation: there are few verbs and clauses, while nearly all important information is packaged in noun phrases. In fact, this register is even more extreme than textbooks in this regard. This same general pattern emerges repeatedly in the following sections and chapters: for a wide range of linguistic features, institutional writing is more complex than any other university register.

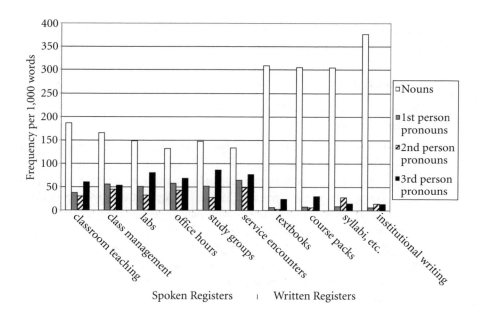

**Figure 4.2**  Nouns and pronouns across registers

## 4.3 Nouns and pronouns

Figure 4.2 shows that spoken university registers rely on pronouns to a greater extent than the written registers. It turns out that all registers have roughly the same number of referring expressions and noun phrases (see LGSWE, p. 578), but these expressions are realized in dramatically different ways: heavily elaborated noun phrases in the written registers (often noun-noun sequences, such as *career objectives, forest land management*), versus a reliance on simple nouns and pronouns in the spoken registers. Text Samples 4.1–4.4 above illustrate these characteristics. Notice in particular how third person pronouns are often substituted for full noun phrases in the spoken registers (e.g., *it, these, they, he*).

First person pronouns (*I, we*) are found in all spoken university registers, although they are slightly less common in classroom teaching. Second person pronouns (*you*) are also found in all spoken registers, although they are most common in class management, office hours, and service encounters. The dense use of first and second person pronouns in service encounters reflects the directly interactive nature of that register, illustrated in Text Sample 4.2 above. Second person pronouns in class management and office hours are often used for directive purposes, as in the following:

> **Text Sample 4.5:** Business Classroom Management, lower division
> (busbacmld_n054)
>
> You're making it too hard, you're making it too hard. and you're doing that in two directions, one is you're doing an awful lot of work that you don't have to do. On the one hand it's good that you know how to do that work and you know how to get the numbers, but as we'll as [unclear] go through this in a second several of you are doing the work, you're doing it wrong, it's right there in front of you, OK you have all the numbers you need, there's nothing to calculate, so some of you are making it too hard by doing a lot of work that's not necessary work – and then you're making it too hard because you're forgetting about the fundamental rule and, you're thinking too much…

Interestingly, second person pronouns are relatively common in written course syllabi and other written class materials, where they serve a similar directive function, for example:

> **Text Sample 4.6:** Engineering Syllabus, upper division (cmeng2.syl)
>
> In this course you will learn how to develop instructional software and articulate the issues involved in using the computer for instruction. This can only be achieved if you are actively engaged in lesson development. Therefore, most of your instruction will consist of reading relevant documentation on the computer and completing assigned projects on your own. […] While this instructional for-

mat is interesting and rewarding, it requires that <u>you</u> be more responsible for <u>your</u> own learning than in the lecture-test format <u>you</u> may be used to. Not everything <u>you</u> need to know will be told to <u>you</u>. <u>You</u> will need to access available resources to find answers to <u>your</u> questions and be willing to ask when <u>you</u> can't find them.

## 4.4 Semantic classes for nouns

Figures 4.3–4.5 show the breakdown of nouns across semantic domains. Figures 4.3 and 4.4 are based on a semantic classification of all nouns occurring more than 20 times per million words in the T2K-SWAL Corpus; the full list of nouns is given in Table A.8 (in Section 4.4 of Appendix A). While the classification of individual nouns can be problematic (because some nouns have multiple meanings from different semantic domains), this perspective is useful for comparing the general patterns of use across registers.

Figure 4.3 shows that many of the common nouns in university registers have abstract/process meanings: nouns that refer to intangible, abstract concepts or processes, like *system, factor, design, difficulty,* and *problem*. Abstract/process nouns are especially prevalent in the written registers, where they constitute over 50% of all nouns. As the following extract from an upper division syllabus shows, com-

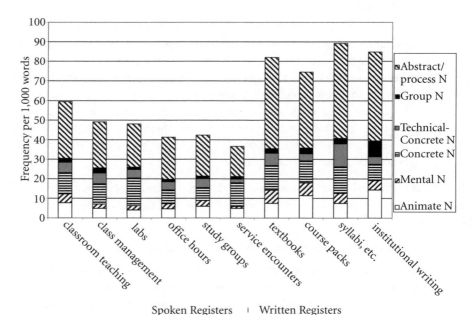

**Figure 4.3**  Breakdown of common nouns across semantic domains, by register

mon abstract/process nouns (marked in **bold**) often co-occur with less common nouns from the same semantic domain (underlined), nouns like *sophistication, complexity, functionality*:

> **Text Sample 4.7:** Business Syllabus, upper division (cmbus2.syl)
>
> Comprehensive **System** Sophistication: **Factors** we will look for related to judging sophistication include the total number of tables; the complexity represented in the **design** and functionality of the **system**; and the **difficulty** of the original **problem** (e.g., did you tackle a trivial or complex **problem** to begin with?). Part of the grading of this **project** will be based on my judgment of and perceptions about the overall sophistication of the **system**; therefore there is clearly a subjective component.

It is interesting that the spoken registers also rely heavily on abstract/process nouns. In fact, abstract/process nouns account for c. 50% of common nouns in all registers. (Only service encounters show a slightly lower proportion.)

There are also interesting patterns for some of the other noun classes. For example, animate nouns and group nouns are especially prevalent in institutional writing, where they are used to refer to the students, instructors, and institutional entities in academic programs. The following examples are taken from university catalogs and program brochures (animate nouns are underlined; group nouns are in **bold**):

> The chair of the Retention **Committee** will prepare a report of the faculty decision for the chair of the **department** and the student. The student will receive a copy of the faculty's decision by certified mail.

> The **College** of Education offers admission to applicants who hold baccalaureate degrees from regionally accredited **institutions**.

> CPS 9660 Applied Practice III: Students work in an appropriate psychological counseling with clients under supervision. Pre: consent of instructor.

> Students are only reserved a place in a particular class section by making arrangements with the **department** Graduate Advisor.

Figure 4.4 shows that there are also systematic differences across academic disciplines in their reliance on particular noun classes. For example, mental nouns (e.g., *decision, experience, conclusion, expectation, observation, recognition, assumption*) are somewhat more common in business and humanities textbooks than in the other disciplines. Abstract/process nouns – describing intangible, abstract concepts or processes – are especially prevalent in business and engineering textbooks. Surprisingly, concrete nouns are also common in engineering texts, but animate nouns are especially rare in this discipline. This combination reflects the dual focus in engineering on everyday entities described in technical terms. For example:

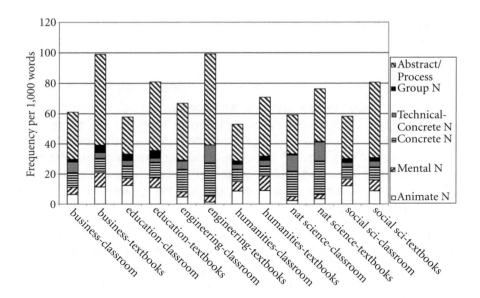

**Figure 4.4** Breakdown of common nouns across semantic domains: classroom teaching and textbooks, by academic discipline

> **Text Sample 4.8:** Engineering Textbook, graduate level (tbmce3.gvd)
> Abstract/process nouns are <u>underlined</u>; concrete nouns are in **bold**.
>
> **Automobiles** travel at high <u>speed</u>, and as a consequence experience a broad <u>spectrum</u> of <u>vibrations</u>. These are transmitted to the passengers either by tactile, visual, or aural <u>paths</u>. The <u>term</u> "<u>ride</u>" is commonly used in <u>reference</u> to tactile and visual <u>vibrations</u>, while the aural <u>vibrations</u> are categorized as "<u>noise</u>." [. . .] The <u>vibration</u> <u>environment</u> is one of the more important <u>criteria</u> by which people judge the <u>design</u> and <u>construction</u> "<u>quality</u>" of a **car**. Being a judgment, it is subjective in <u>nature</u>, from which arises one of the greatest <u>difficulties</u> in developing objective engineering <u>methods</u> for dealing with <u>ride</u> as a <u>performance</u> <u>mode</u> of the **vehicle**.

Figures 4.3 and 4.4 show the distribution of 'common' nouns across semantic classes, that is, nouns that occur more than 20 times per million words in the T2K-SWAL Corpus. Some of these nouns are specialized, even though they occur with high frequencies. This is especially the case with abstract/process nouns (e.g., *application, argument, development, function, method, process, criticism, evolution*) and technical-concrete nouns (e.g., *cell, gene, wave, ion, electron, chromosome, element*).

Rare nouns are even more likely to be highly specialized and technical in meaning, as noted in Chapter 3. One approach to studying rare nouns is to consider the nouns that occur in only one text. Figure 4.5 compares the use

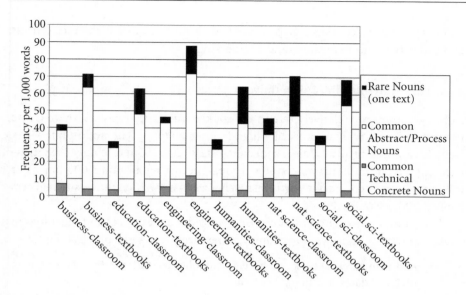

**Figure 4.5** Breakdown of specialized nouns (i.e., nouns that occur in only one text) versus common technical nouns across disciplines

of these rare nouns with common technical nouns across disciplines. Interestingly, business and engineering textbooks show the greatest reliance on common abstract/process nouns, but humanities and natural science textbooks show the greatest reliance on rare specialized nouns (see also the vocabulary distributions discussed in Section 3.3.2 in the last chapter). For example, the first few pages of a chapter on deconstructive criticism (from a graduate level humanities textbook on literary criticism; tbeng3.llc) include the following highly specialized nouns:

> *phenomenology, deconstruction, grammatology, phenomenologists, hermeneuticists, logocentrism, phonocentrism, semiology, archicriture, signifieds, signifiers, solidifications, ontotheology.*

Chapter 3 (Section 3.3.2) discussed how many of the specialized words in Humanities referred to entities and concepts that could be readily described with a fuller phrase that combines common words. In contrast, the above list of 'rare' words – occurring in a single Humanities text – are abstract and highly technical, with meanings that cannot be defined by a simple equivalent expression.

In summary, a detailed study of noun use in spoken and written registers is informative because much of the referential information of academic language is packaged in noun phrases. Taken together, these patterns indicate that textbook prose can vary widely across academic disciplines: for example, having a greater reliance on rare, highly specialized (abstract and technical) nouns in humanities and natural science, versus a greater reliance on more common abstract/process and concrete nouns in business and engineering.

### 4.4.1 The noun *thing* in spoken university registers

Although nouns are relatively rare in the spoken university registers, there is one noun that occurs with an especially high frequency: *thing*. The noun *thing* is extremely common in all academic spoken registers (classroom teaching, class management talk, office hours, and study groups), occurring around 3,000 times per million words. In contrast, *thing* is relatively rare in all written university registers (only c. 300 per million words).

The noun *thing* occurs with an extremely wide range of uses and meanings in spoken university registers. Surprisingly, *thing* rarely refers to a physical object:

> And then he came back and his wife brought figs stuffed with nuts, and more fruit, and dates, and <u>things</u> like that.

Rather, *thing* usually refers to 'actions' or 'ideas'. The fixed expression *things like that* is often used for both meanings:

> OK, I grew up in a neighborhood, where like, you had a number of occupational choices when you grew up – you could go to prison, you could join the marine corp. uh, you know, <u>things</u> like that.

> We're not interested in comparing blue eyed people and brown eyed people. Right? That would be vertical differentiation. It's meaningless. It's irrelevant. It's not important, right? We're not talking about <u>things</u> like that.

In classroom teaching, these two uses of *thing* are extremely prevalent. In the first meaning, *thing* is used to refer to 'actions', 'activities', or 'events', as in:

> Terrible <u>things</u> can happen to you at an early stage of development and still you come out all right later on.

> So the only <u>thing</u> that could be done in that situation or that was done was you call in the local shaman – who performs an exorcism

> I should have known all along that she was a topless go-go dancer. Look at the way she used to dress. Look at how she used to dance at parties. You know, that kind of <u>thing</u>.

The second major use of *thing* refers to ideas or informational points to consider, as in:

> Well I, I think two <u>things</u> are going on. Again, it has in part to do with, public education, you know just what's common kind of quote on quote common knowledge or mythology in the public. And number two uh, the way it actually

gets promoted by educators . . .

I mean the first <u>thing</u> you guys all said was paranoid

This use of *thing* is especially important in classroom teaching because it helps to structure the flow of information. Often the word *thing* is used to identify the points of information that will be covered in a teaching session:

I'm not really going to lecture in your textbook on this chapter. I want to go through some <u>things</u> in the textbook though just to talk about them a little bit

I'm going to lecture on some of the <u>things</u> I want to talk about here.

But that – those are <u>things</u> that we'll discuss when we talk about the actual colonial period

Instructors also use *thing* to signal the introduction of new topics:

The country is big and strong, we have a good economy. OK. Now, one final <u>thing</u> about these – about these population questions. How do we stack up compared to other parts of the world?

So. Um. We have to talk about some basic concepts in here it says here. It says more basic concepts. And um, one of the <u>things</u> I want to talk about in terms of basic concepts is, classes. Let's call them class intervals. What we're, talking about is, grouping data.

This use of *thing* to signal informational packaging is commonly combined with an evaluative adjective, which reflects the instructor's stance towards a topic (e.g., *the interesting thing*). In many cases, instructors use *thing* in the focus construction:

*the ADJECTIVE thing is + that*-clause

This construction emphasizes the evaluative stance indicated by the adjective while focusing on the information provided in the clause after the copula *is*. For example:

Um, <u>the brilliant thing is</u> [that the I.M.F. is voting to give money to the only ally Serbia has].

And as you know they went to Tennessee, and <u>the good thing is</u> [that when they moved to Tennessee, they improved the living standard of the people in the area enormously]

Now, <u>the interesting thing</u> about this study, which just came out last year, <u>is</u> [that it questions that].

This use of *the thing* has become conventualized, so that even when it occurs without an evaluative adjective, it still has the sense of identifying an important consideration:

Now. <u>The thing</u> about Porfirio Villas is that he was a liberal. OK?

See that's <u>the thing</u>, because, because, uh, you would think everything would hinge on how he does as mayor but because it's an internal party decision, it's, it's, it's, his people are the people doing the voting within the party.

## 4.5 Semantic classes of verbs

As discussed in Appendix A, verbs can also be grouped into major semantic classes (building on the corpus-based investigations reported in LGSWE). Figure 4.6 shows that there are interesting differences across registers in their reliance on particular verb classes. The most obvious difference is between the spoken and written registers. Figure 4.1 (above) showed that verbs are much more common in the spoken registers than the written registers. Figure 4.6 shows that this frequency difference is largely due to an extremely heavy reliance on two semantic domains in the spoken registers: activity verbs and mental verbs. In contrast, the other four semantic classes (communication verbs, causative verbs, occurrence verbs, and as-pectual verbs) are used with roughly the same frequency in the spoken and written registers.

Activity verbs are especially common in class management talk and in ser-vice encounters. Participants in service encounters are directly involved in phys-ical activities, or in giving directions about future activities, as in Text Sample

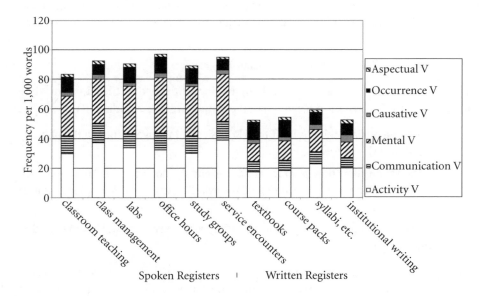

**Figure 4.6** Breakdown of common verbs across semantic domains, by register

4.2 (above). Classroom management talk similarly involves discussion of future activities, for example:

> **Text Sample 4.9:** Education Classroom Management Talk, upper division (edubecmud_n133)
> Activity verbs are <u>underlined.</u>
>
> | | |
> |---|---|
> | Instructor: | I'm going to be at Killup um, when you've <u>signed</u> up for your pre-sentation on December first and December third and, um, I encourage you to get people involved in the activities, um, also, I'd also like to <u>invite</u> people to <u>bring</u> food. I was wondering if we could have the people who are not presenting, <u>bring</u> some snacks. Um, is that a good way to <u>do</u> it? |
> | Student: | Sure. That's fun. |
> | Instructor: | <u>Get</u> lunch that way. If it's not your turn to present, um, in that last week. And really that's great. |
> | Student: | Are you just going to <u>leave</u> a box up by your office? |
> | Instructor: | Yeah, you can just [unclear mix of voices] |
> | Student: | OK. |
>
> [general conversation and mixed voices]
>
> | | |
> |---|---|
> | Student: | Cause I <u>put</u> mine like in the [unclear] |
> | Instructor: | There's a black thing on my door. Just <u>stick</u> it in there |

In contrast, mental verbs are especially common in office hours, where they are used for problem solving and giving advice:

> **Text Sample 4.10:** Natural Science Office Hour (natgloh_n0005)
> Mental verbs are <u>underlined.</u>
>
> | | |
> |---|---|
> | Instructor: | Yeah I <u>think</u> I finally, got Sarah, on a direction in her thesis is gonna go now, so I <u>think</u> we've got that <u>figured out</u>. |
>
> [...]
>
> | | |
> |---|---|
> | Student: | OK. Great. |
> | Instructor: | Mhm. |
> | Student: | I-I <u>guess</u> that's it then. [unclear sentence] |
> | Instructor: | Have you done any more on your grad school? |
>
> [...]
>
> | | |
> |---|---|
> | Student: | And, that <u>reminded</u> me, I'm totally glad you asked because I would have <u>felt</u> quite stupid, um if, if you wouldn't <u>mind</u>, I'd <u>appreciate</u> it, if you could, write a um, letter of recommendation for me. |
> | Instructor: | Mhm. Yeah just be sure to give me at least two weeks' notice. |
> | Student: | Yeah. Got plenty of time. |
> | Instructor: | OK. So what's the deadline? |
> | Student: | Uh, January sixth. |

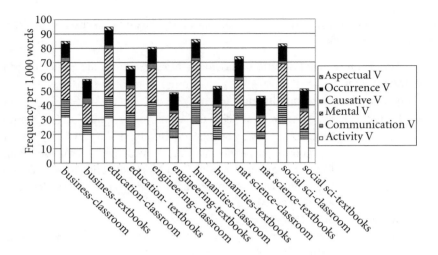

**Figure 4.7** Breakdown of common verbs across semantic domains, by discipline

> Instructor:    OK. That's what's critical is that I <u>know</u> that. Actually the other thing
> I was gonna recommend too is to uh, uh, give me a, if you <u>want</u> me
> to look at it sometime, your uh, your cover letter...

Similar to the patterns described in the last section for noun classes, these verb classes are also used in different ways across academic disciplines. For example, Figure 4.7 shows that Education exhibits the most frequent use of verbs, in both classroom teaching and in textbooks. The majority of these are mental verbs and activity verbs, with communication verbs also being relatively common. For example:

> **Text Sample 4.11:** Education Classroom Teaching (edubelegrmn188)
> Activity verbs are <u>underlined</u>; mental verbs are in **bold**; communication verbs are in *ITALIC CAPS*.

> Instructor: So we're *TALKING* about <u>working</u> together to **solve** problems. So when I <u>approached</u> this I **wanted** to <u>develop</u> a curriculum piece that would also be hands on and they would be **solving** a problem and <u>working</u> together to do it. So, to <u>go</u> into the problem. The problem was, well, oh, I **forgot** one important part, the community involvement. Um, you can't really <u>develop</u> as an Anglo teacher uh lessons on, you **know**, the culture of [unclear words] about it so I <u>brought</u> community members in to <u>help</u> me um **decide** what to <u>do</u>. I **chose** an area and it was area and perimeter, and I <u>went</u> to community members and I *SAID* let me **know** about area perimeter and how Navajo people <u>use</u> it. One woman *SUGGESTED* grazing areas and um that sounded like it would be interesting. But then um another parent *SUGGESTED* um hogan and that actually went with a problem

I had um kind of <u>worked with</u> for another conference, um basically **seeing** if the kids could **figure out** what shape has the biggest area within a perimeter.

Occurrence verbs (i.e., verbs that report events that occur apart from any volitional activity) are also relatively common in most of these disciplines. They are especially important in natural science teaching:

> **Text Sample 4.12:** Natural science classroom teaching (natbileldmn062) Occurrence verbs are <u>underlined.</u>

> Instructor: Antibiotics are not for viruses, the viruses don't <u>become</u> resistant. Humans don't <u>become</u> resistant – bacteria <u>become</u> resistant. And uh uh a minor [unclear] kind of important point was that the the bacteria do not <u>mutate</u> in response to the, to the antibiotic some of them just <u>happen</u> to already have a mutation and that kind of question for sure will <u>come up</u> on your test so things, just keep it in your mind – things don't <u>mutate</u> in response but they're randomly <u>mutating</u> and some of them <u>happen</u> to have that mutation. Um and that's that's what in fact is <u>happening</u> is that with this with this dispensing antibiotics so freely they are <u>becoming</u>, the bacteria are <u>becoming</u> much more immune.

## 4.6 Variation in the verb phrase

Another perspective on the use of verbs in university registers is to consider variation in the marking of tense, aspect, and voice. Past tense is the marked choice in all university registers. This pattern is consistent in the spoken registers, which all use past tense verbs less than 20% of the time. The dis-preference for past tense is more variable in the written registers, ranging from 20% past tense in textbooks to less than 5% past tense in course syllabi and institutional writing.

Figure 4.8 shows that there are also interesting differences across academic disciplines in the extent to which they use present and past tense. At one end, only about 10% of the verbs in engineering and natural science classroom teaching are past tense. Engineering textbooks show the most extreme pattern, with past tense verbs accounting for only about 5% or all verb phrases. At the other extreme, past tense verbs are relatively common in education and humanities textbooks: over 30% of all finite verb phrases in education, and over 40% of all finite verb phrases in humanities. Text Sample 4.8 (in Section 4.4 above) illustrates the absence of past tense verbs in engineering textbooks. In contrast, Sample 4.13 illustrates the style of discourse common in education textbooks, which incorporate relatively frequent past tense verbs to report past events, often in association with personal narratives. (Sample 4.11, in Section 4.5 above, illustrates the similar use of past tense verbs for narrative purposes in education classroom teaching.)

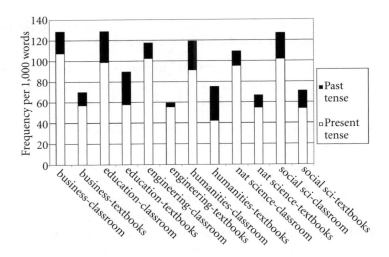

**Figure 4.8** Verb tense across academic disciplines (classroom teaching and textbooks)

**Text Sample 4.13:** Education Textbook (tbele2.jpd)
Past tense verbs are in **bold**; non-finite verbs are <u>underlined.</u>

In one high school where I **was working**, one of the most respected English teachers **amazed** her colleagues when during training she **shared** a description of the first three days of the semester in her English class. As soon as the students **entered** the room, they **were given** a form upon which they **were** to <u>put</u> their name, address, and phone number. Any students who **did** not **have** pencils **were given** them with a private message that this <u>would be</u> the last pencil that they <u>would</u> ever <u>be given</u> and that they <u>would be expected</u> to <u>bring</u> their own pencil and paper in the future. As this task **was nearing** completion, with an overhead projector the teacher **showed** the class a list of basic rules for her class to <u>be copied</u> onto the first page of each student's notebook.

Humanities textbooks also use past tense verbs to report past events, but these tend to be historical recounts rather than personal narratives. Text Sample 4.14 illustrates this style of discourse in a history textbook.

**Text Sample 4.14:** History Textbook (tbhis2.kis)
Past tense verbs are in **bold**, and non-finite verbs are <u>underlined.</u>

Avid colonialists though they **were**, the British never **mastered** the art of decolonization. After finally <u>granting</u> India its freedom, the British **created** Pakistan in 1947 by <u>carving</u> off the Moslem areas.
Pakistan **had** two segments, <u>separated</u> by a thousand miles of Hindu dominated India between them. West Pakistan, <u>inhabited</u> largely by Punjabis, politically **dominated** the poorer East Pakistan, <u>inhabited</u> mainly by Bengalis. The only

bond that **tied** the two Pakistans **was** their shared Islamic faith, which <u>could</u> not fully <u>subsume</u> their economic and ethnic differences.

Such historical recounts are often used to introduce a topic, as in the following passage from a textbook on technical writing. Notice how the historical background to the topic is presented with past tense verbs, while the switch to present tense verbs marks the transition to the more informational discussion of the topic.

> **Text Sample 4.15:** English Textbook, technical writing (tbrpc2.rte)
> Past tense verbs are in **bold**, present tense verbs are in *italics*, and non-finite verbs are <u>underlined.</u>

> When technical communication **emerged** as a career specialization during World War II, the typical technical document **was** mostly words. Furthermore, the page **was packed** with words. Narrow margins, scant interlinear spacing, and the lack of headings **let** the words <u>crowd</u> the page. Technical documents *have changed* dramatically since then as writers *have discovered* the power of graphics and format. Writers *use* typography and space to <u>enhance</u> comprehension and access, and documents without visuals *are* rare. Some documents *are* wholly visual, with illustrations <u>substituting</u> for text. The term illustrations *is* comprehensive: it *refers* to tables, . . .

A related grammatical distinction is the marking of verb aspect. Simple aspect is overwhelmingly the preferred option, in both spoken and written registers. Around 90% of all verb phrases are simple aspect in all spoken registers, while over 95% of all verb phrases are simple aspect in all written registers. Most text excerpts in the preceding sections illustrate these patterns.

When marked aspect is used, progressive aspect is somewhat more common than perfect aspect, especially in the spoken registers. Text Samples 4.3, 4.11, and 4.12 (above) illustrate the mixed use of simple and progressive aspect in classroom teaching. The following sentence, repeated from Sample 4.11 above, illustrates the typical mixing of aspects (simple aspect verb phrases are <u>underlined</u>; progressive aspect in **bold**):

> So when I <u>approached</u> this I <u>wanted</u> to <u>develop</u> a curriculum piece that would also <u>be</u> hands on and they would **be solving** a problem and **working** together to <u>do</u> it.

Here simple aspect verb phrases are used to narrate the researcher's intentions and a stative description of the situation, while progressive aspect verb phrases are used to describe the actions of participants that continue over an extended period of time.

In comparison to the other spoken university registers, progressive verbs are most common in lab sessions (almost 8% of all verb phrases). Lab sessions rely on task-focused language, where participants are actually performing actions and observing events at the same time that they are talking about those actions and events. For example:

> **Text Sample 4.16:** Natural Science Lab Session (natcmlbudhn276)
> Progressive aspect verb phrases are <u>underlined.</u>
>
> Instructor:    It looks like <u>we're still getting</u> a single line with some. This is pretty interesting . . see <u>it's starting</u> to emerge the hydroplane splitting <u>is starting</u> to emerge but it's not – you're still probably at least a factor ten away in terms of concentration but see the bumps on this
>
> Student:    oh yeah
>
> Instructor:    so now <u>you're starting</u> to – that tells me almost certainly that the line you saw before was broadened by electron transfer. Between radical and neutral molecule and so now <u>we're starting</u> to bring this up the splittings must [be] relatively small
>
> Student:    so in other words this is too concentrated still
>
> Instructor:    still now you can see the effect that <u>we're now starting</u> to
>
> Student:    [unclear words]
>
> Instructor:    <u>we're starting</u> to resolve
>
> Student:    closer, <u>we're getting</u> closer [. . .] and <u>they're attracting</u> [unclear words]

In contrast to the relative preference for progressive aspect in the spoken registers, both marked aspects are rare in the written registers. However, perfect aspect verb phrases are occasionally used in course packs and textbooks (4–5% of all verb phrases), where they describe past events that have continuing consequences. For example:

> **Text Sample 4.17:** Course Pack, lower division social science (cpami1.211)
> Perfect aspect verb phrases are <u>underlined.</u>
>
> In the Western world, where mind <u>has been separated</u> from body, where man <u>has been extracted</u> from nature, where affect <u>has been divorced</u> from "fact," where the quest for and focus upon the manipulation and accumulation of things <u>has led</u> man to exploit rather than to respect and admire the earth and her web of life, it is not surprising that art would be divorced from the more practical affairs of business and government and the more serious matters of science, philosophy, and theology.

Transitive verb phrases in English also allow a choice between active and passive voice. Similar to the preference for simple aspect described above, active voice is the unmarked choice in all university registers. All spoken registers use active voice verb phrases over 95% of the time. In contrast, the written university registers show a greater reliance on passive voice: c. 20% passive voice vs. c. 80% active

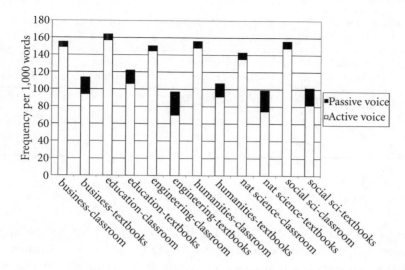

**Figure 4.9** Active and passive voice across disciplines (classroom teaching and textbooks)

voice. Surprisingly, there is little variation across registers within speech or within writing: passive voice is extremely rare in all spoken university registers, while it occurs with moderate frequencies in all written registers, regardless of the particular settings or typical communicative purposes.

However, Figure 4.9 shows that there are some interesting differences across academic disciplines in the extent to which they use passive voice verb phrases. Engineering textbooks (and to a lesser extent natural science textbooks) show the most frequent use of passive voice: almost 30% of all verb phrases. These forms are used to focus on actions, and the entities affected by actions, in cases where the agent is understood or unimportant. In many cases, the agent is simply understood to be the author or the general consensus of researchers in the field, for example:

> **Text Sample 4.18:** Textbook, upper division engineering (tbmce2.iht)
> Passive voice verb phrases are <u>underlined.</u>
>
> The heat flux from a horizontal nichrome wire to saturated water <u>was determined</u> by measuring the current flow 1 and potential, drop E. The wire temperature <u>was determined</u> from knowledge of the manner in which its electrical resistance varied with temperature. This arrangement <u>is referred</u> to as power-controlled heating, wherein the wire temperature, Tx (hence the excess temperature Te) is the dependent variable and the power setting (hence the heat flux qs) is the independent variable. Following the arrows of the heating curve of Figure 10.3, it is evident that as power <u>is applied</u>, the heat flux increases, at first slowly and then very rapidly, with excess temperature.

**Table 4.1** Distribution of discourse markers across spoken registers (each '*' represents 1,000 occurrences per million words)

|      | Classroom Teaching | Class Management | Office Hours | Study Groups | Service Encounters |
|------|-----------|-----------|-----------|-----------|-----------|
| OK   | ***** | ******** | ******** | ****** | ******** |
| well | ** | ** | **** | *** | ** |
| now  | ** | * | * | * | * |
| so   | ***** | ***** | ************** | ************ | **** |

## 4.7  Discourse connectors

Discourse connectors are devices used to bridge between turns (in speech) and sentences, indicating the logical relations among the parts of a discourse, and providing an interpretive framework for the listener/reader. There are two major classes of discourse connectors: discourse markers and linking adverbials. Discourse markers – forms like *ok, well,* and *now* – are restricted primarily to spoken discourse. These forms have distinct discourse functions, but it is difficult to identify the specific meaning of the word itself. In contrast, linking adverbials – forms like *however, thus, therefore, for example* (*e.g.*), and *that is* (*i.e.*) – are found in both spoken and written registers, and they have greater inherent meaning than discourse markers. (The form *so* is intermediate, sometimes functioning more like a discourse marker and sometimes more like a linking adverbial. It is grouped with the discourse markers in the description below.)

### 4.7.1  Discourse markers in spoken university registers

Discourse markers rarely occur in written university registers, but they are common in all spoken university registers. Table 4.1 shows the distribution of these devices across spoken registers.

The discourse marker *so* is the most common, especially in office hours and study groups. (*So* can have other functions, for example as an emphatic. However, well over 90% of the occurrences of *so* in these two registers are functioning as discourse markers.) The discourse marker *ok* is also very common, again in office hours and also in classroom management. Interestingly, *ok* is the only discourse marker used with a high frequency in service encounters. *Well* is considerably less common than *so* and *ok*, but this discourse marker is also more common in office hours than the other spoken registers.

Text Sample 4.19 illustrates the dense use of these discourse markers in an advising session taken from an office hour:

**Text Sample 4.19:** Office hours (advising session), Business Administration (busbaoh_n156)

Discourse markers are <u>underlined</u>

| | |
|---|---|
| Advisor: | <u>all right</u> <u>so</u> say again what's the problem |
| Student: | <u>well</u> I planned on getting out in December |
| Advisor: | are you going to go to summer school? |
| Student: | yes |
| Advisor: | mhm |
| Student: | and but management four thirty five, which I need, is not offered this summer or in the fall |
| Advisor: | you're sure |
| Student: | I'm – <u>well</u> it's not in the books |
| Advisor: | yeah <u>well</u> then it's not in if if they should happen to offer it then you would pick it up at the time |
| Student: | <u>well</u> obviously |
| Advisor: | I don't know – I don't know if that's going to happen |
| Student: | <u>well</u> my question is is it – I don't know if it's being offered right now but if it is I wanna know why I'm not in it |
| Advisor: | we'll substitute something for management four thirty five |
| Student: | we can do that |
| Advisor: | I can do it |
| Student: | <u>OK</u> |
| Advisor: | yeah |
| Student: | <u>OK</u> um what I have here for this the BA three forty and three ninety six I plan on taking it in the fall [. . .] |

[. . .]

| | |
|---|---|
| Student: | and then also BA four ninety and uh |
| Advisor: | history three eighty |
| Student: | yes |
| Advisor: | <u>OK</u> for BA four ninety by the time that second summer session rolls around will you be all done with the core other than BA four ninety. will you be all done with these courses above BA four ninety |
| Student: | all these are done let's see I got that's done uh three oh one I'm taking this summer |
| Advisor: | <u>OK</u> I I I see that |
| Student: | and three sixty yes <u>so</u> everything above four ninety |

[. . .]

| | |
|---|---|
| Advisor: | <u>all right</u> you're done with that <u>OK</u> um |
| Student: | <u>so</u> really I have – I want to take four this summer and then four in the fall is how it's working out |

In the above excerpt from an advising session, almost half of all turns begin with a discourse marker. Although these forms do not have precise meanings, they serve to structure the overall discourse. For example, contrast the functions of *ok* and *well*. *Ok* is often used as a simple response, indicating that the speaker has understood and accepted the preceding utterance, as in:

> Advisor:    I can do it
> Student:    <u>OK</u>

In other cases, *ok* marks a transition to the next step in the discussion, initiating a new sub-topic, as in:

> Student:    <u>OK</u> um what I have here for this . . .

or

> Advisor:    <u>OK</u> for BA four ninety by the time that second summer session rolls around will you be all done. . .

The discourse marker *all right* is relatively rare, but it is similar in being used to initiate a new topic:

> Advisor:    <u>all right</u> <u>so</u> say again what's the problem

In contrast, the discourse marker *well* almost always marks a response to some previous utterance, rather than initiating a new sub-topic. Beginning the response with *well* often indicates that the information in the utterance is somehow counter to the expectations raised by the preceding utterance. For example, when the advisor asks whether the student is sure, she responds <u>*well*</u> *it's not in the books* (that is, she's not absolutely sure, but there's no indication that she's wrong). In another example, the advisor gives a directive to the student, but the student responds instead by showing him her notes:

> Advisor:    just tell me summer ninety nine what do you have
> Student:    <u>well</u> I have I have it written down in here

As noted above, the form *so* often functions more like a linking adverbial than a discourse marker. This use is prevalent in academic office hours, where *so* has a resultative meaning (similar to the meaning of *therefore*). For example:

> Instructor: But China had this incredibly powerful culture that said we're the center of universe, and <u>therefore</u> nobody else matters. And they considered the rest of the world as being, the rest of the world as being, uh basically, barbarians, [. . .] And they had no interest in learning anything from them – they said just, stay away from us. <u>So</u> the Europeans would come and say hey you know we want to trade we want to learn these things from you, and they would say, you know, you're inferior to us. Go away. <u>So</u> the Europeans just came back, you know, and

said OK, now you're going to do what we want you to do, you know. Cos you don't
wanna play nice.

This resultative meaning can also be detected in other uses of *so*, even when it is not
used as part of an extended logical argument. For example, the first turn in Text
Excerpt 4.19 initiates this discussion, and thus the form *so* here cannot indicate
that this is a logical consequence of a preceding utterance:

Advisor:      all right so say again what's the problem

Rather, this use of *so* indicates that the advisor is aware of the general circumstances, and as a result, aware that there is a problem.

Similarly, in the last turn from this excerpt, the student uses *so* to initiate a
statement that summarizes the results of the preceding negotiations:

Student:      so really I have – I want to take four this summer and then four in
              the fall is how it's working out

Notice that *ok* could have been used in this context instead of *so* to initiate the
summary statement, but that discourse marker would not have carried the same
resultative implications. However, because both of these discourse markers serve
turn-initiating functions, they are commonly used together, as in:

Student:      OK so I'm not that off base
Instructor:   well on the contrary you seem to be very much on base

The discourse marker *now* is considerably less common than the other forms, but
it is the only form that occurs more commonly in classroom teaching than in the
other spoken registers. *Now* can be used as either a place adverbial or as a discourse
marker; thus compare:

Time adverbial:
but for right now we'll restrict ourselves to conductors

Discourse marker:
Uh now the first aspect I want to talk about is convenience of the Internet.

(The frequencies reported in Table 4.1 include only occurrences functioning as a
discourse marker.)

In classroom teaching, *now* is commonly used to initiate a new topic, usually
as the next step in a logical progression. In many cases, *now* and *ok* could be used
interchangeably for this function. However, *now* more consistently marks the introduction of a major new topic, and it is this function that results in the greater
use of *now* in classroom teaching. For example:

Instructor: When you think about the proposition that lying is wrong, or one
has an obligation to keep a promise, the mature mind, will see that this is self-

> evidently true. <u>Now</u>, remember the distinction he makes between prima facie duties and actual duties. The prima facie duties being the conditional duties. . .

Surprisingly, *now* is also occasionally used as a discourse marker in textbooks, as in:

> <u>Now</u> to find p*(T) you need only find T on the new abscissa scale.

> <u>Now</u> let's suppose that the observation had been made in a correlational study rather than in an descriptive one.

By adopting this spoken feature in textbook language, authors seem to be suggesting to the student reader that the material is not too difficult if they just follow along step by step. This message is reinforced in the above examples by the direct references to the reader: *you need only* and *let's suppose*.


### 4.7.2 Linking adverbials in written university registers

Linking adverbials can be considered as a parallel system to discourse markers. Both sets of features function to connect propositions in discourse. However, linking adverbials are primarily characteristic of the written registers. The linking adverbials *therefore, for example*, and *that is* are used occasionally in classroom teaching (about 200 times per million words), and *for example* is used with roughly the same frequency in office hours and study groups, but otherwise these forms are rare in the spoken registers. In contrast, Table 4.1 shows that linking adverbials are relatively common in the written university registers.

Linking adverbials are much less frequent in absolute terms than discourse markers. The most common linking adverbials – *however* and *for example* – occur c. 1,000 times per million words in textbooks. In contrast, Table 4.1 shows that the most common discourse markers – *ok* and *so* – are 10 times more frequent in the spoken registers.

Linking adverbials further differ from discourse markers in that they have more specified meanings and functions:

| | |
|---|---|
| Contrast | *however, in contrast, on the other hand, alternatively* |
| Result/inference: | *thus, therefore, consequently,* (*so*) |
| Apposition/exemplification: | *that is, for example, for instance, in other words* |

Table 4.2 gives the frequencies of the most common linking adverbials in university registers. Textbooks show by far the greatest use of these devices, although they are also surprisingly common in course syllabi. In contrast, institutional writing has a much lower use of these forms (except for the contrastive adverbial *however*).

The more frequent use of linking adverbials in textbooks reflects the primary purposes of informational presentation in this register: contrasting arguments

**Table 4.2** Distribution of linking adverbials across written university registers (each '\*' represents 100 occurrences per million words)

|  | Textbooks | Wr. Course Management | Institutional Writing |
|---|---|---|---|
| however | ********** | ******* | ***** |
| for example/e.g. | ************ | ******* | ** |
| thus | ******* | ** | * |
| that is/i.e. | **** | **** | * |
| therefore | **** | *** | * |

**Table 4.3** Distribution of linking adverbials across disciplines, textbooks only (each '\*' represents 100 occurrences per million words)

|  | Business | Engineering | Humanities | Natural Science | Social Science |
|---|---|---|---|---|---|
| however | *************** | *********** | ******** | ********** | ********** |
| for example/e.g. | *************** | *************** | ******* | ********** | ********** |
| thus | ********* | *********** | ***** | ******** | ******** |
| that is/i.e. | **** | ********* | ** | *** | *** |
| therefore | **** | ******* | **** | ***** | *** |

(*however*), exemplifying a concept (*for example, that is*), and presenting logical inferences (*thus, therefore*). For example:

> The value of p\*(t) will be located at the same abscissa value, and the curve of p\* versus Pr\* may then be used to determine p\*(T). Notice, <u>however</u>, that there is no longer a need for the p\* scale, since once you find T on the abscissa you can proceed directly to the curve. The p\* scale can <u>therefore</u> be omitted.

> People, especially young ones, get better at a lot of things as they get older. <u>For example</u>, we would expect kindergarten students' vocabularies to increase over the course of time whether we gave them special vocabulary lessons or not. <u>Thus</u>, if a researcher reported that kindergarten students increased their vocabularies by 15% when they were exposed to an enrichment program for a year, we wouldn't know whether to be impressed or not. [. . .] <u>That is</u>, we would need to measure vocabulary gains over the same period in a control group of students who did not have the enrichment program.

It is interesting to further compare textbooks from different academic disciplines for their reliance on linking adverbials (see Table 4.3). Business and Engineering textbooks show the greatest reliance on linking adverbials. In both disciplines, linking adverbials are most common in technical discourse that explains the derivation or application of mathematical formulas or procedures. The following excerpt, from a graduate level economics textbook, shows the use of several less common linking adverbials working together with the more common forms listed in Table 4.3. In this style of discourse, nearly every sentence is linked with an adverbial specifying the logical relationship to the other sentences in the discourse:

> **Text Sample 4.20:** Textbook, graduate business (economics; tbecn3.dec)
> Linking adverbials are <u>underlined.</u>
>
> <u>Hence,</u> from our theoretical standpoint, (2.5) suffers from the same drawbacks as does the Friedman model. Note, <u>however,</u> that the two models are not identical. [. . .] there is nothing in utility theory used as a descriptive device that precludes interactions between the behavior and tastes of different consumers. <u>On the contrary,</u> it seems unrealistic to suppose that preferences' are exogenous, God given, and unchangeable. <u>Rather</u> they are socially inherited and-conditioned and are governed by the conventions of technology and social institutions. <u>At the same time,</u> goods have social functions, particularly in communicating between people, see <u>for example</u> Becker <(1974)>. Individuals need to define themselves vis a vis others and to communicate these definitions so that they are treated as they would wish; a consumption life style is <u>thus</u> part of this definition of identity. Since belonging to certain social groups and not belonging to others is part of the sense of identity, it is inevitable that, to some extent, households will pattern their consumption and market behavior on that of other households. <u>Conversely,</u> there will be some kinds of behavior from which a household will consciously wish to dissociate itself.

## 4.8  Dependent clauses

Dependent clauses are often considered to be a type of linguistic complexity, and as a result, they have been associated with writing rather than speech. However, Figure 4.10 shows overall patterns of use that run exactly opposite to these prior expectations, with dependent clauses overall being more common in the spoken university registers than in the written registers. When we consider the different structural types of dependent clause, we find that the patterns are more complex: relative clauses are much more common in the written registers, while adverbial clauses and complement clauses are much more common in the spoken registers.

### 4.8.1  Relative clauses

Relative clauses have two primary functions: to specify the reference of the head noun, or to provide elaborating information. In many cases, a single relative clause will serve both functions. As Figure 4.10 shows, relative clauses are much more common in written university registers than in the spoken registers, as exemplified in the following.

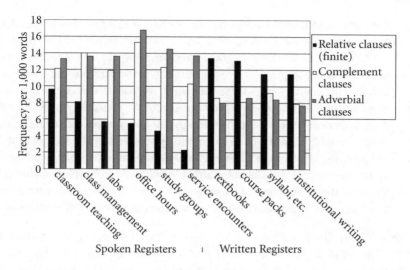

**Figure 4.10** Dependent clause types across registers

Relative clauses specifying the reference of the head noun:

> Each gene has a regulatory region upstream from the sequence **which determines the structure of the protein**. [Natural science textbook]

> In another detail from this manuscript are the same curious geometric rock forms **that we saw at Ajanta**. [Humanities textbook]

Relative clauses that provide elaborating information (in addition to specifying the reference of the head noun):

> This isolation from the effect of selection is also true of some introns and pseudogenes **[which are able to accumulate changes [which have no effect on either the phenotype of the organism or the function of the DNA]]**. [Natural science textbook]

> Most firms use hybrid structures, **in which two of the three departments typically report to the same executive**. [Business textbook]

In addition, there are also frequent 'reduced' (nonfinite) relative clauses in the written registers; these clauses often have passive voice verbs. The following textbook excerpt illustrates the dense use of both types of relative clause:

> **Text Sample 4.21a:** Textbook, graduate social science (tbsoc3.sjh)
> Finite relative clauses are in **bold**; passive voice nonfinite relative clauses are underlined

> As we shall see below, the structural components of the lifeworld become subsystems of a general system of action, **to which the physical substratum of the**

**lifeworld is reckoned along with the "behavior system."** The proposal **I am advancing here**, by contrast, attempts to take into account the methodological differences between the internalist and the externalist viewpoints <u>connected with the two conceptual strategies</u>. From the participant perspective of members of a lifeworld it looks as if sociology with a systems, theoretical orientation considers only one of the three components of the lifeworld, namely, the institutional system, **for which culture and personality merely constitute complementary environments**. From the observer perspective of systems theory, on the other hand, it looks as if lifeworld analysis confines itself to one societal subsystem <u>specialized in maintaining structural patterns</u> (pattern maintenance); in this view, the components of the lifeworld are merely internal differentiations of this subsystem **which specifies the parameters of societal self maintenance**.

Although relative clauses are a major feature distinguishing between spoken and written registers, they are also relatively common in some spoken registers. In particular, the academic classroom registers – classroom teaching and class management talk – use relative clauses to a greater extent than the interpersonal academic registers (labs, office hours, and study groups). The following text excerpt illustrates the relatively dense use of relative clauses in classroom teaching:

> **Text Sample 4.22:** Classroom teaching, upper division, natural science (natglleudln105)
> Finite relative clauses are in **bold**; sentence relatives are in ***bold italics***.
>
> So [. . .] eventually we're going to lose a lot of water **that's stored in the system**. Now, why is this an issue? Well, [. . .] you might be concerned with does Arizona have a water supply **which is sustainable** ***which means the general definition is will there be enough to meet the needs of the present without compromising the ability of the future to have the availability to have the same resources.*** [. . .]
> The Colorado river is no longer sustainable, the system **that used to depend on the discharge of the Colorado river down the gulf** is no longer sustainable. So I think it's really inappropriate term to call the Colorado river a sustainable resource. It may be for humans but it's not for other parts of the earth's systems **that were dependent on the Colorado river**. So we've got to think about all parts of our systems when we look at sustainability just not the human dimensions ***which is what this term safe yield considers.***

Many of the relative clauses in classroom teaching are 'sentence relatives'. These are actually a type of adverbial clause rather than a postnominal modifier (see LGSWE, p. 867). That is, sentence relatives provide a comment on a whole proposition, rather than modifying a particular head noun. Sentence relatives are often used for clarification, as in Sample 4.22 above. (The first sentence relative provides a

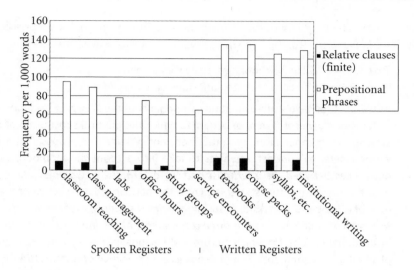

**Figure 4.11** Relative clauses and prepositional phrases across registers

definition of the term 'sustainable'; the second sentence relative clarifies the use of the term 'safe yield'.)

In addition, sentence relatives are often used to express personal attitudes, as in the following examples from classroom teaching:

> And underneath his clothes he had on a union suit, long underwear, one piece. [He] Stripped it off, used that as a rope, lowered it down to Powell, and pulled him up by his longjohns, OK? **Which I always thought was a great story**. [upper division humanities; humhileudmn084]

> Um, the way, it sounds, it's, not as much as it should be. Or, they would like it to be. **Which I guess is not saying a whole lot because that's always the way it is**. [upper division humanities; humenleudhi087]

The more frequent use of relative clauses in the written university registers is related to the general reliance on noun phrase structures in those registers (see Figures 4.1 and 4.2 above). Prepositional phrases are another feature that occurs commonly with noun phrases in informational, written prose. Similar to relative clauses, prepositional phrases are commonly used to modify a head noun, identifying the reference or providing elaborating information. However, as Figure 4.11 shows, prepositional phrases are actually much more common than relative clauses. (Prepositional phrases can also function as adverbials. However, their use as noun modifiers is considerably more common than their use as adverbials in expository written registers; see LGSWE Chapters 8 and 10.) Sample 4.21b repeats Sample 4.21a above, highlighting the use of prepositional phrases as nominal modifiers. The majority of these forms are *of*-phrases, but other prepositions (such as *with, between*) function in similar ways to modify a head noun.

> Text Sample 4.21b: Textbook, graduate social science
> Prepositional phrases as nominal modifiers are in **bold italics**.
>
> As we shall see below, the structural components ***of the lifeworld*** become subsystems ***of a general system of action***, to which the physical substratum ***of the lifeworld*** is reckoned along with the "behavior system." The proposal I am advancing here, by contrast, attempts to take into account the methodological differences ***between the internalist and the externalist viewpoints*** connected with the two conceptual strategies. From the participant perspective ***of members of a lifeworld*** it looks as if sociology ***with a systems, theoretical orientation*** considers only one ***of the three components of the lifeworld***, namely, the institutional system, for which culture and personality merely constitute complementary environments. From the observer perspective ***of systems theory***, on the other hand, it looks as if lifeworld analysis confines itself to one societal subsystem specialized in maintaining structural patterns (pattern maintenance); in this view, the components ***of the lifeworld*** are merely internal differentiations ***of this subsystem*** which specifies the parameters ***of societal self maintenance***.

Although they are less noticeable, prepositional phrases are much more pervasive than relative clauses in academic written registers. Further, because they are so compact, prepositional phrases are often used in sequence, resulting in highly complex noun phrases with multiple modifiers. The head nouns in these structures are often relatively general terms, while the important new descriptive information is usually provided in the following prepositional phrases. For example:

> This **patterning** [of behavior] [by households] [on other households] takes time.
>
> Each new **level** [of system differentiation] opens up **space** [for further increases [in complexity]], that is, [for additional functional specifications and a correspondingly more abstract integration [of the ensuing subsystems]].
>
> This may indeed be **part** [of the reason [for the statistical link [between schizophrenia and membership [in the lower socioeconomic classes]]]].

Learning to understand, and eventually to produce, such structures is one of the main linguistic challenges that students encounter as they progress through a university education and learn to deal with written academic registers.

## 4.8.2 Adverbial clauses

Unlike relative clauses, adverbial clauses are overall more common in spoken university registers than in the written registers (see Figure 4.10). There are many specific meanings expressed by adverbial clauses, depending on the choice of ad-

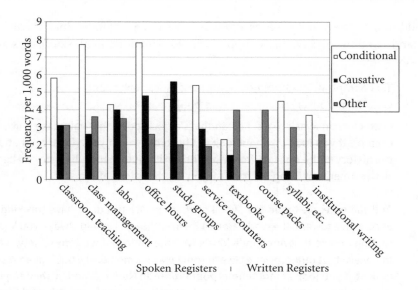

Figure 4.12 Breakdown of finite adverbial clause types across registers

verbial subordinator. The present analysis divides these into three major meaning domains: conditional (*if*), causative (*because*), and other (e.g., *after, before, while, until, as, since, so that*).

Figure 4.12 shows the breakdown of finite adverbial clauses across these semantic classes. Conditional clauses are by far the most common, especially in class management talk and in office hours. These registers can be very directive, and conditional clauses cushion the force of these directives by providing possible options and anticipating alternatives. For example:

> **Text Sample 4.23:** Office hours, business (busbaoh_n156)
> Conditional adverbial clauses are **in bold**.
>
> Instructor:   Now here's what you should do **if you want me to go over your graduation papers** you gotta do it this semester because **if you wait until the summer or the fall**
>
> Student:   uh huh
>
> Instructor:   then you'll have to go through somebody else and it'll just take longer
>
> Student:   yeah so I can do that then and what do I – do you just file
>
> Instructor:   go down to Rosemary's office and get the papers, two sets of papers one for the college of business and one for NAU.
>
> Student:   and I can do it now
>
> Instructor:   mhm you can do it this semester and **if she says no**, you tell her why
>
> Student:   OK [unclear]

In addition, office hour sessions often involve intensive individualized teaching, and conditional adverbials support the explanations in those discussions. For example:

> **Text Sample 4.24:** Office hours, business (socpooh_n222)
> Conditional adverbial clauses are **in bold**.
>
> Instructor: Um, yeah that's, I mean that's a good point that you make – like for example **if you look in**, **if you look in Chaco canyon**, **if you**, **if you read about the history of the Anasazi**, from what little of it I understand, uh, there had been, Native Americans living in Chaco canyon for, thousands of years
> [. . .]
> And some people argue that, you know other societies don't have this kind of perspective toward, the world around them, although I would always, you know, caution people that often individuals who are critical of western society, want to believe that other societies live in some way harmoniously, but I mean **if you look at**, **if you look at indigenous populations in Native America**, they engage in all kinds of desertification and they, I mean **if you, you know, why did Chaco canyon fail** well **if you go to Chaco canyon** and you talk to them, you'll find that they cut down all the trees in the area and that didn't help very much.

It is interesting to note that almost 50% of all conditional clauses in office hours begin with 'if you. . .'. In directive contexts, this is a polite way of telling the student what to do, but this form is used more commonly in teaching contexts, encouraging the student to adopt a particular point of view or supposition for the sake of the argument.

Among the written registers, conditional adverbial clauses are most common in written course management (syllabi, etc.) and in institutional writing. Many of these clauses also begin with 'if you' and serve directive functions similar to classroom management talk and office hours:

Examples from course management writing:

> None of the questions are intended to be tricky, please ask if you have questions.
>
> If you work in a group, be sure to indicate which student's input numbers you used.
>
> Show your work! If you don't show your work, or you have errors in the work, I may take off points even if you have the correct answer.

Examples from institutional writing:

> If you believe you qualify, obtain a Request for Application Fee Waiver form from the Graduate Center.
>
> If you have not completed the writing proficiency requirement at CSUS or another CSU campus, you should do so during your first semester. If you have

questions regarding when the writing proficiency exam is offered throughout the school year, contact the Testing Office or visit their home page.

Causative adverbial clauses are generally less common than conditionals. However, study groups are exceptional here: Figure 4.12 shows that causative adverbial clauses are actually more common than conditionals in this register. Students often partake in intense negotiations in study groups, and causative adverbial clauses are used to provide supporting arguments or justifications for proposed answers or explanations; for example:

> Text Sample 4.25: Study Group, natural science (natcmsgldgn016)
> Causative adverbial clauses are in **bold.**
> A: So it would be seconds squared times seconds
> B: yeah times seconds **because it should be joules seconds.**
> [. . .]
> A: Doesn't that just make it one second?
> B: Yeah he wants [unclear] yeah it makes it one second.
> A: OK.
> B: Yeah it makes it one second.
> A: Alright.
> B: **Because the one cancels it out over there.**
> A: OK
> B: There. **Cos that cancels th- cancels – cos the top, you're making this.**
> [. . .]
> A: Actually that I rounded it that's probably why I got a different answer. And then I multiplied that by one minute over sixty seconds and I got two point five minutes. Maybe its just cos of my rounding. [long pause] I think so **because I see I you have to ch- she told me to change miles**
> B: OK. So 3S would have
> A: So 3S would – could have most it no it could have at the most two electrons. **Cos in each orbital you can have the two.**

The 'other' adverbial clauses (e.g, *as, since, while*) are more common in the written registers, especially textbooks and course packs. Interestingly, these dependent clauses are often vague or imprecise, because they begin with adverbial subordinators that have multiple meanings. For example, the subordinator *as* can express manner, reason, or time meanings; the subordinator *since* expresses reason and time meanings; and the subordinator *while* expresses concession/contrast and time meanings (see LGSWE 846-50). Subordinators like *so that* and *such that* express the circumstances or result of an event. All of these subordinators are found most commonly in the written academic registers; the following examples are from textbooks:

As you will see in this chapter, many behavioral differences among organisms, both within and across species, correspond to genetic and other biological differences.

The process continues interminably, as the signifiers lead a chameleon-like existence, changing their colours with each new context.

For one thing, such an agreement could be very costly since similar agreements would have to be negotiated with all users.

The sparse matrix can be represented as a graph, such that each node represents a row or column of the matrix [. . .]

In addition, non-finite adverbial clauses – especially *to*-clauses expressing purpose meanings – are found more commonly in the written registers; the following examples are from a course pack:

In order to understand designs you will need to learn their explanations as well as their identifications.

To really understand a design we must make sure we are thinking about what it was intended to be. . .

### 4.8.3  Complement clauses

Similar to adverbial clauses, complement clauses are considerably more common in the spoken university registers than in the written registers. In fact, Figure 4.10 (above) shows that complement clauses are even more common than adverbial clauses in the interactive spoken registers (office hours, study groups, and service encounters).

When we consider the different types of complement clause, we find a more complicated pattern. Figure 4.13 shows that the overall greater frequency of complement clauses in speech is mostly due to a single clause type: *that*-clauses. WH-clauses are also much more common in speech than in writing, but the overall frequencies of WH-clauses are much lower than *that*-clauses. In contrast, *to*-clauses are about equally common in the spoken and written registers.

Most of these complement clauses are controlled by verbs. *That*-clauses and *to*-clauses controlled by adjectives and nouns have much lower frequencies, and they have the opposite distribution: more frequent in the written registers.

There are even more specific differences in the use of complement clauses across registers. For example, in office hours *that*-clauses usually occur without the complementizer *that*; the controlling clause usually has the pronoun *I* as subject; and the main verb is *think, mean,* or *guess.* These constructions are used to

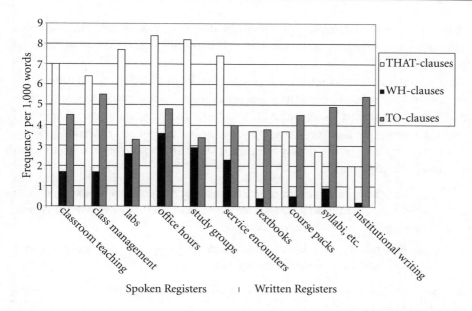

Spoken Registers    ˌ    Written Registers

**Figure 4.13**  Breakdown of complement clause types across registers

express a generalized kind of hedging or lack of certainty about the proposition contained in the *that*-clause:

> **Text Sample 4.26:** Office Hour, natural science (natgloh_n003)
> *That*-clauses are marked in [ ]; the controlling main clause is <u>underlined</u>; <0> marks omitted complementizers.
>
> Student:    <u>I mean</u> [<0> if you were going to be running the test for four days you'd look at it for four days] and <u>I think</u> [<0> that's what you said in class] <u>is</u> [that you should do it at least as long as you're going to run the test].
>
> Instructor:    Yeah .. yeah <u>I guess</u> [<0> <u>I just hadn't seen</u> when I read it [that um you defined those two things very well] ], but um but um <u>I guess</u> [<0> you could have meant that].
>
> [. . .]
>
> Student:    P4 is right here, which is pretty close to the D2. Yeah D9. So <u>I think</u> [<0> those are the only ones that match]. The only P that's on here is P, well P3 and P4.
>
> Instructor:    mhm, and where are they plotted on your paper?
>
> Student:    There's P4. <u>I think</u> [<0> that's the only one on there].

*That*-clauses have somewhat different characteristics in classroom teaching: the complementizer *that* is usually retained, and the complement clauses occur with a much larger set of controlling verbs in the main clause (e.g., *argue, assume, believe, claim, decide, feel, find, hope, mean, notice, realize, see, show, think*). Three of these controlling verbs are especially common in classroom teaching: *know, say*, and the copula *BE*.

The combination *know* + *that*-clause in classroom teaching is used most commonly with the subject pronouns *we* or *you*. This structure introduces statements that have the status of background information. That is, the statements have the implicit assumption that they do not require further supporting evidence. In some cases, these statements are simply reminding students about information that has previously been presented:

> We don't like to work with conductances or admittances, we like to work with resistances, and impedances, but sometimes we have to work with the other one, we – you know [that conductance is one over R].

> If we're talking about break-even in units, we know [that each one of the units has a contribution margin of twenty-four dollars].

In other cases, these constructions are used to identify cultural background knowledge that students should share:

> Now we know [that in our classrooms that kids come to the classroom from many different homes].

> Most of you know [that once, once a trial is underway jurors are not supposed to discuss the case among themselves until the point of deliberation]

In the above examples, the instructor presents the information in the *that*-clause as if it were established fact that the students should already know. Because it has this function, instructors can further exploit this complement clause construction to present their own knowledge and beliefs, giving the statements the status of accepted fact that should not be challenged, even in cases where the student might not already 'know' the proposition. For example:

> Now we know [that multi-ethnic literature is important for students from all backgrounds]. We know [that multi-ethnic literature helps students of diverse backgrounds gain pride and confidence . . .]

> Are people really always reporting accurately what's happened? Well we know [that varies a lot depending on the nature of the survey, the kinds of questions asked, even the way the questions are worded].

*That*-clauses controlled by the verb *SAY* have somewhat different functions. In most spoken registers, these constructions are used to simply report what someone has 'said', as in the following example from a study group (reconstructing what the instructor had said in class):

> She said [we have until the last week to get it done].

However, in classroom teaching, *say* + *that*-clause is usually used in to rephrase an idea or to present a hypothetical position, rather than actually reporting previous speech:

> if I value something as a means to something else, <u>we could also say</u> [that is has instrumental value]

> if I were to combine all of those together add all those numbers up <u>we can say</u> [that the series combination of all those resistors together behaves in exactly the same way]

> Look if you want to compare it <u>you can say</u> [that um the rate of female uh victimization by homicide is about one point five per hundred thousand.

> So let me start to ask you some questions along these lines – <u>let's say</u> [that we know that these are social perception categories] – <u>let's say</u> [<0> we haven't been particularly effective in the past] and <u>let's say</u> [<0> we're trying to make change in schools relative to working with these kids] – why is change coming so . . hard? why is change so slow?

The copula *BE* is also extremely common as a controlling verb with *that*-clauses in classroom teaching. This construction is used for information packaging and the expression of 'stance': The subject of the main clause identifies the status of the information (e.g., an 'explanation', 'argument', or 'claim'), and then the new information itself is presented in the *that*-clause following *BE*. For example,

> <u>An alternative explanation is</u> [that muscle movement may simply be an overflow from a cortex].

> <u>The other argument is</u> [that people moved around in mass like they do now]

> <u>The basic claim is</u> [that these unlearned behaviors that are relatively universal within a species are instincts].

> <u>Sartre's point here is</u> [that we confront the world in a questioning mode]

> but <u>the only issue here that we're talking about is</u> [that observability depends only on the A matrix and the C matrix]

In textbooks and course packs, *that*-clauses occur with lower frequencies, but they are used with a wider array of different controlling verbs. For example, the following verbs all occur with moderate frequencies controlling *that*-clauses in course packs: *admit, argue, assert, assume, believe, claim, conclude, decide, demonstrate, estimate, find, imply, is, know, maintain, mean, note, realize, recognize, remember, report, require, say, show, state, suggest, suppose, think, understand.* That-clauses are comparatively rare in course management writing and institutional writing.

WH-clauses are generally less common than *that*-clauses, but they are similar to *that*-clauses in being primarily a feature of spoken registers. WH-clauses are especially common in office hours, occurring with controlling verbs like *believe, explain, know, remember,* and *see*:

> You know [what I'm saying]?
>
> I didn't know [how to put together the points], well cos that's [what you gave me] and I I I didn't I didn't know [how to connect em].

The verb *BE* is the most common form controlling WH-clauses in office hours. This construction usually occurs with a demonstrative pronoun as subject and functions to focus attention on the new information contained in the WH-clause:

> Ah, OK. So we need to, OK, so this is [what we needed to do].
>
> So what things were important to us? Well one of the things was naval power, and that's [why we had that conference], to help control naval power.

*To*-complement clauses are relatively common in both spoken and written registers. They are most common in the directive registers which share the primary purpose of telling students what they should be doing: classroom management, course syllabi and assignments (written course management), and institutional writing. *To*-clauses are actually one of the major linguistic devices used for giving directives. However, the specific forms used vary across registers.

In spoken classroom management, only a few verbs are commonly used controlling a *to*-clause – *get, is, would like, try/trying,* and especially *want*:

> You're supposed to make a survey, an interview, to get [to know a child]. Next September, you're gonna have twenty-five charges in front of you. Lisa, when the kid walks in the room, you're gonna have to get [to know the child].
>
> and so one of the last, uh topic or the last requirement is [to do a movie review]
>
> Uh what I would like [to do with you today] is try [to jump ahead about one week and get caught up].
>
> I want [to remind you again that Tuesday we will not be meeting]
>
> You might want [to jot this will down for future reference].
>
> For next class I want you [to do two things], and we can start talking about them today.

Most of these same verbs can also be found controlling *to*-clauses in written course management and institutional writing (except the verb *get* + *to*-clause, which is restricted to speech). Of these, the copula *be* is especially common with this function in the written directive registers.

Course syllabi and assignments:

> Your job is [to explain the code as fully as possible].

> Attempting the homework is one way to gain practice and confidence in the material. <u>Another way is</u> [to attempt homework problems not assigned].

Institutional writing:

> <u>The goal of the program is</u> [to help keep students in the University through graduation].

> <u>The purpose of our doctoral residency requirement is</u> [to provide you with opportunities for conferences, seminars . . .]

This construction functions in a similar way to other complement clause constructions controlled by the copula *BE*. In this case, the grammatical subject identifies how this information is relevant to the student (e.g., *your job, the goal, the purpose*), while the new information is given in the *to*-clause following *BE*.

Many other verbs can control *to*-clauses in the written registers, with similar directive functions, including: *choose, continue, desire, expect, fail, intend, plan, seek,* and *wish*.

Course syllabi and assignments:

> <u>Students should expect</u> [to spend approximately six to eight hours each week. . .]

> <u>You may choose</u> [to work with her book and your questions, probings, and ponderings of what she has to say].

Institutional writing:

> <u>You should not plan</u> [to support yourself by working while enrolled].

> International <u>students who desire</u> [to pay all or a portion of their non resident tuition fees on the installment plan] must visit the CSUS Billing Services Office. <u>Students wishing</u> [to pay on an installment basis] <u>will be required</u> [to execute an agreement at the time of registration at the Billing Services Office].

> Biological Sciences <u>majors who intend</u> [to pursue a teaching credential] must complete the science subject matter program which is described in this catalog. [. . .] <u>The Science Teaching Credential allows</u> graduates [to teach all four of the sciences . . .]

Passive verbs are also common controlling *to*-clauses in the written directive registers: *be allowed, be asked, be authorized, be designed, be encouraged, be expected, be intended, be permitted, be required*.

Course syllabi and assignments:

> <u>You are encouraged</u> [to take advantage of this service].

> <u>Students are expected</u> [to arrange their schedules to leave time for the all too normal delays that one encounters on Atlanta's highways].

> <u>You are required</u> [to attend all of the final project oral presentations].

Institutional writing:

> <u>All students are invited</u> [to become involved with the student media organizations on campus].
>
> <u>All new international students are required</u> [to attend a formal orientation program just before the beginning of the semester; <u>the program is designed</u> [to welcome you to the University . . .]
>
> <u>All students are required</u> [to earn a high school diploma on or before their original graduation date . . .]

I return to the directive functions of these complement clause constructions in Chapter 5, which focuses on the expression of stance in university registers. Similarly, complement clauses controlled by nouns and adjectives are used mostly to express stance, and so they are also described in Chapter 5.


## 4.9  Chapter summary

This chapter has surveyed linguistic differences across university registers and disciplines with respect to a number of grammatical and syntactic features. Additional descriptions of individual linguistic features are provided in the investigations of stance (Chapter 5) and lexical bundles (Chapter 6). Chapter 7, then, investigates how these linguistic features work together to define systematic patterns of variation among university registers.

The present chapter has shown that even at the level of basic grammatical features – content word classes; noun and verb semantic categories; variations in verb tense, aspect, and voice; discourse connectives, and dependent clause types – different registers and different disciplines at the university manipulate the linguistic resources of English in quite different ways, reflecting a range of important functional considerations.

CHAPTER 5

# The expression of stance
# in university registers

## 5.1 Introduction

Many of the lexico-grammatical features described in Chapter 4 can be used to indicate the personal **stance** of the speaker or writer: 'personal feelings, attitudes, value judgements, or assessments' (LGSWE, p. 966). Stance expressions can convey many different kinds of personal feelings and assessments, including attitudes that a speaker has about information, how certain they are about its veracity, how they obtained access to the information, and what perspective they are taking.

According to one idealized representation of university language, there would be no need for stance expressions. Rather, lecturers and textbook writers would communicate only the facts and propositional information that students need to know. However, this ideal is far from reality; in fact, in some cases speakers and writers in university registers seem more concerned with the expression of stance than with the communication of 'facts'.

Considering the goals of academic registers helps to explain why stance is centrally important in these registers. A crucial aspect of liberal education is the ability to assess the status of information, being able to discriminate among a host of epistemic distinctions, from 'speculation' to 'fact'. These distinctions reflect the reliability of a statement, as well as the possibility that statements are offered from a particular perspective. In addition, instructors and authors take advantage of their positions of power to convey their own opinions and attitudes. Thus, in addition to simply conveying propositional information, teachers shape the ways that students approach knowledge, helping them to assess how statements are to be interpreted (e.g., whether they should be adopted as fact, criticized, or understood from a particular perspective).

Over the last several years, linguists have become increasingly interested in the linguistic mechanisms used by speakers and writers to convey their personal feelings and assessments. Such investigations have been carried out under several different labels, including 'evaluation' (Hunston 1994; Hunston & Thompson 2000), 'intensity' (Labov 1984), 'affect' (Ochs 1989), 'evidentiality' (Chafe 1986; Chafe & Nichols 1986), 'hedging' (Hyland 1996a, b, 1998), 'modality' (Palmer

1986; Bybee & Fleischman 1995), and 'stance' (Barton 1993; Beach & Anson 1992; Biber & Finegan 1988, 1989; Biber et al. 1999: Chapter 12; Conrad & Biber 2000; Precht 2000, 2003). Other studies in this area have taken a diachronic perspective, either documenting the patterns of use in a particular historical period (e.g., Fitzmaurice 2002, 2003; Kytö 1991; Myhill 1995, 1997), or tracking historical patterns of change across periods (e.g., Biber 2004a, b; Biber, Conrad, & Reppen 1998: Chapter 8; Krug 2000; Leech 2003). These investigations of personal expression have been conducted with a variety of complementary methodologies, ranging from detailed descriptions of a single text sample to empirical investigations of general patterns in large computer-based corpora.

The present description of stance adopts the framework developed in LGSWE, Chapter 12. Section 5.2 below summarizes the major aspects of that analytical framework. Then, Section 5.3 uses that framework to survey the use of stance features across university registers, while Section 5.4 describes the overall stance of selected registers.

## 5.2  A framework for the study of stance

### 5.2.1  Grammatical, lexical, and paralinguistic marking of stance

Stance can be expressed to differing extents through grammatical devices, value-laden word choice, and paralinguistic devices (see LGSWE, p. 966–969). Grammatically marked stance – the focus of the present chapter – is overt, where a distinct grammatical structure is used to express stance with respect to some other proposition. For example, two common grammatical devices used to mark stance are adverbials and complement clause constructions. Stance adverbials express the attitude or assessment of the speaker/writer with respect to the proposition contained in the matrix clause. The following examples are from study groups:

> **Obviously** the money has to come from somewhere and they're not getting it from selling Girl Scout cookies.
>
> **Unfortunately** it's not a matter of what we decide.

With complement clauses, the matrix clause verb expresses a stance with respect to the proposition in the complement clause:

> I **doubt** [that there will be a lot on the test].
> I **hope** [we do better on this test].

A different kind of stance can be conveyed through value-laden word choice, as in:

> Oh my gosh I **hate** this stuff.
> I **love** this dictionary.

Affective or evaluative word choice differs from grammatical stance marking in that it involves only a single proposition. If I say *I love this dictionary*, I am not communicating any other information apart from my love for the dictionary. With such value-laden words, the existence of a stance is inferred from the use of an evaluative lexical item, usually an adjective, main verb, or noun. In contrast, grammatical stance marking involves the expression of stance relative to some other proposition. For example, if I say *I doubt that there will be a lot on the test*, I am communicating a proposition – *there will be a lot on the test* – and also expressing my stance towards that proposition (in this case 'doubt').

Many of the most common words in English are evaluative and used for lexical expressions of stance. For example, the most common predicative adjectives in conversation include *good*, *nice*, *right*, and *sure* (see LGSWE, 516–518, 968). These forms are typically used to express positive feelings about the general situation (usually referred to with a pronoun), as in:

> Yeah that's very **good.**
> Yeah that's **right**.
> We don't have to know the chapter eight names, which is kind of **nice.**

Some of these same forms can also be used as attributive adjectives to express some evaluation of the head noun:

> They were very **good** people at that time.

At one level, almost any choice among related words can be seen as evaluative. Such lexical expressions of stance depend on the context and shared background for their interpretation. There is nothing in the grammatical structure of these expressions to show that they mark stance. Rather, stance is embedded in these structures, depending on the addressee's ability to recognize the use of value-laden words. In contrast, grammatical stance marking includes two distinct grammatical components, one presenting a personal stance, and the other presenting a proposition that is framed by that stance.

In addition to grammatical stance and value-laden word choice, stance can be conveyed through paralinguistic devices. In speech, paralinguistic devices include pitch, intensity, and duration, which can be coupled with other modifications of articulation (such as hissing or whispering). Paralinguistic devices can also be accompanied by non-linguistic indicators of stance, such as body position, facial expressions, and gestures. In writing, the resources for paralinguistic marking of stance are much more limited, including italics, bold face, or underlining. Writers can also use manner of speaking adverbs to suggest a paralinguistic stance. In the T2K-SWAL Corpus, these adverbs are rare; the following examples are from textbooks:

> Nixon **angrily** denounced the votes. . .
> Some Marxists have quarreled **bitterly** over purely theoretical issues. . .

The descriptions below focus exclusively on the grammatical marking of stance. While value-laden word choice and paralinguistic devices can also reflect underlying attitudes or feelings, they are less explicit and they do not overtly express an evaluative frame for some other proposition. Further, it is extremely difficult to operationalize value-laden word choice. Nearly any word could be analyzed as reflecting an evaluation, making it hard to identify a closed set of words used to convey specific attitudes and evaluations. For these reasons, lexical and paralinguistic stance marking are excluded from the descriptions in 5.3 and 5.4.

### 5.2.2 Attribution of stance

A second limitation of the analysis here is that it focuses only on devices that can be interpreted as direct expressions of speaker/writer stance. Grammatical stance devices range along a continuum, from those that are explicitly attributed to the speaker/writer (1st person), to those that are explicitly attributed to a 2nd or 3rd person. Stance structures with a 1st person subject are the most overt expressions of speaker/author stance:

> 1st person pronoun + stance verb + *that*-clause:
> **I know** I'm going to hit my knee on that thing.
> **I hope** you guys slept in separate tents.

> 1st person pronoun + stance adjective + *that*-clause:
> **We are becoming increasingly certain** that the theory has far reaching implications. . .

In addition, stance structures with a 1st person object, or even a 1st person possessive pronoun, can often be attributed directly to the speaker/author:

> Stance adjective + *me* + *to*-clause:
> That'd be **good for me** to do.

> Stance adjective or stance verb + *me* + complement clauses:
> It was **interesting to me** that this sort of big deal public lecture thing **seemed to me** to be the least well thought out.

> *Our* + stance noun + *to*-clause:
> This reemergence represents an increase of **our ability** to detect and identify infections

In contrast, stance expressions that are attributed to the addressee (2nd person) or to a 3rd person are excluded from the study. Although such structures express some kind of attitude or evaluation, they do not necessarily reflect the personal stance of the speaker/writer. For example:

> Do **you think** we'll get this on the test?
> Yeah I know **you want** to condense it down to a title.
> **She didn't realize** that you are a stranger.
> **They needed** to rebuild the entire government system.

In between these two extremes are a number of grammatical stance devices with no explicit attribution; in many cases, the normal inference is that these devices express the stance of the speaker/writer. These devices include modal verbs, stance adverbials, and extraposed complement clauses. For example:

> Modal verb:
> Accountants **should** be more accurate.
> Both of those things **might** be true.

> Stance adverbial (with modal verb):
> **Maybe** someone mentioned this in speaking about it.
> **Probably** there **might** be some homework assigned.

> Stance adjective controlling extraposed *to*-clause:
> **It seems fairly obvious** to most people that Watson tremendously oversimplified the learning process.
> **It is important** to distinguish between describing sensations using modality and duration and intensity and decomposing sensation into those.

The present study includes analysis of these implicit devices that are readily attributed to the speaker/writer, in addition to more explicit expressions of grammatical stance.

## 5.2.3 Stance features included in the present study

Grammatical stance devices have two main elements: the stance marker and the proposition that the stance marker frames. Grammatical stance devices come from different structural levels: they can be words (e.g. *unfortunately*), phrases (e.g. *in all probability*), or clauses (e.g. *as we all know*).

The analysis here focuses on three major structural categories: modal verbs (and semi-modals), stance adverbs, and stance complement clauses. Table 5.1 lists the most common controlling words included in each of these categories. The actual analyses include all controlling words that occurred commonly in the LSWE Corpus (taken from the LGSWE, Chapter 12), as well as any other words that were attested in the T2K-SWAL Corpus with this function.

**Table 5.1** Common lexico-grammatical features used for the stance analyses

1.    **Modal and semi-modal verbs** (See LGSWE, pp. 483ff.)

    –    possibility/permission/ability: *can, could, may, might*
    –    necessity/obligation: *must, should, (had) better, have to, got to, ought to*
    –    prediction/volition: *will, would, shall, be going to*

2.    **Stance adverbs** (See LGSWE, pp. 557–558; 853–874)

    –    **Epistemic:**
        **Certainty:** *actually, always, certainly, definitely, indeed, inevitably, in fact, never, of course, obviously, really, undoubtedly, without doubt, no doubt*
        **Likelihood:** *apparently, evidently, kind of, in most cases/instances, perhaps, possibly, predictably, probably, roughly, sort of, maybe*
    –    **Attitude:** *amazingly, astonishingly, conveniently, curiously, hopefully, even worse, fortunately, importantly, ironically, rightly, sadly, surprisingly, unfortunately*
    –    **Style:** *according to, confidentially, frankly, generally, honestly, mainly, technically, truthfully, typically, reportedly, primarily, usually*

3.    **Complement clauses controlled by stance verbs, adjectives, or nouns**
3.1.    **Stance complement clauses controlled by verbs**
3.1a.    **Stance verb + *that*-clause** (See LGSWE, pp. 661–670)

    –    **Epistemic verbs:**
        **Certainty:** *conclude, demonstrate, determine, discover, find, know, learn, mean, notice, observe, prove, realize, recognize, remember, see, show, understand*
        **Likelihood:** *assume, believe, doubt, gather, guess, hypothesize, imagine, predict, presuppose, presume, reckon, seem, speculate, suppose, suspect, think*
    –    **Attitude verbs:** *agree, anticipate, complain, concede, ensure, expect, fear, feel, forget, hope, mind, prefer, pretend, require, wish, worry*
    –    **Speech act and other communication verbs:** *announce, argue, assert, claim, contend, declare, emphasize, explain, imply, insist, mention, promise, propose, recommend, remark, respond, say, state, suggest, tell*

3.1b.    **Stance verb + *to*-clause** (See LGSWE, pp. 693–715)

    –    **Probability (likelihood) verbs:** *appear, happen, seem, tend*
    –    **Cognition/perception verbs (likelihood):** *assume, believe, consider, expect, find, forget, imagine, judge, know, learn, presume, pretend, remember, suppose*
    –    **Desire/intention/decision verbs:** *agree, choose, decide, hate, hesitate, hope, intend, like, love, mean, need, plan, prefer, prepare, refuse, want, wish*
    –    **Verbs of causation/modality/effort:** *allow, attempt, enable, encourage, fail, help, instruct, manage, oblige, order, permit, persuade, prompt, require, seek, try*
    –    **Speech act and other communication verbs:** *ask, claim, invite, promise, remind, request, be said, show, teach, tell, urge, warn*

**Table 5.1** (*continued*)

**3.2.  Stance complement clauses controlled by adjectives**

**3.2a.  Stance adjective +** *that*-**clause** (See LGSWE, pp. 671–674; many of these occur with extraposed constructions)

- **Epistemic adjectives:**
  **Certainty:** *apparent, certain, clear, confident, convinced, correct, evident, false, impossible, inevitable, obvious, positive, right, sure, true, well-known*
  **Likelihood** (extraposed): *doubtful, likely, possible, probable, unlikely*
- **Attitude/emotion adjectives:** *afraid, amazed, aware, concerned, disappointed, encouraged, glad, happy, hopeful, pleased, shocked, surprised, worried*
- **Evaluation adjectives:** *amazing, appropriate, conceivable, crucial, essential, fortunate, imperative, inconceivable, incredible, interesting, lucky, necessary, nice, noteworthy, odd, ridiculous, strange, surprising, unacceptable, unfortunate*

**3.2b.  Stance adjective +** *to*-**clause** (See LGSWE, pp. 716–721; many of these occur with extraposed constructions)

- **Epistemic (certainty/likelihood) adjectives:** *apt, certain, due, guaranteed, liable, likely, prone, unlikely, sure*
- **Attitude/emotion adjectives:** *afraid, ashamed, disappointed, embarrassed, glad, happy, pleased, proud, puzzled, relieved, sorry, surprised, worried*
- **Evaluation adjectives:** *(in)appropriate, bad/worse, good/better/best, convenient, essential, important, interesting, necessary, nice, reasonable, silly, smart, stupid, surprising, useful, useless, unreasonable, wise, wrong*
- **Ability or willingness adjectives:** *(un)able, anxious, careful, determined, eager, eligible, hesitant, inclined, obliged, prepared, ready, reluctant, (un)willing*
- **Ease or difficulty adjectives:** *difficult, easier, easy, hard, (im)possible, tough*

**3.3.  Stance complement clauses controlled by nouns**

**3.3a.  Stance noun +** *that*-**clause** (See LGSWE, pp. 648–651)

- **Epistemic nouns:**
  **Certainty:** *assertion, conclusion, conviction, discovery, doubt, fact, knowledge, observation, principle, realization, result, statement*
  **Likelihood:** *assumption, belief, claim, contention, feeling, hypothesis, idea, implication, impression, notion, opinion, possibility, presumption, suggestion*
- **Attitude/perspective nouns:** *grounds, hope, reason, view, thought*
- **Communication (non-factual) nouns:** *comment, news, proposal, proposition, remark, report, requirement*

**3.3b.  Stance noun +** *to*-**clause** (See LGSWE, pp. 652–653)
  *agreement, decision, desire, failure, inclination, intention, obligation, opportunity, plan, promise, proposal, reluctance, responsibility, right, tendency, threat, wish, willingness*

Within each structural category, I distinguish among several semantic classes expressing particular kinds of stance. To the extent possible, I have tried to use the same semantic distinctions for the different linguistic types of stance. For example, epistemic meanings (certainty and likelihood) can be expressed by stance adverbs; the verbs, adjectives, and nouns controlling *that*-clauses; and the verbs and adjectives controlling *to*-clauses:

> **Epistemic – certainty and likelihood – stance devices**
>
> Adverb:
> That's **certainly** a major cause of absenteeism.
> Now these schools might **possibly** be able to afford this special fund.
>
> Verb + *that*-clause:
> Lashly **found** [that retention of a maze habit is directly proportional to the amount of brain tissue remaining after extirpation].
> Therefore there is no reason to **suspect** [that the two means are different].
>
> Adjective + *that*-clause:
> It is **evident** [that by 1925 Gandhi had fully worked out his approach to, and explanation of, the text].
> If there is inflation, and the cost of the automobile goes up, then it's quite **likely** [that the interest rate will also go up].
>
> Noun + *that*-clause:
> Supporting the experimenters' quantitative results was their general **observation** [that the town dwellers were noticeably more friendly and less suspicious than the city dwellers].
> There's some **indication** [that prenatal development has an influence on life-span development].
>
> Verb + *to*-clause:
> Our best evidence **seems** [to suggest that if you control for size, the more international you are, the less risk you have].
>
> Adjective + *to*-clause:
> These "control failures" are **certain** [to happen occasionally].

Similarly, attitudes and evaluations can be expressed by stance devices from several different grammatical types:

> **Attitude and evaluation stance devices**
>
> Adverb:
> **Amazingly** the archivists at the national archives are under a extreme amount of pressure.
>
> Verb + *that*-clause:
> I really **hope** [that it doesn't take that long to put the whole thing together].
>
> Adjective + *that*-clause:
> We are **pleased** [that you are considering graduate study at Northern Arizona University].

Adjective + *to*-clause:
Jane's question is not **appropriate** [to discuss in marketing class].

In addition, there are some more specific stance meanings expressed by these devices. For example, communication verbs (e.g., *say, ask, tell*) controlling complement clauses are included as a kind of stance because they distance the speaker/writer from the truth of the proposition in the complement clause. That is, this proposition presents new information, but it is packaged as what somebody else reported, rather than as a direct unmodified assertion. Further, the specific choice of communication verb implies differing degrees of commitment to that proposition. For example, compare:

In 1986 Harding **asserted** [that a shared assumption in feminist scholarship and practice was that there existed multiple feminist standpoints].

Some analysts **contend** [that while position diagrams are satisfactory tools for analysis when options are European, this is not true when options are American].

## 5.3 Distribution and functions of stance features

The frequency of the three major structural classes of stance features is shown in Figure 5.1. In general, stance is overtly marked to a greater extent in the spoken registers than the written registers. Modal verbs are used much more frequently than the other markers of stance, but stance adverbs and stance complement clauses also occur more commonly in the spoken registers than in the written registers.

At the same time, Figure 5.1 indicates that the use of stance features sometimes cuts across the spoken/written distinction, instead being associated with particular communicative purposes. For example, the directive registers in both spoken and written modes – classroom management and course management (syllabi, etc.) – make extensive use of stance features, especially modal verbs. These patterns are discussed further in the sections below.

### 5.3.1 Modal verbs as stance markers

As noted above, modal verbs are by far the most common grammatical device used to mark stance in university registers (see Figure 5.1). Modals are especially common in the spoken registers, but they also show a strong association with directive purposes, whether in speech (class management) or in writing (course management: syllabi, homework assignments, etc.).

Figure 5.2 shows that there are several interesting differences in the use of particular modal classes across registers. Prediction/volition modals (e.g., *will, would*) are the most common modal class, although the possibility/permission/ability

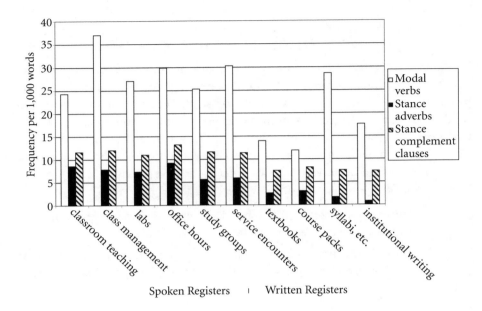

**Figure 5.1** Major stance features across registers

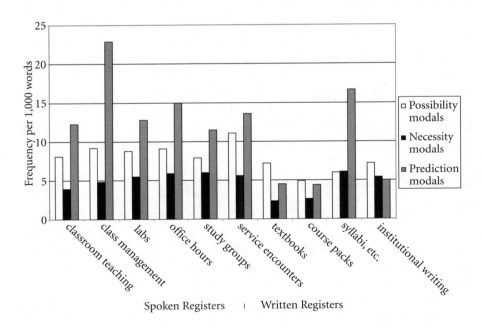

**Figure 5.2** Modal verb classes across registers

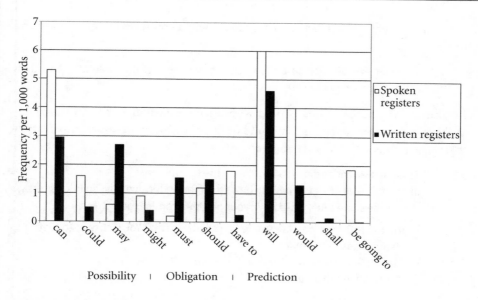

**Figure 5.3**  Modal and semi-modal verbs across modes

modals (e.g., *can, could*) are also very common in the spoken registers (especially service encounters). In textbooks, the possibility modals are actually the most common class, although modals overall are less common than in the spoken registers. The necessity/obligation modals (e.g., *must, should*) are the least common class overall. However, institutional writing is especially interesting in this regard, where the necessity/obligation modals account for nearly 1/3 of all modals.

Figure 5.3 provides more detailed information, comparing the rate of occurrence for each individual modal verb between spoken registers (all registers combined) and written registers. Prediction/volition modals are especially common in class management and written course management (syllabi, etc.), accounting for the exceptionally frequent use of modal verbs overall in those two registers. Figure 5.3 shows that the modal *will* is especially common, but the modal *would* is also extremely common in the spoken registers. The semi-modal *be going to* is considerably less common and restricted primarily to the spoken registers.

In most cases, the modal *will* is used to announce future class actions/events, as in:

> When we get into chapter seventeen we **will** start talking about something called the pecking order theory of raising money.

These verb phrases often occur with personal subjects, referring directly to the instructor's own intended future actions or to events that the students will be experiencing (e.g., *we will not be meeting, you'll get your final exam*). *Will* also occurs with impersonal subjects serving the same general function of announcing future events:

> So, what I've decided to do is have the peer review on – Monday and then assignment six **will** be due Tuesday.

In contrast, the modal *would* is used with a counterfactual future meaning, describing future events/actions that could occur, but with no necessary implication that those events actually will happen:

> Student: Depends what you require on the take-home.
> Instructor: Well, it **would** have to be a little more extensive than an in-class essay. Um, at the same time, you'd have your notes in front of you.

> Instructor: Is that what you want to be called? – Scott? You'll answer to that?
> Student: I'll answer to that.
> Instructor: But what **would** you prefer? He-man?!
> Student: Um, no that's all right.

Most instances of *would* in classroom management occur with a first person subject (*I*) and have a specific directive function. The directive force is very polite and indirect, because of the counterfactual underlying meaning, but the speaker (usually the instructor) clearly intends that these utterances be understood as directives. This pattern occurs most commonly with the main verb *like* and the modal *would* contracted to the grammatical subject: (*I'd*):

> I**'d** like you to bring some food.

> I**'d** like for you to do problem 1-A.

> I**'d** like you to review your quizzes, your mid terms immediately, and let me know if we did something wrong.

However, a wide range of main verbs expressing desire or encouragement co-occur with *would* expressing a directive function; for example:

> I **would** encourage you to add this to your stack of materials.

> I **would** suggest reading it.

> I **would** prefer actually if we could try to find an evening where everybody could get together at my house.

> OK, I**'d** also recommend reading all these books vertically.

The modal *will* can similarly be used in directives, but the underlying force is less polite and more direct. While *would* has an underlying counterfactual force, *will* simply announces future events/actions, implying that it is a foregone conclusion that the actor (i.e. the student) intends to carry out the action:

Um, on the tenth you **will** do chapters nine and ten.

Um. After, well, let me do the days here. So, Monday, on the first of March, these people **will** be here. And, the first five people **will** speak. And in this order. Andy **will** be speaking first. . .

Service encounters differ from classroom management in that possibility modals are nearly as common as prediction modals. *Can* is the modal most commonly used for requests in this register. In some cases, *can* clearly questions whether something is possible:

Hey. I need to pay for my registration and dorm. **Can** I pay for both here?

In other cases, though, there seems to be an expectation of compliance, although the use of *can* acknowledges that the request might not be granted:

Student: Hi **can** I get an application?
Service provider: Sure.

The modal *can* readily shifts between possibility and permission meanings in service encounters; the following example is from the front office for a dormitory:

Student: Hi, **can** I get toilet paper? [possibility/ability]
Service provider: Yeah
Student: **Can** I just take these?      [permission]
Service provider: Yeah go for it

In many cases, it is difficult to distinguish between possibility and ability meanings of *can*:

Service provider: OK. This one's, marked that it's due back on the fifteenth. I **can** check it in and then check it out.
Student: **Can** you do that?
Service provider: Sure.
Student: Yeah do that so I that I **can** bring it back either Friday or –
Service provider: OK and **can** I get your I.D.?
Student: Yeah. And I **can** bring them back either, tomorrow late evening or, Friday?

In textbooks, the possibility/permission/ability modals are by far the most common class, with *can* and *may* being especially common. The modal *may* is one of two modal verbs that occurs more commonly in writing than in speech (see Figure 5.3). Although both *can* and *may* tend to occur with inanimate subjects, they differ in their typical functions: the modal *can* often expresses both ability and possibility meanings, while *may* usually expresses only possibility meanings.

> The origins of such misperceptions **can** be traced back to the comprehension stage of information processing.
>
> International negotiation **can** also help to avoid a trade war.
>
> Discrete MOS **can** occur at a variety of locations.

versus:

> It **may** therefore be in the interest of a politician to adopt positions that are against the interest of the typical voter. . .
>
> The packing material **may** be spheres, cylinders, or various kinds of commercial packing for contacting apparatus.
>
> State and local guidelines and mandates **may** limit what particular schools and teachers choose to teach,

Possibility/permission/ability modals are also the most common class in institutional writing. However, in contrast to the typical uses of these modals in textbooks, institutional writing relies heavily on the permission meaning of *may* to spell out rules and requirements for students:

> If a person is under 18 years of age, he or she **may** register as a resident student only upon a showing that his or her supporting parent or guardian has been a legal resident [. . .] If a parent or legal guardian of a minor changes his or her legal residence to another state following a period of legal residence in Georgia, the minor **may** continue to take courses [. . .]

Institutional writing also uses the possibility meanings of *may* to inform students of potential rules or required actions:

> Depending on the program, as little as a minor (18 hours) or as much as a major **may** be required to prepare for your graduate study. At the discretion of your departmental adviser, you **may** also be required to have as a prerequisite to graduate study any undergraduate course that is normally required of undergraduate majors in the field.
>
> You **may** be asked to provide U.S. income tax returns, the worksheets in this booklet, and other information. If you can't or don't provide these records to your college, you **may** not get Federal student aid. If you get Federal student aid based on incorrect information, you will have to pay it back; you **may** also have to pay fines and fees. If you purposely give false or misleading information on your application, you **may** be fined $ 10,000, sent to prison, or both.

Some institutional writing is intended to educate and inform students, rather than setting out rules and requirements; in these texts, possibility *may* is used in combination with the possibility/ability meanings of *can*:

> A person who has HIV **may** be susceptible to diseases most healthy people **can** resist. People infected with HIV **can** look and feel healthy and **may** not even know that they are infected. Even though they don't look or feel sick, they **can** infect others. When symptoms do appear, they **can** be like those of many common illnesses, and **may** include swollen glands, fever, and diarrhea.

Finally, the obligation/necessity modals are especially prevalent in institutional writing, accounting for c. 30% of all modals in that register. The modals *must* and *should* are the most common individual modal verbs, explicitly specifying the obligations of students:

> You **must** fill out this form accurately.

> You **must** complete an enrollment form, and it **must** be postmarked to Wellmark Blue Cross and Blue Shield of Iowa by September 8, 1998.

> You **must** present evidence that you can pay all expenses at NAU for one year.

> You **should** not plan to support yourself by working while enrolled.

The modal *must* is one of two modal verbs that are more common in writing than speech (see Figure 5.3). *Must* can be used to convey two major kinds of meaning: personal obligation and logical necessity. The first meaning expresses our personal responsibility to carry out some action, while the second meaning expresses a logical conclusion based on evidence available to the speaker/writer. Thus compare:

> We **must** be careful to avoid several logical pitfalls. (textbook; personal obligation)

> It **must** have something to do with the government. (study group; logical necessity)

Classroom instructors generally avoid *must* altogether (see Figure 5.3). However, when they do use this modal, instructors express both kinds of meaning (see also Keck & Biber 2004). Classroom teaching uses the logical necessity meaning of *must* and the personal obligation meaning of *must* with about the same frequency. In contrast, *must* is overall much more common in textbooks, and textbook authors rely heavily on the personal obligation meaning rather than the logical necessity meaning (c. 80% of all occurrences of *must* in textbooks have a personal obligation meaning).

This distribution is surprising: The linguistic descriptions elsewhere in this book show that the spoken university registers rely heavily on linguistic features that express (inter)personal functions and meanings, while the written university registers rely heavily on linguistic features that express informational functions and meanings. However, the patterns of use for the modal *must* are exactly the opposite: textbooks strongly prefer the personal (obligation) meaning, while class-room teaching shows equal preference for both the logical (necessity) meaning and personal (obligation) meaning (although the overall use of this modal is relatively rare).

The explanation for this pattern comes from the extremely strong directive force of the modal *must* when it is used with the personal obligation meaning. This use leaves no room for negotiation or avoidance of the directive. In face-to-face spoken situations, this modal use can be perceived as face threatening and impolite, and thus it is generally avoided. In contrast, textbook authors often discuss actions that <u>somebody</u> should feel obligated to perform, without directly stating that the student reader should feel this obligation; for example:

> To find sites subjected to thousands and even millions of years of these natural processes of deposition, we **must** dig.

In some cases, the author clearly identifies other parties that should be responsible, as in:

> Employers with federal contracts **must develop** a list of action steps they will take toward attaining their goals to reduce underutilization. The company's CEO **must make it clear** to the entire organization that the company is committed to reducing underutilization, and all management levels **must be involved** in the planning process.

In other cases, passive verbs are used to make the expression of obligation more indirect, even though the intent is that the student reader should be (partly) responsible for some action. For example:

> An important factor that **must** be taken into account in using faunal analysis to reconstruct prehistoric diet is taphonomy.

> As indicated, not everything we call "theory" contains all these elements, so the definition **must** be regarded as a desideratum rather than a description.

In these constructions, the *by*-phrase is omitted, so the agent of the verb is not overtly stated; however, it is often possible to infer that these agents include 'the student reader'. That is, both students and researchers should feel a responsibility to 'take taphonomy into account' and 'regard the definition as a desideratum'.

These same patterns are found in classroom teaching when the personal obligation meaning of *must* is expressed:

> 3rd party obligation:
> The jury has to reach some agreement on how many dollars for this kind of (hurt). And they all have to agree. Or in a certain case a majority **must** agree.

Passive verb used to avoid identification of the responsible party:
**When problems arise, corrective action must be taken**

Rarely, when an instructor is feeling especially confrontational, we find the use of personal obligation *must* that directly identifies the student as the responsible party:

**I don't care how you do it, I am not picky, but you must cite your references. OK?**

In addition, classroom instructors use *must* to express logical necessity meanings, as in:

**So a hydrogen iodide bond is longer, versus a hydrogen chloride bond, so if the bond is longer it must be weaker.**

**Instructor: It's bad when I've got to explain the jokes. OK? I must have really sucked.**
**Students: [laughter]**
**Instructor: OK, that must have really been bad.**

As noted above, the modal *must* is generally rare in classroom teaching (and the other spoken university registers). Instead, there is a strong preference for the semi-modal *have to*, which occurs over 10 times more frequently than *must* in the spoken registers. *Have to* also expresses both logical necessity and personal obligation meanings, although the directive force of *have to* is less strong and somehow less face threatening than *must*. For example:

Logical necessity:
**Could there be a way that this did not have to occur?**

**So what does the exponent have to be?**

Personal obligation:
**So you have to be a little bit careful of how you handle that.**

**You don't just stick a firewall in a system and expect it to do your work. You have to continually tweak and feed your monitor.**

## 5.3.2 Stance adverbs across registers

As described in Section 5.2.3 above (Table 5.1), four major semantic classes of stance adverbs are distinguished here: certainty, likelihood, attitude, and style. Figure 5.4 shows that stance adverbs are generally much more common in the spoken registers than in the written registers. Epistemic stance adverbs are the most common; certainty adverbs (e.g., *actually, in fact*) are especially common, but likelihood adverbs (e.g., *possibly, probably*) are also very common. Style adverbs (like

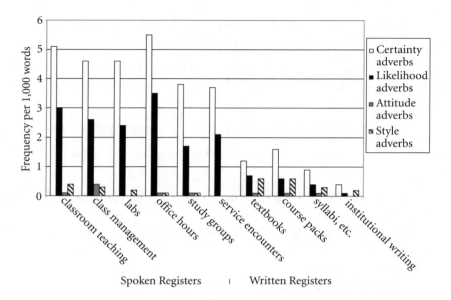

**Figure 5.4**  Semantic classes of stance adverbs across registers

*generally, typically*) are relatively rare overall, but they are the only adverb category that is more common in writing (textbooks and course packs) than in the spoken registers. Attitude adverbs (e.g., *amazingly, curiously*) are the least common overall; classroom management is the only register with a moderately frequent use of them.

Certainty adverbs are common in all spoken university registers. They are used mostly by instructors (rather than students), to identify information as factual and beyond dispute:

> Office hours – Anthropology
> They lacked the sort of complementary animals, so they had some but they may not have had enough to make it a, a, to make an incentive for them to be sedentary. I mean, **obviously** there were societies around here that were **clearly** very sedentary. I mean if you, you look at the Sinagua and you look at the Anasazi culture and, and you, you go up to Wapatki or, or wherever you look around here you see examples of, **clearly** these individuals lived in in these areas and they were sedentary, but, I think the distinction that Diamond would make is that, that, and **obviously** they built huge cities throughout Latin America. That's not the, that's not the problem.

Certainty stance adverbs are also used to emphasize the expected activities of students and the instructor:

> But, what I **really** have to do though is to keep the total time frame for each person, almost exact, to fifteen minutes.

> Well we need the equal sign here so I can **actually** look that up in the table.

Likelihood adverbs (e.g., *probably* and *maybe*) are used for similar purposes, indicating events and actions that are likely to occur (or should be done). Likelihood adverbs are especially common in office hours, where they are used to suggest actions and events that would be desirable or likely:

> OK what I'll **probably** have to do then is just have you drop this one.

> and uh um I guess **probably** the best thing to do would have been for me to go over and meet everybody over there over Christmas time but I'm not going to get a chance to do that so, in in case that doesn't happen what I was going to say **maybe** if we can't all travel let's **maybe** try a conference call.

Style adverbs are generally much less common than certainty and likelihood adverbs. In textbooks and course packs, however, these adverbs are relatively salient, being almost as common as likelihood adverbs. Many of these adverbs are used to indicate that a statement describes the usual case, rather than an invariable fact. For example:

> The first permanent housing to be constructed consisted of wooden houses, which are still in use today, and are inhabited **generally** by the young married couples.

> In other words, characterizations of medical interactions **typically** tend to contrast the action repertoire of doctors and patients.

> Among foraging peoples, occupational specialization (assigning particular tasks to particular people) exists to varying degrees and depends **mainly** on gender and age.

In other cases, style adverbs and adverbial phrases identify the source of a claim, with the implication that some people consider the statement to be true, but that it is not necessarily accepted as fact:

> Since poisonous Amanita species **reportedly** taste good and because amatoxins are slow to act, the unfortunate person who has consumed the poisonous material initially has no idea that he or she is in jeopardy.

> **According to** Wallerstein, this system works to the advantage of core nations and the disadvantage of periphery nations.

Finally, the class of attitudinal adverbs is by far the least common overall. However, these adverbs are moderately important in class management talk, where they are

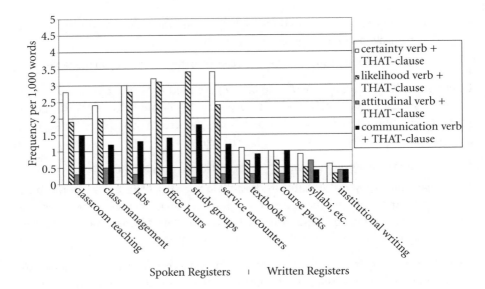

**Figure 5.5**  Semantic classes of controlling verb with THAT-clauses

slightly more common than the style adverbs. They are usually used by instructors to mark personal attitudes:

> so **hopefully** it'll just get you a little bit more feedback and you can make some changes before you hand it in to me

> more **importantly** there's a few things like the way Jupiter rotates and the way the red (clot) spins the way magnetic fields uh go around these objects and so forth that you really get best from a moving image rather than in still slides.

> Um, **unfortunately** there is no perfect way of evaluating performance in a classroom setting.

### 5.3.3  Stance complement clauses across registers

#### A. Stance verb + *that*-clause
Figure 5.5 shows that the semantic classes of stance verb + *that*-clause are distributed in different ways across the university registers. In general, these stance constructions are much more common in the spoken university registers than in the written registers. Certainty verbs and likelihood verbs are the two most common classes controlling *that*-clauses. Certainty verbs are more common than likelihood verbs controlling *that*-clauses in the teacher-centered academic registers (classroom teaching and class management), while likelihood verbs + *that*-clauses are more common in the student-centered academic registers (especially study groups). Thus compare:

Certainty verbs + *that*-clauses in class lectures:

Instructor: How do I **know** it's Y plus two over nine?
Students: [unclear words]
Instructor: Because I got to have fifty-four. I **know** that – remember I **know** they're independent, I **know** that F of X Y is equal to this [. . .]

We **recognize** that it's a real error [unclear words] because he pursues the ideal out of this world.

And if this confidence interval spans the value one covers it, then it is reasonable to **conclude** that the evidence does not support different variances.

And if we're English teachers, too, we **see** that much of this popular culture does involve the English language really on a global scale.

Likelihood verbs + *that*-clauses in study groups:

A:   and basically what the interaction process analysis, I **guess** he did interaction process analysis and then socio-emotional and instrumental leaders now I don't know if it's on here. No it's not. but instrumental leadership is on here. but I **think** for socio-emotional, I don't **think** that he terms it socio-emotional. he terms it something else, um
B:   whoa whoa wait –
A:   I **think** it's expressive
B:   I **think** that he did something on S.E.S.?
A:   We don't need these A's then. Right? We don't need these A's.
B:   No, we don't need them.
A:   Right.
B:   I don't **think** we [unclear] put em.
A:   I **guess** we **thought** that you still had to have them even though like we're only looking at four bits, we **thought** you had to fill like the eight bits.

Interestingly, students interacting in university service encounters follow a very different pattern of use from study groups: in service encounters, certainty verbs are considerably more common than likelihood verbs with *that*-clauses.

I **know** that they will let faculty members check them out for a couple of hours if they want to copy them in their offices or something like that.

Let me look here, well I don't **show** that you have a credit at all so I don't **see** that there's money that there's extra money

Communication verbs are moderately common with *that*-clauses across university registers, but they are most common in study groups. Students use these constructions to identify the source of information: often the instructor or the author of course readings:

> Actually he **said** they can be either one but they prefer to be called justices.
>
> And then, to figure out our T. score, our actual T. score, you go to the table, and it **says** the sample size is nine.

Attitude verbs are the least frequent overall with *that*-clauses, but their register distribution is interesting: Unlike the other verb classes with *that*-clauses, attitude verbs are used mostly for the specific purpose of directive discourse. Thus, these constructions are most common in written course management (syllabi, etc.), although they are also common in institutional writing and spoken classroom management. For example:

> Written course management:
>
> I **expect** that you will put in three hours a week in class. . .
>
> It is **expected** that you will bring to MIS 101 the "statistical maturity" and basic skills commensurate with your successful completion of the prerequisite course.
>
> Success in this course will **require** that you spend time studying for it!
>
> I **hope** that by the end of the quarter you will have gained a facility for reading and commenting critically upon such materials, both in class and in your written work.
>
> Institutional writing:
>
> Even though we provide assistance with your academic planning, please be aware that the ultimate responsibility for completing graduation requirements remains with you, so you must **ensure** that you have adequate information to do so.
>
> I **hope** that you will take advantage of the variety of campus involvement opportunities that are available through the Division of Student Affairs. I strongly **recommend** that you seek assistance from Georgia State staff and faculty when you need direction regarding academic or personal goals.

## B. Stance verb + *to*-clause

Figure 5.6 shows that *to*-clauses as stance markers are more evenly distributed across spoken and written registers than *that*-clauses. Verbs of desire (e.g., *want, like*) are the most common class controlling *to*-clauses, especially in the spoken registers. Verbs of causation/effort (e.g., *help, try*) are also relatively common, and they are equally frequent in written and spoken registers. Mental verbs (e.g., *is assumed, is believed*) and probability verbs (e.g., *seem, tend*) are less frequent overall, but when they are used, they tend to be found in the written rather than spoken registers. Finally, communication verbs (e.g., *ask, advise*) are generally rare with *to*-clauses.

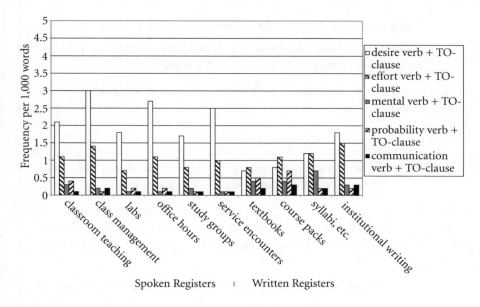

**Figure 5.6** Semantic classes of controlling verb with TO-clauses

Verbs of desire with *to*-clauses are found in all spoken registers, but they are especially common in class management, office hours, and service encounters. Among the written registers, these verbs are most common in institutional writing and course management. These stance devices are used to express desires, but they are usually intended as an indirect directive. That is, some action or outcome is identified as being desirable to the speaker, but this action usually entails joint action between speaker and listener, or it actually functions as a way of directing the listener to do the action.

These functions can be illustrated from class management talk. At one end of the continuum are utterances that seem to simply identify the desires of the speaker:

> What I'd **like** to do is say just a couple of things about language development
>
> There are maybe a few things I want, I **want** to emphasize as important
>
> I **need** to talk to you sometime about when to footnote, how to footnote.

In these cases, the speaker – usually the instructor – expresses a personal desire, but that desire is usually for the benefit of the student and requires the active participation of the student.

In many other cases, the expression of speaker desire includes an overt identification of the listener and the action that that person should perform:

> I'd **like** you to read it first to see if you can read at a very interpretive level.
>
> um, for this Thursday I **want** you to write just a brief handwritten paragraph to me proposing, what you think your subject and topic will be.

Finally, there are some cases where a speaker uses desire verbs with a second person subject to tell the listener what their needs are (and therefore direct the listener to carry out the action):

> you **need** to be here at eight oh clock, uh, you **need** to be here pretty frequently, the class is based generally on lectures. Most of the test will be over lectures and so you will find that if you're not here, it will hurt your grade.

Verbs of desire are also used with *to*-clauses for similar functions in institutional writing and written course management texts. However, these registers are more consistently explicit about the intended directive meaning than classroom management:

> You **need** to register with the office to make sure of graduation requirements
>
> The admission procedures for students who are not U.S. citizens are complex, so you should **plan** to make inquiries well in advance of the semester or summer session in which you wish to enroll.
>
> The students can **choose** to use these services or continue with the method you are currently using.
>
> Biological Sciences majors who **intend** to pursue a teaching credential must complete the science subject matter program which is described in this catalog.

Causation/effort verbs are less common than desire verbs, but they are generally found in the same registers. In the written registers, causation/effort verbs are almost as common as desire verbs. In institutional writing and course management writing, these constructions often have directive functions (causation/effort verbs are in **bold underline**; other directive stance devices are underlined):

> Before you go to look at a place, you might <u>want</u> to ask yourself if you really <u>want</u> to live in off campus housing. **Try** to compare the difference between living in your own home or in these apartments near the campus.
>
> If you **fail** to file your application or pay the graduation fee by the time specified, we may have to schedule you for graduation at a later date.
>
> During your academic career at the University, you will work with a faculty member who will **help** you select courses that will meet your individual education and career goals.
>
> We do **permit** you to use coffee makers, water warmers, and microwave ovens under 700 watts.

> Once again, it will be <u>necessary</u> for you to obtain the Health Insurance electronic registration hold clearance before the CASPER system will **<u>allow</u>** you to attempt your first semester's registration at CSUS.

In course packs and textbooks, these verbs serve more informational purposes, identifying events and actions that are possible, and the circumstances that facilitate their occurrence:

> Such studies increase our general knowledge of language acquisition because they **<u>allow</u>** us to gain a better understanding of the conditions upon which it relies.

> The difficulties arise when we **<u>try</u>** to understand precisely what this means, for the diversity of Hinduism is truly vast and its history long and complex.

> Knowing the techniques of production, or processes of manufacture, **help** us to understand why they look the way they do and how they have been intended to function.

> Opening valves or stopcocks too fast can **<u>cause</u>** joints to blow apart.

Other verb classes are generally less common with *to*-clauses and restricted mostly to the written registers. Mental verbs + *to*-clause are moderately common in course management. It is interesting that these constructions are also used for directive functions:

> I **<u>expect</u>** you to be prepared and to actively participate in the classroom discussion if the opportunity arises.

> Other than the group assignment, students are **<u>expected</u>** to do their own work and to abide by the Policy on Academic Honesty discussed in the GSU General Catalog.

> **<u>Remember</u>** to spell check and grammar check!

> Reminder: Do not **<u>forget</u>** to convert the original data to SI.

Finally, probability verbs + *to*-clauses are moderately common only in textbooks and course packs. This combination is used for epistemic hedging, marking information as uncertain to some extent:

> Many Deep Ecologists of today **<u>seem</u>** to define human beings as an alien presence on the earth.

> Electrons **<u>tend</u>** to repel each other...

> The funds for the site and construction **<u>appear</u>** to have come from the French government

C. Stance adjective/noun + complement clause

In contrast to verb + complement clause constructions, adjectives and nouns are rare controlling a complement clause. In the spoken registers, *that*-clauses controlled by adjectives are used with first person pronouns to express personal attitudes, as in the following examples from office hours:

> yeah I was, **I was afraid** [that you know maybe the the flowery type stuff wouldn't be what they wanted]

> **I** wanted to make **certain** [that you you know sort of got up to date]

In the written registers, *that*-clauses controlled by adjectives are usually used in impersonal, 'extraposed' constructions. These constructions function to characterize the status of information in textbooks and course packs, while they serve directive functions in syllabi and institutional writing:

> Course packs – characterizing the status of information:

> With regard to the two different views of art contrasted above, **it is not surprising** [that Navajo society is one of artists . . .]

> Yet though they admired each other deeply, **it is also clear** [that their cordiality and mutual respect was enhanced rather than hampered by the geographical distance between them].

> Syllabi – directive functions:

> If you have any concerns related to this policy, **it is important** [that you contact your Area Chair, or call the Office of Student Life. . .]

> **It is imperative** [that you come prepared to discuss and debate these materials. . .]

*That*-clauses controlled by nouns are also relatively rare and restricted primarily to the academic registers: classroom teaching, textbooks, and course packs. The nouns label the status of the information presented in the *that*-clause, including *argument, assumption, case, claim, idea, knowledge, notion, possibility, reason, sense.* The following examples are from classroom teaching:

> I started out with the **assumption** [that consciousness is complete with the on-tological proof].

> He dispels the **notion** [that the government is this overwhelming entity that can simply control us all].

Only one noun – *fact* – is relatively common controlling a *that*-clause:

> I can come up with a new business, but I don't like the **fact** [that there's not flex-ibility in that].

> I think they were frustrated by the **fact** [that most of the second language teaching started too late].

*To*-clauses controlled by adjectives and nouns are somewhat more common than *that*-clauses, especially in the written registers. In textbooks and course packs, *to*-clauses occur with adjectives like *best/better, desirable, difficult, easy, hard, important, (im)possible, (un)likely, necessary*. These constructions usually evaluate the likelihood of information, or the desirability/possibility of some action or event. The following examples are from textbooks:

> A hunting and gathering people in this area are **likely** [to have used such resources at one time or another].

> Even fairly recent specimens are **unlikely** [to have any of the radioactive isotope left to be measured].

> It is still scarcely **possible** [to distinguish between an identity, securing core of tradition and a periphery open to revision].

> The general feeling is that it is **best** [to proceed from the general to the specific in constructing questionnaires].

> It is very **difficult** [to determine the beginning of the exploration in human ecology in the USSR].

> It is also **important** [to consider the tectonic framework of entire continents. . .]

In course syllabi, *to*-clauses are used with adjectives like *acceptable, happy, important, necessary, permissible, possible, sure, willing, (un)able*, serving the directive purposes of that register. For example:

> It is **permissible** [to work on homework with other people or to receive assistance]

> I would also be **happy** [to talk with you about your diagrams . . .]

> Be **sure** [to cite your text or reading as a source . . .]

In contrast, institutional writing differs from all other registers in its relatively heavy reliance on noun + *to*-clause constructions. Many of these controlling nouns are nominalized equivalents of verbs and adjectives that can control *to*-clauses: *failure, intent, invitation, permission, plan, ability*. For example:

> If you have **plans** [to leave the country for a short visit], you must have your I20 and IAP66 forms signed. . .

> Your **ability** [to make smart decisions] is lessened when you are drunk or high.

Other nouns controlling a *to*-clause have no equivalent verb or adjective, such as *effort* and *right*. The two most common nouns controlling a *to*-clause in institutional writing are of this type: *opportunity* and *responsibility*:

> Students have an **opportunity** [to learn all phases of museum work] . . .
>
> It is the student's **responsibility** [to consult with the instructor regarding official or unofficial absences].

One interesting aspect of these noun+*to*-clause constructions is that they are often completely impersonal. That is, although these structures are usually used for directive purposes, they often provide no overt indication of who should be acting on the directed course of action. For example:

> **Failure** [to do so] may result in cancellation of enrollment, credits earned, or both.
>
> Under this policy, **intent** [to plagiarize] is not required, although intentional plagiarism will be considered a more serious offense.
>
> The course provides the **opportunity** [to learn and apply various systems] . . .
>
> **Permission** [to enroll for less than the normal number of units] should be obtained from the O.I.P.

## 5.4  Comparing the stance of university registers

The sections above have surveyed a wide range of linguistic features used to express stance meanings in university registers. Two general patterns emerge: (1) stance features are used much more commonly in the spoken registers than in the written registers; and (2) the management and advising registers – whether spoken or written – all tend to use stance features frequently for directive functions. In general, epistemic stance meanings are more prevalent in academic university registers, while the directive stance meanings are common in the management and advising registers. The sections below further describe the expression of stance in these two major register categories.

### 5.4.1  Academic registers

The academic university registers included in the study – classroom teaching, lab sessions, study groups, textbooks, and course packs – all share the primary communicative purpose of conveying information. Even though instructors and textbook authors are also concerned with providing their own perspectives on information, epistemic stance expressions are much more common in these registers than attitudinal expressions. For example:

Epistemic stance devices in classroom teaching:
but I **certainly** don't **think** these data **indicate that** we are more lenient to women uh but I also **think** they raise a serious question about whether or not we're more punitive to them too.

Epistemic stance devices in a textbook:
As we **indicated** in the beginning of this section, the interpretation of an observation depends on the kind of study in which it was made. In the descriptive study, the observation provided only a **suggestion that** the argument course **might** be related to students' higher critical thinking scores. In the correlational study, the observation provided **evidence** that the argument course was related to the students' higher critical reading scores. . .

Attitude stance devices (generally rare) in classroom teaching:
Well to put it together I think, um, first place I was **shocked** to find out that women, were not really up front in affirmative action

However, a closer consideration of stance features in the spoken academic registers shows that they are often used for functions other than the expression of epistemic or attitudinal meanings. First, stance features are commonly used for directive/obligation functions in academic spoken registers. That is, interspersed with the discussion of informational content, we find classroom instructors commonly telling students what they *can* do (i.e. what they **are able to** accomplish), what *I want you to* do; and what they *should*, *have to*, or *need to* do. For example:

If you think about it in chunks you **can** do it.

The following equation, is extremely simplified, but I **want you to** sort of **be able to** think in these terms.

So you **have to** go back and think about which ones did we choose.

You don't **need to** write this part down.

Looking at the use of stance features across the full range of university registers, we can conclude that the management of student activities is almost as important as conveying informational content, in both the 'academic' and the 'management' registers. The only exception to this general pattern is the written academic registers (textbooks and coursepacks), which rarely use stance features for student management functions.

A second surprising general characteristic of stance features in the spoken academic registers is that they are frequently used for discourse organization rather than the more expected epistemic or attitudinal meanings. For example, prediction modals are often used to structure a spoken lecture, identifying the upcoming steps in the presentation (or the course overall):

> OK, um I'm now **going to** talk about language and verbal communication.
>
> And what we **will** begin to understand as I go through these different ap-
> proaches, to government, you **will** begin to understand and **I'll** make it com-
> pletely clear at the end, that some of these approaches are used most often
> by cities.

Reporting verbs with complement clauses often have the opposite function in spoken academic registers – reminding students of what was 'said' in previous class
discussions. This use differs from the typical function of reporting verbs in the
written academic registers, where they are used to provide historical perspectives
or inform students about previous research studies. Thus compare:

> Classroom teaching:
>
> So here again, if they ask you for break-even in sales dollars, remember last time
> **we said,** you can talk about it in terms of number of units that you have make and
> sell in order to break-even, or the dollar amount of sales revenue has to (gener-
> ated) to break-even, you get that sales dollars two ways.
>
> Of course **we said** last time the Mohave Desert the [unclear] desert of the
> southeastern interior according to Los Angeles and San Diego is basically (the)
> Great Basin.
>
> This cancels out, so the current density J is equal to E over S, but **we said** S is one
> over sigma so this is sigma.

versus

> Textbooks:
>
> Basing his argument on the states rights view of federalism, Martin **said**
> the power to incorporate a bank is not expressly delegated to the national
> government.
>
> Rosenzweig (1984; Renner & Rosenzweig 1987) **reported** being so surprised by
> these effects of experience on brain tissue that he repeated the experiment sev-
> eral times before publishing his findings.

The subsections below illustrate these general characteristics of stance in specific
academic registers.

## A. Classroom teaching

In classroom teaching, instructors are motivated by several different purposes relating to stance, including: conveying information (and guiding students through
the steps of complex explanations); indicating the extent to which information is
known or doubtful; providing historical contexts (and indicating the source of in-

formation); and conveying personal attitudes about course content. Text Sample 5.1 illustrates many of the stance features that are typical of classroom teaching.

> **Text Sample 5.1:**  Business statistics lecture (busmsleudms055)
> Stance features are in **bold**
>
> **Instructor:** Now you people in the back **have to** arrange to get these things. [...]
> now to properly interpret these grades or these scores, I **have to know** whether it is **legitimate to** combine the scores of all four. For example, if the people in section ten – you people – are just a whole lot smarter than those in section eleven, then it **would** not be scientifically **honest to** combine the scores. If the uh questions on the blue form differ remarkably from the questions on the yellow form, then we **should** not combine them. now I'm **going to** illustrate a number of tests here using stat graphics, that will add up to the **fact that** there is no significant difference with respect to mean or variance in any of the comparable groups such as section ten yellow section ten blue.
> [...]
> You**'ll** be **able** to complete all of the other all of the other uh columns by considering the four that you have there. Now the first thing we're **going to** do, uh I'm not **going to** drag you through using two systems to do this. So we **will** use stat graphics.
> [...]
> And if the standard deviations are equal then we **can** move the data together to get a pooled standard deviation three point seven three six six one, which **could** be applied to both samples.
> [...]
> and if this confidence interval spans the value one covers it, then it is **reasonable to conclude that** the evidence does not support different variances. So what line is it that tells you you **can presume that** the variances are the same between the populations [unclear word] sample one and sample two? it's this confidence interval here. now, now we **know** which uh mean test to uh interpret up here for the difference of mean. we**'ll** be dealing with equal variances.
> [...]
> now by either route you get the **conclusion that** the underlying means are the same between the two samples.
> [...]
> I **want you to** get started with stat graphics. OK. so, now this uh line down here, hypothesis test, it reads this way H subzero, you all **know that** means null hypothesis.

Modal verbs are the most common stance feature used in classroom teaching, but they are the least explicit in terms of their stance meanings. As noted in 5.3 above, the most common modal verbs in classroom teaching are often used for functions other than expressing the core stance meanings. For example, Text Sample 5.1 illustrates the modal verbs *will* and *be going to* used for discourse packaging – announcing the next topic in the discourse – rather than stereotypical stance functions:

> now I'm **going to** illustrate . . .
> so we **will** use stat graphics . . .

Similarly, the modal *can* usually indicates someone's ability to carry out an action, rather than expressing core stance meanings relating to epistemic possibility or personal permission; for example:

> we **can** move the data together
> you **can** presume

Epistemic meanings, relating to certainty and likelihood, are usually expressed in classroom teaching using stance adverbs and complement clauses. One interesting pattern, found across the spoken registers, is the general tendency for instructors to express certainty more than likelihood or possibility; in contrast, students tend to express likelihood more than certainty. Text Sample 5.1 illustrates this heavy reliance on certainty expressions (e.g., *fact that, conclude that, conclusion that, know that*).

Text Sample 5.2 illustrates this contrast, with the student using possibility stance features (e.g., *maybe* and *I think*), while the instructor uses certainty stance markers (*you know, actually*).

> Text Sample 5.2:  Education classroom teaching (edubelegrhn138)
>
> **Student:** there's, there's a book I just finished reading it's about the fourth grade reading level, **maybe** fifth grade, and it's titled Morning Girl, **I think**.
> **Instructor:** by Michael Dorris.
> **Student:** yeah OK
> **Instructor:** OK
> [. . .]
> **Student:** Uh, like **I think** it gives the perspective of the people um who were welcoming Columbus and the people on the boat. And it was an interesting perspective.
> **Instructor:** OK, **you know** another resource is the diaries of Columbus. And he kept extensive diaries and there are **actually** some secondary sources written for kids

Other common certainty adverbs used by instructors are *in fact* and *of course*:

> **In fact** you'll see some additional ones in chapter nine of this text.

And **in fact** the attorneys who defend most of these defendants will be attorneys hired by the insurance company.

The myth **of course**, there's this big myth **of course** that uh that Montezuma sort of rolled over, didn't know what to do because he thought Cortez was the return of the uh of the uh feathered serpent god, Quetzalcoatl.

Many occurrences of *know* are in the fixed expression *you know*, which often functions more like a discourse marker than a stance feature. However, the combination *we know* is also commonly used by instructors, to identify information that should be clearly understood by the class, and therefore assumed as background knowledge. This use is especially prevalent in the teaching of technical/quantitative methods, as in:

OK, and **we know** that the per unit relationship is still, OK, the same percentage

I mean **we know** it's going to be X plus one

**we know** that that has to be equal to one-half C of that squared and V squared

As noted in 5.3 above, classroom teaching often uses directive stance expressions like *I want you to*. These phrases are usually used to direct student activities, make assignments, or tell students about course expectations. However, these expressions are also often incorporated into the teaching of content, to emphasize some aspect of a lecture that the instructor regards as especially important:

This is, because, one of the things we're gonna work with, today, and **I want you to** make this distinction, is between grouped, [WRITING ON BOARD], and ungrouped.

OK um. All of this is to lead us toward, kind of the underbelly, of where public policy comes from. **I want you to** have, a a a sort of an intuition about public policy.

This is common sense we know that she doesn't, you know uh judge people based on the color of their skin, but **you need to** realize that this is a part of our history

## B. Study groups

At one level, study groups are a genuinely student-centered academic register: students are on their own, outside the classroom context, fully controlling the discussion. However, from another perspective, even student study groups are to a large extent controlled by instructors, who have helped to establish the parameters of discussion in their earlier classroom teaching. As a result of these mixed characteristics, two kinds of stance features are especially prevalent in study groups: communication verbs, used to report what instructors said in class; and likelihood epistemic markers, indicating a lack of certainty about course content. The excerpts in Sample 5.3 illustrate these two kinds of stance markers and show how they often occur together in the same interactions:

> **Text Sample 5.3:** Excerpts from study groups, illustrating the use of communication verbs and likelihood stance markers
>
> Student 1: **I thought he said** it wasn't supposed to change unless you changed it
> Student 2: yeah that's what **he said**.
> Student 2: what do **you think he'll ask** on those though like, just give us options or how-
> Student 1: he'll just give us those **like**-
> Student 2: how can you ask questions on that stuff-
> Student 3: he **might** just give us a, **I'm thinking maybe** for the course, like a multiple choice type thing,
> Student 1: yeah
> Student 3: like he'll just like U.S. supreme court, U.S. court of appeals, U.S. district court, **you know** he'll list all the courts then **say**, this court has, nine justices, and
> Student 1: what's the jurisdiction of an original appellate or something. piece a cake.
> Student 3: if **he asks** anything on it. **I don't know** how specific he can get.
> Student 1: yeah

## C. Textbooks and course packs

As noted above, textbooks and course packs contain relatively few markers of stance in comparison to the spoken academic registers. When stance is overt in these registers, it typically expresses either epistemic meanings or the perspective that information is presented from. Although no individual feature is especially common, a wide range of different stance devices is used to express these meanings, including epistemic devices (e.g., possibility modals, certainty adverbs, certainty verb/adjective + *that*-clause) and perspective or point of view devices (e.g., style adverbs, communication verbs + *that*-clause). For example:

> **Of course**, it is very **difficult** to estimate scenario probabilities **accurately**.

> We must be sensitive, however, to the **fact that** the use of stimulus factors is not without risk.

> **Clearly**, the **tendency to** engage in proactive ways-to seek opportunities and develop them, and, **more generally**, "to make things happen," – **may** also be related to performance of many other jobs and to the success of entire organizations.

> A palmately lobed leaf is **usually** also palmately veined with a primary vein in each lobe. Lobing **should** be considered separately from marginal features or

blade shape, as **should** be obvious from the figures. A lobed leaf **may** have entire margins such as white oak and sassafras or serrate margins as in red oak and striped maple.

For, on this record, it is **apparent that** the State's purported concern with local control is offered **primarily** as an excuse rather than as a justification for interdistrict inequality.... [If] Texas had a system **truly** dedicated to local fiscal control one **would** expect the quality of the educational opportunity provided in each district to vary with the decision of the voters in that district as to the level of sacrifice they **wish to** make for public education. **In fact**, the Texas scheme produces **precisely** the opposite result.

Consumer researchers have **typically** focused on elaboration in the form of semantic or verbal elaboration.

Remick **argues that** an operational definition of comparable worth hinges on the application of a single evaluation system across job families.

Stockard and Wood (1984) **claimed that** female underachievement as measured by grades is a myth, since they **found** in student records of seventh through twelfth graders **that** females were **less likely** than males **to** have English and mathematics grades that were lower than **would** be predicted by standardized ability tests.

However, in many cases, textbook language is packaged as a simple reporting of information, often with no indicators of personal stance; for example:

Text Sample 5.4: Geology textbook (tbgeo1.msg)

The Jura are hills that separate France from Switzerland. Partly wooded, partly farmland, long inhabited, the Jura derive their name from *juria*, the Latin word for "forest."

The rocks of the Jura are fossiliferous limestones. They are famous for fossils of extinct sea creatures called ammonites that lived in coiled shells resembling the modern coiled nautilus. In the early nineteenth century, when European geologists started to arrange fossils in the sequence in which they had lived, fossils in the Jura were selected as the types characterizing certain ammonites and rocks containing ammonites were selected as the examples of Jurassic sedimentary rocks, named after the Jura hills.

## 5.4.2 Management/advising registers

The management/advising registers are different from the academic registers in the expression of stance. First of all, both spoken and written management registers rely on the relatively dense use of stance features (in contrast to the relative absence of stance features in academic writing). And second, stance in these registers usually expresses directive rather than epistemic or attitude meanings. For example, modals are used in the management registers to describe obligations and future intentions. These can be short term – e.g. in a single class session – or long term – over a semester or an entire degree program. For example,

> So, Monday, on the first of March, these people **will** be here. And, the first five people **will** speak.
>
> So you **have to**, you **have to** tabulate these items.
>
> Students **MUST** turn in the exam to me before leaving class or they **will** receive a zero for the exam.

Complement clause constructions also commonly express directive rather than epistemic meanings in the management registers; e.g.:

> and I think from your perspective you really do **want to** get that knocked out next week.
>
> uh you will need the book. uh I'll rely on it a lot in lecture, I**'d like you to** bring it to class everyday, because I'll refer to a lot of figures in there.
>
> **You will need to** access available resources to find answers to your questions and be willing to ask when you can't find them.

The following subsections provide more detailed descriptions of the expression of stance in particular management/advising registers.

### A. Classroom management

Classroom management talk, as it has been defined in the present study, occurs when an instructor discusses course requirements and student expectations. It is thus not surprising that stance in this register focuses on human behavior: what the instructor will do (or will try to do), and what students should do.

As noted above, modals are common in this register expressing prediction / intention meanings (*will, be going to*), obligation meanings (*should, have to*), and ability or permission meanings (especially *can*). Stance adverbs are also common in this register, especially certainty adverbs. These are often used for emphasis (e.g., *what I _really_ have to do. . .*), to identify points of information that students should pay special attention to. The stance adverb *actually* is used to identify statements that are true but surprising because they are counter to prior expectations (*I tried to not be redundant, but, __actually__ it was amazing to me how parallel all your input was*). Verbs of desire and effort are commonly used controlling a *to*-clause. In many cases, these describe the desires or efforts of the instructor:

> There's really not enough time to cover what I **want to** cover.
>
> I'll **try to** do it Monday.

Text Sample 5.5 provides an extended excerpt from class management talk, showing the dense use of these features working together to express a range of stance meanings:

**Text Sample 5.5:** Class management talk – Instructor in Education class:

**Instructor:** OK. I **want to** remind you again that Tuesday we **will** not be meeting because I'**ll** be in Killup. Um, You **can** turn in your thematic unit to my office and then, um, on the first and third, lost my chalk, I'**d like you to** bring some food, some snacks. I'**ll** bring, um, I'**ll** bring something healthy, like carrots or fruit. First and third, so if you, you're not presenting, I'**d like you to** bring some snacks for the rest of the group. And you'**ll** get your final exam on December first, and its due December ninth or earlier if **you want to** turn it in.
[...]
Thank you for asking that. Just to reclarify that. The hard copy portfolio that you leave with me, I **will** be pulling this up on your portfolio. You'**ll** only receive one rubric back, and that **will** be from me, I, uh, what we'**ll probably going to have to** do because all of you **obviously** are giving me different times and, your schedules are all different, is that, when I finish evaluating your, um, I'**ll** have a box outside my office door, where they **can** be picked up at your convenience.
[...]
And if you put that, references, available upon request, I **will** accept that. What you **really** do **need to** do is have some reference, to references, so even if some of you are [3 sylls] and you've-you've done that, that's fine. Some of you have **actually** visited the contact uh, names addresses and phone numbers of references.
[...]
A lot of-a lot of things are pretty self explanatory aren't they? If I put in an award or certificate whatever it says on that, **really** tells what it **needs to** I **would** think about that. So you **have to** use your judgment if you **think** additional explanation is needed. Or, if it's something that may be **fairly**, um, lengthy, in narrative style, and you **think that** someone **might really want to** read the entire document, then that **might** be a reason to have a summary overview.
[...]
I **tried to** not be redundant, but, **actually it was amazing** to me how parallel all your input was.

## B. Office hours

Office hours serve a dual purpose: individual tutoring on academic content and student advising. Some meetings with students combine both purposes, but more often a meeting will have one or the other focus. A wide range of stance devices are used for directive functions in office hours. Many of these are explicit in meaning, including obligation modals (*should, have to, got to*):

> now here's what **you should** do if you want me to go over your graduation papers **you gotta** do it this semester
>
> you **have to** say your name, your year, and your major.

However, other features are more indirect, even though the directive force is usually clearly understood by students. For example, the modals *will* and *can* are often used to indirectly express directives in office hours:

> you guys**'ll** it have to support it on your own as far as, you know because I don't think the school **will** support a non-Dell computer.
>
> this one you **will** just turn in
>
> You **can** make it up during spring break
>
> Oh, well you **can** take uh, next fall you **can** take six ninety two.

Desire verbs controlling *to*-clauses are also commonly used for directive functions in office hours. Similar to the use of modals, these constructions can be explicit and direct, or they can function as indirect instructions to carry out some action. For example:

> Explicit directives:
>
> **Instructor:** yeah all right what **I want you to** do is to come back um on Thursday
>
> **Instructor:** OK so that's what **you need to** work on – get that in before midnight today all right
>
> Indirect directives:
>
> **Instructor:** all right **we want to** stay away from the negative
> **Student:** OK
> **Instructor:** just stay away from the "not unable unfortunately however's" – OK **we want to** write positively
>
> **Instructor:** OK now uh .. so what **we need it to** do is, **we need to** get rid of a negative eleven ah and a negative twelve.

Interestingly, students (as well as instructors) commonly use desire verbs controlling *to*-clauses during office hours. In many cases, these constructions simply express the desires and needs of the student, as in:

> **Student: I want to** take four classes this summer
>
> **Student:** And I've got a list of classes or an idea of classes that **I would like to** take next semester
>
> **Student: I need to** take accounting 350

In other cases, students express their own needs/desires as an indirect attempt to issue a directive to the instructor; for example:

> **Student:** um **I want to** talk about my exam first.
>
> **Student:** there's some stuff **I'd like to** know one way or the other before I leave town
>
> **Student:** what all right so **I need to** know [laughing] I'm not gonna be here next Thursday that's the thing

## C. Written course management

Written course management – syllabi and assignments – is similar to classroom management and office hours in being highly directive, but these texts are in some ways more explicit in the expression of this function. Obligation modals (*must, should*) are probably the most explicit and face-threatening directive devices. These modals are rarely used in speech, but they commonly occur together with the second person pronoun *you* to express strong directives in written course management. Fuller expressions such as *I expect you to...* or *it is essential that you...* perform similar functions.

In addition, indirect stance expressions are also commonly used, such as the modal *will* in constructions that state the requirements, rules, and consequences associated with a course. These are usually impersonal statements that do not explicitly identify students as the people who are expected to follow the rules. In fact, these constructions often occur with a passive voice main verb, so neither the instructor (the enforcer of the rule) nor the student (expected to comply with the rule) are explicitly identified; for example:

> The grade **will be lowered** for poor grammar and poor spelling.
> Late reports **will not be accepted** [...]

Of all university registers, course syllabi are probably the most marked for the dense use of directive stance expressions, with the least concern for politeness. This is probably because the syllabus serves as a kind of contract between the instructor and student, specifying the expectations and requirements of a course. However, the resulting prose can often end up being intimidating. Text Sample 5.6 below is from a syllabus for a business course, illustrating the extremely dense use of forceful directive expressions in this register:

> **Text Sample 5.6:** Course syllabus – prediction modals are **<u>bold underlined</u>**; obligation modals are in ***bold italics***. Related directive expressions are <u>underlined</u>.

ADDITIONAL INFORMATION:

Each chapter lists Learning Objectives that indicate what **you should** <u>be able to</u> accomplish after completing the chapter. These Learning Objectives **should** guide your study and sharpen your focus.

Although assigned problems are not collected, <u>it is essential that you</u> complete all problems before I present and discuss them in class. ... <u>It is preferable for you</u> to work problems yourself incorrectly and learn from your mistake than it is to merely copy problem solutions from the board. **You should** study the material and attend my office hours on a chapter by chapter basis, rather than "cramming" before exams.

Although class attendance is not an explicit component of the course evaluation, successful completion of the course <u>requires your attendance</u> at each and every class. I frequently distribute handouts and additional information at class. If you do not attend a class at which I distribute materials, <u>it is your responsibility</u> to obtain those materials.

D. Course Grade:

Your final grade <u>**will**</u> be based on your class performance, exams, and the overall evaluation of your performance. [. . .]

I <u>**will**</u> assume that if you attend class, you are prepared. [. . .]

Final Exam:

The final exam <u>**will**</u> consist of tasks to be performed using the computer. **You must** perform the tasks and store the results on your floppy disk to receive any credit.

Makeup examinations <u>**will**</u> not be given unless (1) adequate documentation is provided by the student AND (2) the instructor is notified by telephone prior to the start of the examination.

Grades <u>**will**</u> be available only during office hours. Your exam disk <u>**will**</u> NOT be returned to you at the end of the course or the end of the semester.

One of the few concessions to politeness in this syllabus is the use of *should* rather than *must*, indicating a desirable rather than absolutely necessary obligation. However, course syllabi do also use *must* for strong statements of course requirements or rules:

Students <u>**must**</u> turn in the exam to me before leaving class or they will receive a zero for the exam.

The modal *will* is the most common device used to state explicit rules and expectations in course syllabi (see Sample 5.6 above). In this case, the expectation is stated as a simple fact about the future, rather than overtly expressing strong obligation:

> Students <u>will</u> work together on a computational project (on programs ATLAS or TLUSTY). The group <u>will</u> be responsible for running a specific model...
>
> For this portion of the assignment, you <u>will</u> select a rhetorical situation for a technical description of your object...

At the other extreme, course syllabi and written assignments can also include extremely indirect directives, sometimes simply telling students what would be good for them and assuming that students will understand the directive force. For example:

> Warning: they [i.e., electronic versions of help manuals] are long. **You might want to** transfer them to a disk rather than printing them out.
>
> **You may want to** switch to orthographic view to input the points that define the outline.

## D. Institutional writing

Overall, institutional university writing has fewer expressions of stance than course syllabi. There are relatively few epistemic stance features, and few indications of personal attitudes in this register. However, the stance of obligation is commonly expressed to describe the rules, requirements, and expectations of student life at the university. In many cases, institutional writing includes statements of what a student might want (or desire) to accomplish, followed by a description of the rules or expectations required to achieve that goal. These stance functions are performed mostly by modal verbs and *to*-clauses (controlled by verbs, nouns, or adjectives), expressing meanings related to obligation, permission, desire, and ability. For example:

> Thus, students **desiring to** add a certain course but **unable to** do so through CASPER or CASPER Plus **should** attend the class and mention his/her interest to the instructor. The instructor **may be able to** offer guidance and/or suggestions.
>
> Students **wishing to** accelerate their program **may** enroll for a maximum of twenty one units in a semester. Students whose university record justifies a course of study in excess of twenty one units **may** petition **to be allowed to** carry extra units. The petition **must** be recommended by their advisor and approved by the Department Chair and School Dean. Only students with superior academic records **are allowed to** enroll for more than the maximum unit load.

Student rules and expectations are presented with a wide array of stance structures in institutional writing. In most cases, these structures are different from the typical stance constructions found in spoken discourse. The expression of obligation is usually overt in institutional writing, but these statements are often less explicit that the reader (i.e. a student) is the person who should abide by these requirements. Further, there is usually no reference to the person or institution that enforces the requirement or expectation.

Obligations are often stated as a general requirement for all students; that is, with the noun *students* as the grammatical subject. Many of these clauses occur in the active voice, even though the meaning is usually that some unspecified authority is requiring the students to perform some action. For example:

> Students **need to** be aware that the last day of Phase III is the last day for any schedule change.

> Transient <u>students</u> **may** attend for only one fall or spring semester.

> Students **wishing to** be considered for a subsequent term **must** submit a Reactivation Form and any required credentials by the application deadline date for that particular term.

> When <u>a graduate student employee</u> **needs to** be absent either for personal reasons or illness, the supervisor should be understanding and accommodating to that need. At the same time, <u>the graduate assistants</u> **should attempt to** plan personal leave so that it does not interfere with or cause neglect of the duties associated with his or her appointment.

It is even more common to use passive voice with *students* as the grammatical subject. In these statements, the *university* is usually understood to be the authority functioning as the agent, setting the expectations and requirements, and encouraging students to behave in specified ways; for example:

> All students **are expected to** purchase Student Liability Insurance . . .

> All students **are required to** earn a high school diploma on or before their original graduation date

> Students **will be required to** complete placement assessments under the following conditions: [. . .]

> Students **are also encouraged to** demonstrate involvement in their affiliated organizations.

> Students **are strongly encouraged to** consult with an advisor prior to registration.

> The students **are urged to** attend [. . .]

These two grammatical strategies can occur together, even in the same sentence. The following example begins with the active voice to present the student's needs and the student's ability to carry out certain actions, then switches to passive voice to specify what the university requires:

> A student registering through CASPER or CASPER Plus who is either initially **unable to** register for all courses he/she **requires, or desires to** make changes to his/her schedule **will be required to** add/drop courses.

In other cases, no human participants are mentioned at all, resulting in an even more indirect, impersonal expression of student obligations. In some structures, the grammatical subject refers to the performance of the obligation:

> **Failure to** do so may result in cancellation of enrollment, credits earned, or both.

More commonly, extraposed constructions are used to present impersonal obligations. In these structures, the grammatical subject is non-referential (*it*); the predicative adjective presents the stance (e.g., *necessary, advisable, important*); and the following *to*-clause (or *that*-clause) presents the obligation. For example:

> **It is necessary to** apply for a new visa in order to return to the U.S.

> **It is advisable to** keep all receipts of international and domestic transfers.

> **It is important to** purchase a class schedule [. . .]

> **It is strongly recommended that** you meet with a campus academic advisor.

These two impersonal stance strategies can occur together, as in:

> The U.S. visa stamped in the passport grants **permission to** enter the U.S. [. . .] The IAP66 **must** be valid at all times. If a scholar or a family member leaves the U.S. after the visa has expired, or if a status change has been approved by the U.S. Immigration and Naturalization Service, **it is necessary to** apply for a new visa in order to return to the U.S.

Similarly, impersonal statements can occur together with general 'student' statements:

> All payments **must be received** (not postmarked) in the Office of Student Accounts by 7 p.m. on the fee deadline as published for each phase. Students who **fail to** meet the published fee deadline for any phase will lose all classes for which they are scheduled.

At the opposite extreme, institutional writing occasionally adopts a personal style, directly addressing the student as *you*:

> To be an effective leader, you **must be able to** inspire the faith of others in your group.

> If you **can't** or don't provide these records to your college, you **may** not get Federal student aid. If you get Federal student aid based on incorrect information, you **will have to** pay it back; you **may** also **have to** pay fines and fees.

In this more personal style, the university often refers to itself as *we*; for example:

> **We encourage you to** become actively involved in the MSC.
>
> **We expect you to** have adequate undergraduate preparation for your intended major.
>
> If you have hall or roommate preferences, **we make every effort to** meet your request when space is available.

Imperative structures are also used in this more personal style:

> **Meet** with your adviser and develop your program of studies. **Find out** exactly what **you are required to** take and where any previous graduate work will transfer into your program. **You may want to** complete a tentative version of your program of studies because of uncertainties about course offerings. **You should** file your program of studies by your third semester at NAU.

Institutional writing is often produced by committees, with the finished product reflecting the individual stylistic preferences of numerous authors. As a result, institutional documents sometimes switch between a personal style (directly addressing the reader as *you*) and the more impersonal structures that are the preferred style for this register. The combination of these two strategies in close proximity can result in prose that feels almost schizophrenic:

> For **students** who are teaching and **wish to** remain at the same school, **you need to** indicate the county and school name as the first choice.
>
> **Permission to** audit a course will depend, among other considerations, upon the availability of classroom space. [. . .] **You will then be permitted to** complete registration for classes.
>
> To facilitate processing your application and, therefore, receive a quicker admission decision, **you are encouraged to** include all of the required transcripts (in envelopes officially sealed by the issuing institution) with your University application. **Please include** 2 transcripts from all colleges and universities attended. Transcripts already on file with CSU, Sacramento **need not be** resubmitted unless there is additional work to be reported. **It also is not necessary to** submit CSU, Sacramento transcripts. However, **you may need to** supply additional copies of any or all transcripts directly to the program to which you are applying.

## 5.5  Chapter summary

The present chapter has surveyed the use of lexico-grammatical features for a particular function: the expression of stance. It turns out that stance is fundamentally important in university registers, although different registers express stance to differing extents and for different particular functions (e.g., the expression of

epistemic certainty, likelihood, or doubt; the expression of attitudinal and evaluative meanings; or a range of directive meanings). As the following chapter shows,
these same functions are also important for the interpretation of the recurrent
multi-word expressions ('lexical bundles') in these registers.

## Note

1. Adverbial phrases and clauses can also serve stance functions; see LGSWE 853–75.

# CHAPTER 6

# Lexical bundles in university teaching and textbooks

## 6.1 Introduction

As noted in Chapter 1, one approach to the study of classroom teaching has been to consider the functions of longer lexical phrases, chunks, and idioms (see, e.g., DeCarrico & Nattinger 1988; Nattinger & DeCarrico 1992; Khuwaileh 1999; Simpson & Mendis 2003; Schmitt 2004). These studies are part of a growing research tradition focusing on the use of multi-word prefabricated expressions in general (see the reviews in Weinert 1995; Ellis 1996; Howarth 1996; Wray & Perkins 2000; and Wray 2002).

Multi-word sequences have been studied under many rubrics, including 'lexical phrases', 'formulas', 'routines', 'fixed expressions', and 'prefabricated patterns' (or 'prefabs'). These approaches all define the object of study in somewhat different terms, and so they provide different perspectives on the use of multi-word sequences. For example, some studies describe multi-word sequences that are idiomatic (e.g., idioms like *in a nutshell*), while other studies focus on sequences that are non-idiomatic but perceptually salient (e.g., *if you know what I mean*).

A complementary approach, adopted in the present chapter, is to describe the multi-word sequences that occur most commonly in a given register. I refer to these multi-word sequences as 'lexical bundles', defined simply as the most frequent recurring sequences of words. Recurrent word sequences have been investigated in several earlier studies, including Salem (1987), Altenberg and Eeg-Olofsson (1990), Altenberg (1998), Butler (1997), and Schmitt, Grandage, and Adolphs (2004). The term 'lexical bundle' was first used in the Longman Grammar of Spoken and Written English (Chapter 13), which compared the recurrent sequences of words in conversation and academic prose.[1] This framework has been applied in several subsequent studies, including Biber and Conrad (1999), Biber, Conrad, and Cortes (2003, 2004), Cortes (2002, 2004), and Partington and Morley (2004).

The present chapter begins with a description of lexical bundles in the two most important academic university registers – classroom teaching and textbooks – at the same time developing a functional framework for the analysis of bundles.[2] The chapter then compares these patterns to the lexical bundles used in the full range of university registers (classroom management, office hours, study groups, service encounters, course management writing, and institutional writing). Finally, the chapter compares the use of lexical bundles across academic disciplines (for textbooks).

## 6.2  General characteristics of lexical bundles

Lexical bundles are identified using a frequency-driven approach: They are simply the most frequently occurring sequences of words, such as *do you want to* and *I don't know what*. These examples illustrate two typical characteristics of lexical bundles: they are usually not idiomatic in meaning, and they are usually not complete grammatical structures.

The actual frequency cut-off used to identify lexical bundles is somewhat arbitrary. The present chapter takes a conservative approach, setting a relatively high frequency cut-off of 40 times per million words to be included in the analysis. Many of the bundles described here are actually much more common, occurring more than 200 times per million words. To further limit the scope of the investigation, only 4-word sequences are considered here. (However, several of the text excerpts throughout the chapter show that two 4-word lexical bundles sometimes occur together to form a 5-word or 6-word sequence; see Biber et al. 1999:992ff. for discussion of these longer lexical bundles.)[3]

A further defining characteristic is that a multi-word sequence must be used in at least five different texts to be counted as a lexical bundle; this restriction guards against idiosyncratic uses by individual speakers or authors. Most bundles are distributed widely across the texts in a corpus. Even the least common lexical bundles in the analysis of classroom teaching and textbooks (Section 6.3) are usually used in at least 20 different texts, while the more common bundles are distributed even more widely.[4]

I noted above that lexical bundles have two surprising characteristics. First, most lexical bundles are not idiomatic in meaning. Rather, the meanings of bundles like *do you want to* or *I don't know what* are transparent from the individual words. (However, the analysis below shows that bundles typically function as a unit in discourse.)

In fact, most longer idioms are far too rare to be considered lexical bundles. Stereotypical idioms such as *kick the bucket* (meaning 'die') and *a slap in the face* (meaning 'an affront') are rarely attested in natural speech or writing. (Fiction is one of the few registers that uses idioms and fixed formulas with moderately high frequencies; see Biber et al. 1999:1024–1026.) Simpson and Mendis (2003) document important pragmatic functions of idioms in classroom teaching, but they found that these expressions are generally rare, and they are often short noun phrases or prepositional phrases (e.g., *the bottom line* and *the big picture*).

The second surprising characteristic of lexical bundles is that they usually do not represent a complete structural unit. For example, Biber et al. (1999:993–1000) found that only 15% of the lexical bundles in conversation can be regarded as complete phrases or clauses, while less than 5% of the lexical bundles in academic prose represent complete structural units. Instead, most lexical bundles bridge two structural units: they begin at a clause or phrase boundary, but the last words of the bundle are the beginning elements of a second structural unit. Most of the bundles in conversation bridge two clauses (e.g. *I want to know, well that's what I*), while bundles in academic prose usually bridge two phrases (e.g., *in the case of, the base of the*).

Because the research approach used here for the study of lexical bundles is based exclusively on frequency criteria, it is also deliberately exploratory. The investigation starts out by simply asking whether there are chunks of language – sequences of words – that are used repeatedly by speakers and writers in the university. The answer to this question turns out to be 'yes': there are many lexical bundles used with high frequency in texts, and it further turns out that different university registers tend to rely on different sets of lexical bundles. These distributional facts raise a second set of research questions: what are the structural and functional characteristics of these word chunks, and how can we explain their repeated use in discourse?

For the most part, linguists have not noticed these high frequency multi-word sequences, probably because most previous research has focused on idiomatic or structurally complete grammatical phrases and clauses, disregarding the possibility of lexical units that cut across grammatical structures. However, the descriptions below show that lexical bundles have identifiable discourse functions, suggesting that they are important for the production and comprehension of texts in the university.

## 6.3 Lexical bundles in university classroom teaching and textbooks
### Section coauthors: Susan Conrad and Viviana Cortes
### [based on a revised version of Biber, Conrad, & Cortes 2004]

### 6.3.1 Overall distribution of bundles in classroom teaching and textbooks

The present section compares the lexical bundles in classroom teaching and textbooks to those found in conversation and academic prose. (The description here synthesizes the findings reported in LGSWE Chapter 13 with those reported in Biber, Conrad, & Cortes 2004.)

As discussed in previous chapters, classroom teaching is a spoken register, constrained by real-time production circumstances, and marked by speakers' personal concerns and interactions among participants. At the same time, classroom teaching has a primary informational focus, and instructors normally pre-plan the content and structure of their class sessions to achieve their informational goals.

Based on these characteristics, we predicted that classroom teaching would be intermediate between conversation and academic prose in the use of lexical bundles. This general pattern was seen repeatedly in Chapter 4. For example, Figure 4.1 shows classroom teaching being generally similar to other spoken registers in using frequent verbs and adverbs, and relatively few nouns, in comparison to written registers. However, classroom teaching is intermediate in that it uses considerably more nouns than conversational registers like service encounters or study groups.

Surprisingly, classroom teaching does not follow this pattern in the use of lexical bundles: rather than being intermediate, classroom teaching far exceeds conversation in the number of different lexical bundles (using almost twice as many different bundles; see Figure 6.1). At the other extreme, both textbooks and academic prose use relatively few different lexical bundles.

We can begin to explain these patterns by considering the structural characteristics of lexical bundles found in each register. Section 6.2 noted that lexical bundles have strong grammatical correlates, even though they are not usually complete structural units. It is possible to distinguish among three major structural types of lexical bundle.

The first major structural type incorporates verb phrase fragments. These bundles often begin with a subject pronoun followed by a verb phrase (*I'm not going to, it's going to be, that's one of the, and this is a*). These bundles can also begin directly with a verb phrase (e.g., *is going to be, take a look at*) or question fragment (e.g., *are you going to, how many of you*). The second major structural type is similar in that it incorporates verb phrase elements, but these bundles also incorporate dependent clause fragments (e.g., *I want you to, if we look at, what I want to*).

In contrast, the third major structural type of bundle includes only phrasal components. Many of these bundles consist of noun phrase components, usually ending with the start of a postmodifier (e.g., *the end of the, a little bit about, those of you who, the way in which*). Other bundles of this type consist of prepositional phrase components with embedded modifiers (e.g., *of the things that, at the end of*).

Figure 6.1 shows the distribution of these structural types across registers. The previous investigation of lexical bundles in conversation and academic prose, presented in the LGSWE, showed that the grammatical correlates of lexical bundles in conversation are strikingly different from those in academic prose. In conversation, almost 90% of all common lexical bundles incorporate verb phrases. In fact, c. 50% of these lexical bundles begin with a personal pronoun + verb phrase (such

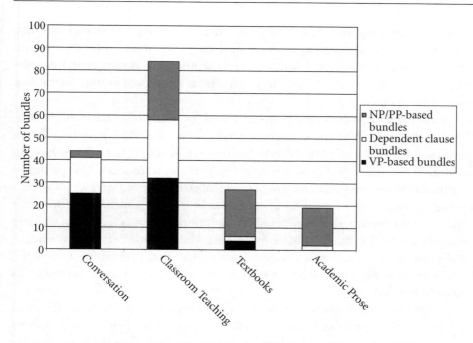

**Figure 6.1** Distribution of lexical bundles across structural types

as *I was going to, I thought that was*). An additional 19% of the bundles consist of an extended verb phrase fragment (e.g., *have a look at*), while another 17% of the bundles are question fragments (e.g. *can I have a*). In contrast, the lexical bundles in academic prose are phrasal rather than clausal. Almost 70% of the common bundles in academic prose consist of noun phrase expressions (e.g. *the nature of the*) or a sequence that bridges across two prepositional phrases (e.g. *as a result of*).

Classroom teaching uses about twice as many different lexical bundles as conversation, and about four times as many as textbooks. The distribution across structural patterns shown in Figure 6.1 helps explain this extremely frequent pattern of use: classroom teaching relies on the lexical bundles associated with both spoken and written registers. Similar to conversation, classroom teaching makes dense use of lexical bundles that incorporate declarative and interrogative clause fragments. At the same time, classroom teaching is similar to academic prose and textbooks in making dense use of noun phrase and prepositional phrase lexical bundles. Thus, the extremely high density of lexical bundles in classroom teaching exists because this register relies heavily on both 'oral' and 'literate' bundles.

This pattern of use is in marked contrast to the general patterns of use for grammatical features described in Chapter 4. That is, classroom teaching is similar to the more colloquial spoken registers (like office hours and study groups) in relying primarily on 'oral' rather than 'literate' grammatical features. In contrast, classroom teaching uses the full range of lexical bundle types with high frequencies. Thus, classroom teaching does not have the productive use of complex noun phrase structures associated with academic writing, but it uses lexical bundles that incorporate complex noun phrase structures to an even greater extent than academic writing.

In addition, classroom teaching has a large inventory of lexical bundles associated with dependent clause fragments, especially conditional adverbial clauses and complement clauses (26 different bundles in classroom teaching, versus 16 in conversation, and only 2 in academic prose, and 2 in textbooks). This pattern is surprising given previous claims that dependent clauses are more typical of written prose than speech (see the survey of research in Biber 1988: Chapter 3). However, it turns out that these lexical bundles are more common in both classroom teaching and in conversation than in the written registers (similar to the general grammatical patterns of use for verb + complement clause constructions; see Chapters 4 and 5; see also Biber et al. 1999: Chapter 9, for a discussion of these constructions in conversation).

Textbooks and academic prose are at the opposite extreme from classroom teaching in the overall use of lexical bundles.[5] It is surprising that textbook authors do not incorporate more lexical bundles in their writing, given the heavy reliance on bundles in classroom teaching. Reasons for this absence might be that textbook authors tend to use fuller expressions, preferring full clauses rather than phrasal lexical bundles, perhaps reflecting the fact that textbook authors are free of the real-time production constraints of face-to-face teaching. A much fuller analysis of textbook discourse structures is required to interpret the relative absence of lexical bundles in that register.

Given that the structural correlates of lexical bundles in these four registers are so dramatically different, it will come as no surprise that their typical discourse functions differ as well. I turn to a discussion of those functions in the following section.

## 6.3.2  Discourse functions of lexical bundles in university classroom teaching and textbooks

To better understand the distribution of lexical bundles, it is important to consider their discourse functions. In Biber, Conrad, and Cortes (2004), we identified functions using an inductive approach. That is, we grouped together bundles that serve similar functions, based on the typical meanings and uses of each bundle (based on concordance listings of each bundle in its discourse contexts). Once the bundles were assigned to groups, we attempted to label the discourse functions associated with each of the groups. Of course this last step was influenced by previous theoretical studies on the discourse functions of linguistic features (e.g., Hymes 1974: 22ff.; Halliday 1978; Brown & Fraser 1979; Biber 1988: 33ff., 1995).

In some cases, even a single occurrence of a bundle can be considered multi-functional. For example, bundles like *take a look at* and *let's have a look* function at the same time as directives and topic introducers. In other cases, a single bundle serves different functions depending on the context. For example, bundles like *the beginning of the* and *at the end of* can function as a time reference, place reference, or text deictic reference. In general, however, most bundles have a primary function. Potentially multi-functional bundles were examined in concordance listings and classified according to their most common use. (Several of these cases are discussed in 6.3.3–6.3.5 below.)

Three primary functions are distinguished for lexical bundles in these registers: (1) stance expressions, (2) discourse organizers, and (3) referential expressions. Stance bundles express attitudes or assessments of certainty that frame some other proposition. Discourse organizers reflect relationships between prior and coming discourse. Referential bundles make direct reference to physical or abstract entities, or to the textual context itself, either to identify the entity or to single out some particular attribute of the entity as especially important. Each of these categories has several sub-categories associated with more specific functions and meanings.

Biber, Conrad, and Cortes (2004) provides a comprehensive list of the most common bundles, grouped by functional category (and showing the frequency in each register). The following subsections describe each of these functional categories in detail.

### 6.3.3  Stance bundles

Stance bundles provide a frame for the interpretation of the following proposition, conveying two major kinds of meaning: epistemic and attitude/modality (see the general discussion of stance in Section 5.2). Epistemic stance bundles comment on the knowledge status of the information in the following proposition: certain, uncertain, or probable/possible (e.g., *I don't know if, I don't think so*). Attitudinal/Modality stance bundles express speaker attitudes towards the actions or events described in the following proposition (e.g., *I want you to, I'm not going to*). Stance bundles can be personal or impersonal. Personal stance bundles are overtly attributed to the speaker/writer (*I*), as in the examples given above. Impersonal stance bundles express similar meanings without being attributed explicitly to the speaker/writer (e.g., *it is possible to, can be used to*).

### 6.3.3.1  *Epistemic stance bundles*

*Personal epistemic bundles:* Most epistemic stance bundles are personal (especially in classroom teaching). Although epistemic stance bundles can express certainty or uncertainty, most of these bundles express only uncertainty, as in:

> That's, kind of hard to tell, but again, the important thing is be resourceful when you do these. <u>I don't know what</u>, <u>I don't know what</u> the voltage is here, so, but, the real point is it's irrelevant.                    [classroom teaching]

Expressions with *I (don't) think* express possibility but a lack of certainty. Thus compare the two bundles in the following:

> <u>I don't know if</u> it will mean revolution in the same sense of the word, <u>I don't think so</u> because I think there are other political factors involved. [classroom teaching]

Several lexical bundles in classroom teaching combine epistemic stance with other functions. For example, bundles with *I think/thought it* serve a dual function of referential identification combined with an uncertain epistemic stance; for example:

> The Wall Street Journal last week or <u>I think it was</u> the Wall Street Journal had something about NASA and this same problem.                    [classroom teaching]

Imprecision bundles like *and stuff like that*, discussed in 6.3.5.1 below, also serve an epistemic function combined with referential identification.

*Impersonal epistemic bundles:* In contrast, impersonal epistemic stance bundles usually express degrees of certainty rather than uncertainty:

> Boys <u>are more likely to</u> be hyperactive, disruptive, and aggressive in class.
>                    [textbook]

> Yet there was irony in <u>the fact that the</u> Russian Revolution, one of the most important Western revolutions, proclaimed itself to be Marxist in aims and character but happened in violation of Marxist historical logic.                    [textbook]

### 6.3.3.2  *Attitudinal/Modality stance bundles*

Attitudinal/Modality stance bundles are also usually personal, expressing speaker attitudes towards the actions or events described in the following proposition. Four major subcategories are distinguished here: desire, obligation/directive, intention/prediction, and ability.

*Desire bundles:* Desire bundles include only personal expressions of stance, which frame self-motivated wishes and desires, or inquire about another participant's desires:

> So I may not want to see her face to face because <u>I don't want to</u> deliver bad news to her.                                    [classroom teaching]

Several lexical bundles that express personal desire in classroom teaching are also used to initiate new topics, including *what I want to do* and *I would like to*; these are discussed in Section 6.3.4.1 below.

*Obligation/directive bundles:* The second subcategory of attitudinal/modality stance bundles expresses obligations or directives. Most of these bundles are personal stance expressions, but they differ from other personal bundles in that they have a second person pronoun (*you*) rather than first person pronoun as subject. However, they are still clearly understood as personal expressions of stance, directing the listener to carry out actions that the speaker wants to have completed. For example,

> Now <u>you need to know</u> how to read these.                      [classroom teaching]

> All <u>you have to do</u> is work on it.                            [classroom teaching]

In some cases, these bundles include verbs of desire with a first person pronoun, directly conveying the speaker's desire that the addressee carry out some action:

> <u>I want you to</u> take out a piece of paper and jot some notes down in these four areas.                                           [classroom teaching]

In other cases, the directive force of these bundles can be very indirect, as in:

> <u>You might want to</u> look at a couple of examples just to remind yourself of how these look.                                       [classroom teaching]

Some directive bundles are used for topic introduction (e.g., *take a look at*); these are discussed in 6.3.4.1 below.

A few obligation/directive stance bundles are impersonal, with no personal pronoun at all, even though they still clearly direct the reader to carry out some action:

> <u>It is important to</u> note that Derrida does not assert the possibility of thinking outside such terms.                               [textbook]

*Intention/prediction bundles:* The third subcategory of attitudinal/modality stance bundles is intention/prediction. Many of these bundles are overtly personal, expressing the speaker's own intention to perform some future action. In most cases, these are expressions of joint action, used to announce the proposed plan of a class session, as in:

> But, right now <u>what we're going to</u> take a look at are ones that are produced that are positive and beneficial.                    [classroom teaching]

Other bundles in this category are impersonal, expressing predictions of future events that do not entail the volition of the speaker. These bundles are usually used when explaining a logical or mathematical process that involves several steps, as in:

> And so if you require a, twenty percent return on investment, this net present value <u>is going to be</u> zero.                    [classroom teaching]

*Ability bundles:*  A few stance bundles express ability in classroom teaching. These bundles often co-occur with a 2nd person pronoun, identifying skills and tasks that students should accomplish:

> I want you <u>to be able to</u> name and define those four curriculum category [sic].
>                    [classroom teaching]

> So encoding's always harder than decoding. cos you have <u>to come up with</u> the word, you have to spell it, you have to use it correctly.       [classroom teaching]

### 6.3.4  Discourse organizing bundles

Discourse organizing bundles serve two major functions: topic introduction/focus and topic elaboration/clarification.

#### 6.3.4.1  *Topic introduction/focus bundles*

Topic introduction bundles in classroom teaching provide overt signals to the student that a new topic is being introduced. Many of these are expressions of intention or desire (see 6.3.3.2 above), but they have the more specialized function of announcing the instructor's intention to begin a new topic:[6]

> But, before I do that, I <u>want to talk about</u> Plato.           [classroom teaching]

> <u>What I want to do is</u> quickly run through the exercise that we're going to do. OK just so you see what it does.                    [classroom teaching]

As the preceding example shows, sometimes two 4-word bundles occur together, in effect creating a longer 5-word or 6-word bundle.

The following example illustrates the use of these longer bundles for procedural instructions, identifying the major steps in the procedure:

> OK? next thing <u>I want to do is</u> - <u>what I want to do is</u> I want to change the back color [...] OK? first thing <u>I want to do is</u> let's set up some colors of the text boxes to start with [...] OK? first thing <u>I want to do is</u> let's make the first text box.
>                    [classroom teaching]

Topic introducing bundles can occur with both first and second person pronouns. The first person plural pronoun *we* as subject seems to invite student participation, although the 'we' often refers to the instructor rather than a collective enterprise:

> Today we are <u>going to talk about</u> testing hypotheses.     [classroom teaching]
>
> Now, we <u>want to talk about</u> getting our sample mean...     [classroom teaching]

Topic introducing bundles with 'if we look at' are more genuine attempts to encourage student participation, as in:

> <u>If we look at</u> Heidegger, Heidegger makes a basic distinction between things in the world and [...] human reality...     [classroom teaching]

Topic introducing bundles with second person pronouns also invite student participation, although the instructor is usually intending collective consideration of the topic:

> <u>If you look at</u> development and the jobs that are created, it says nothing first of all of the type of jobs that are created.     [classroom teaching]

The bundle *if you look at* often has a deictic reference, identifying the props required for a topic. They direct the students' attention to the prop, indirectly introducing a new topic by reference to it:

> <u>If you look at</u> the answers that are given, there's only two answers that have one big M...     [classroom teaching]

Finally, topic introducing bundles with WH-question structures provide the most overt attempts to directly engage students in a new topic:

> <u>What do you think</u> the text is trying to tell us when they call our attention that often conflict doesn't appear suddenly?     [classroom teaching]

### 6.3.4.2 *Topic elaboration/clarification bundles*
The second major subcategory of discourse organizing bundles relates to topic elaboration or clarification. For example,

> Well why is the Navajo Depot, Camp Navajo important today? [...] It <u>has to do with the</u> START talks with the Russians, the START Treaty signed in 1991.
> [classroom teaching]

The discourse markers *you know* and *I mean* are used in sequence as a lexical bundle, usually when the speaker believes that additional explanation or clarification is required:

> When you come to class next time – and I'm gonna look at grammar <u>you know I mean</u> I expect you to have things spelled relatively correctly. . .
>
> [classroom teaching]

The bundles *as well as the* and *on the other hand* are used for explicit comparison and contrast. These two discourse organizing bundles are considerably more common in textbooks than in classroom teaching:

> Section 3.5 [. . .] illustrates how the techniques are employed together <u>as well as the</u> range of resulting execution characteristics that are presented to an architecture, . . .
>
> [textbook]

> We know that if the project is in the same line business as the firm's other projects [. . .] then high stand alone risk translates into high corporate risk [. . .]. <u>On the other hand</u>, if the project is not in the same line business, then it is possible that the correlation may be low . . .
>
> [textbook]

### 6.3.4.3 *Identification/focus bundles*

Identification/focus bundles are common in classroom teaching, focusing on the noun phrase following the bundle as especially important. (As a result, identification/focus bundles were classified as 'referential' rather than 'discourse organizers' in Biber, Conrad, & Cortes 2004.) For example, the bundle *those of you who* identifies the subgroup of students who are in focus:

> For <u>those of you who</u> came late I have the, uh, the quiz.    [classroom teaching]

In most cases, identification/focus bundles have a discourse organizing function. These bundles are often used after a lengthy explanation to emphasize or summarize the main point:

> Schizophrenia typically uh will mean that uh separation from reality uh it can mean uh uh you know extreme periods of euphoria and extreme periods of depression it can mean a lot of things – and <u>that's one of the</u> problems of schizophrenia.
>
> [classroom teaching]

> OK. Uh we create a tri-block for an object of type thread, and there is a built-in thread object that has a method called sleep, and that method called sleep takes a parameter which is the number of milliseconds [. . .] OK? <u>And this is a</u> real simple way, the simplistic way to do animation.
>
> [classroom teaching]

In other cases, identification/focus bundles can be used to introduce a discussion by stating the main point first, and then giving the details:

> <u>One of the things</u> they stress in parenting is to be consistent and particularly with parents um some parents are inconsistent between siblings. Uh fathers are

notorious for letting their little darling girls get away with what they swat the
boys about...                                                      [classroom teaching]

### 6.3.5  Referential bundles

Referential bundles generally identify an entity or single out some particular attribute of an entity as especially important. Four major sub-categories are distinguished: identification/focus, imprecision indicators, specification of attributes,
and time/place/text reference.

#### 6.3.5.1  *Imprecision bundles*
One major subcategory of referential bundles indicates imprecise reference. These
have two specific functions, either to indicate that a specified reference is not necessarily exact, or to indicate that there are additional references of the same type
that could be provided:

> I think really we now have what about, six weeks left in class <u>or something like
> that</u>.                                                        [classroom teaching]

> There are obviously companies that do uh evaluations <u>and things like that</u>
>                                                                  [classroom teaching]

#### 6.3.5.2  *Bundles specifying attributes*
A second subcategory of referential bundles identifies specific attributes of the
following head noun. Some of these bundles specify quantities or amounts:

> You'd <u>have a lot of</u> power.                                [classroom teaching]

> Does it create a lot of wealth? no. It creates <u>a little bit of</u> wealth.
>                                                                  [classroom teaching]

The bundle *a little bit about* usually has the more specialized function of introducing a topic (see 6.3.4 above), apparently to minimize the expectations required
from students:

> So I want to talk <u>a little bit about</u> process control from that point of view.
>                                                                  [classroom teaching]

Other bundles in this category describe the size and form of the following head
noun:

> These figures give an idea of <u>the size of the</u> ethnological community in Russia.
>                                                                  [textbook]

> They are <u>in the form of</u> half-wheels, with concentric bands of representations alternating with bands of scrollwork.    [textbook]

In contrast, some specifying bundles identify abstract characteristics:

> Rather than reading textbooks and solving textbook problems, students must define and constantly refine <u>the nature of the</u> problem...    [textbook]

These abstract specifying bundles are often used to establish logical relationships in a text:

> Fleshy fruits are classified <u>on the basis of</u> the differentiation of the fruit wall (pericarp).    [textbook]

> They are defined <u>in terms of the</u> emotion they elicit.    [textbook]

### 6.3.5.3  *Time/place/text-deixis bundles*

Finally, several referential bundles refer to particular places, times, or locations in the text itself. Three place bundles in the T2K-SWAL corpus refer to the United States, apparently reflecting the narrow focus of textbooks and classroom teaching in the U.S.:

> Children <u>in the United States</u> are not formally employed in farm work, ...
>
>     [textbook]

Text deixis bundles are common only in the written registers, where they make direct reference to figures and graphs contained in the text itself:

> <u>As shown in Figure</u> 4.4, the higher the real estate agents scored in terms of the proactive personality dimension, the more houses they sold ...    [textbook]

Many of these bundles are multi-functional, referring to time, place, and/or text deixis, depending on the particular context:

> So you have to record that, since the asset was sold at <u>the end of the</u> year
>
>     [classroom teaching]

> She's in that.. uh.. office down there.. at <u>the end of the</u> hall  [classroom teaching]

> uh I'm going to start actually with <u>the end of the</u> chapter   [classroom teaching]

### 6.3.6  Register variation in the functional exploitation of lexical bundles

The preceding sections have outlined a taxonomy of the major discourse functions served by lexical bundles in university academic registers. The taxonomy was developed to include functions that can potentially be realized in any register. However, as Figure 6.2 shows, the four registers are strikingly different in

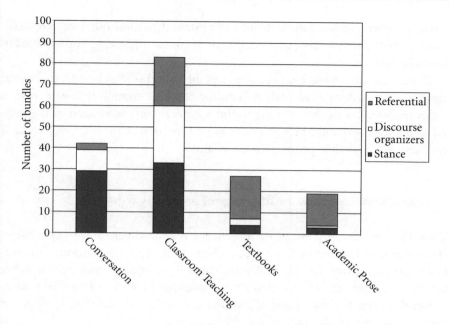

**Figure 6.2**  Distribution of lexical bundles across functional categories

their reliance on particular functional types.[7] The examples presented in Sections 6.3.3–6.3.5 above illustrate the use of these bundles in their characteristic registers. Three general patterns emerge from this analysis:

— Stance bundles are extremely common in both classroom teaching and conversation;
— Discourse organizing bundles are by far most common in classroom teaching (and moderately common in conversation);
— Referential bundles are common in both classroom teaching and textbooks (and to a lesser extent in academic prose).

The patterns of use in classroom teaching are especially interesting here, and they help to explain why lexical bundles are generally so much more common in this register than any other register.[8] Classroom teaching combines characteristics of both conversation (using stance and discourse organizing bundles) and textbooks/academic prose (using referential bundles). However, classroom teaching actually goes beyond these other registers, using bundles in all three functional categories to a greater extent than either conversation or academic writing.

Two major patterns are noteworthy here: First, classroom teaching combines the functional and communicative priorities of involved spoken discourse (shown by the dense use of stance bundles) with the priorities of informational written discourse (shown by the dense use of referential bundles). Second, classroom teaching is structured with lexical bundles to a greater extent than these other registers. This is shown most clearly by the large number of discourse organizing bundles used in classroom teaching.

In fact, classroom teaching actually uses the most bundles in each functional category. This pattern apparently reflects the complex communicative demands of this register. Lexical bundles are useful for instructors who need to organize and structure discourse which is at the same time informational, involved, and produced with real-time production constraints.

## 6.4 Lexical bundles across the full range of university registers

Given the importance of lexical bundles in the core academic university registers (classroom teaching and textbooks, described in the preceding section), it is reasonable to expect that these lexical sequences will be equally important in other university registers like office hours, study groups, and course syllabi. The present section describes the use of lexical bundles across the full range of spoken and written registers included in the T2K-SWAL Corpus.

The findings presented in this section are exploratory because the T2K-SWAL corpus sampling for the non-academic university registers is less representative than for classroom teaching and textbooks: First, the samples for all non-academic registers in the T2K-SWAL Corpus are small for the purposes of lexical bundle analysis. Second, there is considerable variation in the extent to which these registers are represented, ranging from only 11 texts (50,400 words) for office hours, up to 37 texts (151,500 words) for institutional writing.

I used somewhat different criteria for the identification of lexical bundles in the different registers, in an attempt to adjust for these differing sample sizes. For all registers, only lexical bundles that occurred with a rate of at least 40 times per million words were included. However, in the registers represented by the smallest text samples (class management, office hours, and course management), a bundle could occur as few as 3 times and still have a normed rate of occurrence greater than 40 times per million words. For example, a bundle that occurred only 3 times in the office hours sub-corpus (with only 50,400 words) would have a normed rate of 60 per million words:

$$(3 / 50,400) * 1,000,000 = 60 \text{ per million words}$$

To adjust for this inflated rate of occurrence, an additional restriction was imposed for the analysis of those registers: any bundle with a raw count of 3 must be distributed across 3 different texts.

At the same time, when the sub-corpus for a register included only a few different texts, I relaxed the requirement that a bundle must occur in at least 5 different texts. Thus, for class management, office hours, and course management, I included bundles that occurred in only 2 texts, as long as the bundle occurred at least 4 times (a normed count over 70 times per million words). In study groups and service encounters, a recurrent sequence had to occur in at least 3 different texts to be considered a bundle. Institutional writing is represented by a larger text sample, and so it was possible to require occurrence in at least 4 different texts for inclusion in the study.

Although these sliding criteria help to adjust for the differences in representation of the sub-corpora for these registers, the results presented below should still be considered preliminary. A more comprehensive analysis would be based on much larger samples, with the sample design more evenly matched across registers. In particular, it is difficult to say with certainty that a lexical bundle found only 3 or 4 times in a register sample of only 11 texts would actually be found as a frequently recurrent sequence in a much large sample.

However, the goals of the analysis presented in this section are not to focus on individual lexical bundles. Rather, the primary goal here is to compare the overall patterns of lexical bundle use across these registers: exploring the overall extent to which bundles are used, and the major functional associations of bundles, in each of these registers. The T2K-SWAL Corpus and the methods adopted here are adequate for these general purposes. As the following sections show, there are striking differences among non-academic university registers in the overall patterns of use for lexical bundles.

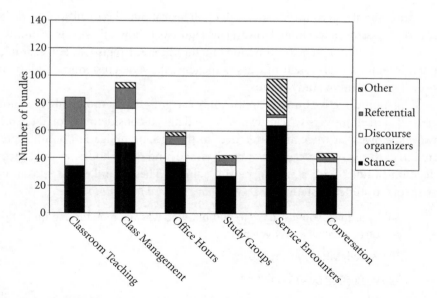

**Figure 6.3** Distribution of lexical bundles across functional categories: All spoken university registers (+ conversation)

### 6.4.1 Lexical bundles in spoken university registers

Figure 6.3 shows the distribution of lexical bundles across functional categories for each of the spoken university registers in the T2K-SWAL Corpus. Classroom teaching and conversation (discussed in 6.3 above) are included here for comparison. Table 6.1 lists many of the most common lexical bundles in these registers, grouped according to major function.

Stance bundles are especially important in the spoken university registers. For example, Figure 6.3 and Table 6.1 show that class management is similar to classroom teaching in using many different lexical bundles from all three major functional categories (stance, discourse organizers, referential). The main difference is that class management uses stance bundles to an even greater extent than classroom teaching. In contrast, referential bundles are somewhat more prevalent in classroom teaching than in class management talk. Discourse organizers are very common in both registers.

Stance bundles are even more strongly preferred in office hours, although there are fewer different bundles used overall (see Figure 6.3). Study groups use the fewest lexical bundles of any of these spoken registers. The functional distribution of bundles in study groups is strikingly similar to face-to-face conversation, indicating that the face-to-face interactive nature of study groups is a more powerful determining factor than the academic content of those sessions. Finally, service encounters are at the opposite extreme, using more bundles than any other of these registers.

Stance bundles account for over half of all lexical bundles in all spoken registers except classroom teaching. However, as Figure 6.4 shows, these stance bundles are used for different specific functions in the different registers. For example, 'desire' bundles are prevalent in class management, while epistemic bundles are especially prevalent in study groups.

Obligation/directive bundles are the only category that is uniformly common across all spoken university registers. A more detailed consideration of Table 6.1, however, shows that there are differences in the specific obligation bundles preferred in each register. In classroom management and office hours, we find many obligation bundles with a second person subject. These bundles are spoken by instructors to students, stating what 'you' *have to/need to/want to do*:

> So if you miss, <u>you just have to</u> find out who was the monitor and go to that person and get whatever you missed.
>
> That's really <u>what you need to do</u>.
>
> <u>So you need to</u> go to the library.

**Table 6.1** Functional classification and distribution of common lexical bundles across spoken university registers

Key to symbols:

| '**' | 40–99 per million words |
|---|---|
| '***' | over 100 per million words |

| | | Class Teach | Class Manage | Office Hours | Study Groups | Service Encount | Conv-ersation |
|---|---|---|---|---|---|---|---|
| **I.** | **STANCE EXPRESSIONS** | | | | | | |
| **A.** | **Epistemic stance – Personal:** | | | | | | |
| | I don't know if | ** | ** | *** | *** | *** | ** |
| | I don't know what | ** | ** | | *** | *** | *** |
| | I don't know how | ** | | | *** | ** | ** |
| | you know what I | ** | | | *** | *** | ** |
| | I don't think so | | | ** | ** | ** | ** |
| | I think it was | ** | | | ** | | ** |
| | I have no idea | | | | ** | *** | |
| **B.** | **Attitudinal/Modality stance** | | | | | | |
| | **Desire – Personal:** | | | | | | |
| | if you want to | *** | *** | ** | ** | *** | ** |
| | I don't want to | ** | ** | | ** | ** | *** |
| | do you want to | | ** | ** | ** | *** | *** |
| | you want to do | | ** | | | ** | |
| | I just wanted to | | | ** | | ** | |
| | I really want to | | ** | | | | |
| | you might want to | | ** | | | ** | |
| | and I just need | | | | | *** | |
| | I just need your | | | | | *** | |
| | **Obligation/directive** | | | | | | |
| | **Personal:** | | | | | | |
| | you don't have to | ** | *** | *** | | *** | ** |
| | don't have to do | | ** | ** | | | |
| | you have to do | ** | | | ** | | |
| | we're going to/gonna have(to) | ** | *** | | ** | | |
| | so you have to | | ** | ** | ** | | |
| | you just have to | | ** | | ** | | |
| | I want you to | *** | *** | ** | | | |
| | you don't want to | ** | ** | ** | | | ** |
| | you want me to | | | *** | | *** | ** |
| | need to do is | | | *** | | | |
| | what you need to | | | *** | | ** | |
| | you need to do | | | *** | | ** | |
| | I just need to | | | | | *** | |
| | I need to pay (for) | | | | | *** | |
| | I'd like you to | | *** | | | | |
| | can I get a | | | | | *** | |
| | take a look at | ** | ** | *** | | | |

Table 6.1  (*continued*)

| | Class Teach | Class Manage | Office Hours | Study Groups | Service Encount | Conversation |
|---|---|---|---|---|---|---|
| **Imperatives:** | | | | | | |
| don't worry about it | | | *** | | ** | |
| make it out to | | | | | ** | |
| just go ahead and | | | | | ** | |
| **Intention/prediction** | | | | | | |
| **Personal:** | | | | | | |
| we're going to do | ** | *** | | | | |
| what we're going to | ** | *** | | | | |
| are you going to | | ** | | | ** | *** |
| you're going to do | | | *** | | | |
| **Impersonal:** | | | | | | |
| it's going to be | ** | | | | *** | ** |
| is going to be | *** | *** | | | | |
| going to be a | ** | ** | | | | |
| not going to be | ** | ** | | | ** | * |
| it's not going to | | *** | | ** | | |
| **Ability/effort – Personal:** | | | | | | |
| to be able to | *** | ** | | | | |
| see if I can | | | ** | | | |
| and then we can | | ** | | | | |
| try to do it | | ** | | | | |
| can I help you (with/please) | | | | | *** | |
| may I help you (with/please) | | | | | *** | |
| **II.    DISCOURSE ORGANIZERS** | | | | | | |
| **Topic introduction/focus** | | | | | | |
| what do you think | ** | ** | | | | ** |
| if you look at | ** | ** | ** | | | |
| if you have a | ** | *** | | | | |
| going to talk about | ** | | | | | |
| want to do is | ** | | | | | |
| you know if you | ** | ** | ** | | | |
| a little bit about | ** | *** | | | | |
| do you know what | | | | ** | ** | ** |
| do you know where | | | | | *** | |
| I wanted to ask | | | ** | | | |
| **Topic elaboration/clarification** | | | | | | |
| at the same time | ** | *** | | ** | | |
| has to do with | ** | ** | | ** | | |
| to do with the | ** | | | ** | | |
| I mean it would | | | ** | | | |
| know what I mean | | | | ** | ** | ** |
| if you have questions | | ** | | | | |
| have a question about | | ** | | | | |

**Table 6.1** (*continued*)

| | Class Teach | Class Manage | Office Hours | Study Groups | Service Encount | Conv-ersation |
|---|---|---|---|---|---|---|
| **Identification/focus** | | | | | | |
| that's one of the | ** | | | | | |
| and this is a | ** | | | | | |
| one of the things | *** | ** | | | | |
| those of you who | ** | ** | | | | |
| of the things that | *** | | | | | |
| some of you are | | ** | | | | |
| the first thing I | | ** | | | | |
| **III. REFERENTIAL EXPRESSIONS** | | | | | | |
| **Imprecision** | | | | | | |
| or something like that | ** | ** | ** | *** | ** | ** |
| and stuff like that | ** | | | *** | | |
| **Specification of attributes** | | | | | | |
| **Quantity specification** | | | | | | |
| have a lot of | ** | | ** | | | |
| in a lot of | ** | | | | | |
| the rest of the | ** | ** | *** | ** | | |
| a little bit more | ** | | ** | | | |
| a lot of you | | *** | | | | |
| how many of you | | *** | | | | |
| **Multi-functional reference** | | | | | | |
| the end of the | ** | *** | | | | ** |
| at the end of | ** | *** | | | | ** |
| **IV. SPECIAL FUNCTIONS** | | | | | | |
| **Politeness and Inquiries** | | | | | | |
| thank you very much | | | ** | | *** | ** |
| what are you doing | | | | ** | *** | ** |
| do you have a | | | | | *** | |
| what's your last name | | | | | *** | |
| **Longer expressions in service encounters** | | | | | | |
| (ok) it's going to take just | | | | | | |
| a minute for that to go through | | | | | *** | |
| go ahead and sign that (for me please) | | | | | *** | |
| and there's your receipt | | | | | *** | |
| do/did you want a bag | | | | | *** | |
| (you) have a good day | | | | | **** | |
| (you) have a nice day | | | | | *** | |
| (hi) how are you doing | | | | | *** | |

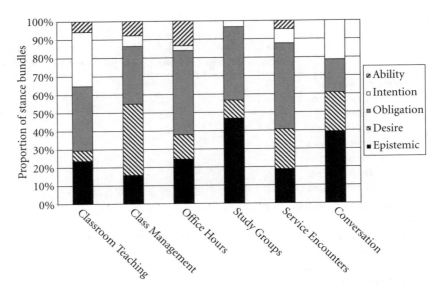

**Figure 6.4** Proportional breakdown of stance bundles across functional categories: All spoken university registers (+ conversation)

In other cases, instructors state their own desire for students to perform some action. These bundles function as both desire and obligation/directive bundles:

So I want you to do problem 1-A.

In contrast, obligation bundles in study groups often have 'we' as subject, as students discuss the course requirements that they all share:

we're gonna have to have time to write this up now.

and then we don't have to worry about this part.

I think we need to know those two definitions.

Obligation stance bundles in university service encounters often have first person 'I' as subject, with no mention of 'you'; these bundles are used by students to identify a required task that they are attempting to complete; for example:

I need to get some of these copied

Do I have to do it in housing?

In addition, service providers express directives to students that incorporate bundles. These usually incorporate a verb of desire (especially *need*) and refer to expected actions; for example:

I just need to see a license or something.

You need to take it over to enrollment

Apart from their shared reliance on obligation bundles, spoken university registers differ in the other kinds of stance bundles that they employ. Intention/prediction bundles are very common in classroom management; many of these bundles are used as macro discourse organizers, announcing class topics and activities ahead of time:

> now here's <u>what we're going to do</u> today…

Desire bundles are also relatively common in classroom management. These are usually used to discuss possible future activities, often taking on an indirect directive function or identifying possible actions that a student could pursue:

> <u>You might want to</u> jot this will down for future reference.
>
> <u>If you want to</u> talk to them about that you need to talk to the other desk.

Office hours use few intention/prediction bundles, but epistemic and ability bundles are more common than in classroom management. Epistemic bundles are often used to hedge claims, as in:

> <u>I don't know if</u> it's being offered right now.
>
> Instructor: Have you changed the gradient any?
> Student: <u>I don't think so.</u>
>
> so like <u>I just kind of</u> like keep track of them and everything

Ability bundles are also used in office hours with an indirect directive function, emphasizing the student's ability to accomplish some assigned task:

> so <u>you should be able to</u> estimate on this when you've got a boundary influence.

Study groups differ from other spoken university registers in that almost half of all stance bundles have an epistemic function. Similar to office hours, though, these bundles usually function to hedge claims rather than asserting certainty; for example:

> <u>I don't know how</u> to define any of that.
>
> <u>I don't know what</u> kind of aggression this one was.
>
> <u>I don't think that</u> he terms it socio-emotional.
>
> <u>I think it was</u> a review.

Finally, service encounters have a greater reliance on desire bundles than the other spoken registers. These usually express the desires of the customer:

> <u>I just wanted to</u> pay my fees.
>
> <u>Do you want to</u> go back there and check?

### 6.4.1.1 *High frequency fixed expressions in service encounters*

In addition to regular 4-word lexical bundles, there are a number of longer fixed expressions that occur with high frequencies. These are composed of several 4-word bundles that occur in an overlapping sequence, as in:

> it's going to take just a minute for that to go through
>
> go ahead and sign that (for me (please))

These longer fixed expressions are found only in service encounters (in the T2K-SWAL Corpus), reflecting the formulaic nature of that register. That is, the providers in service encounters repeat the same actions many times each day, and they use formulaic interactions accompanying those actions: greeting customers, asking if they can help, completing transactions, etc. For example, the following interaction occurs repeatedly in the student business services office. There are minor variations, depending on the particular circumstances, but the overall structure of the interaction is relatively fixed:

> Provider: hello. hi.
> Student: I need to pay this
> Provider: OK. [types on keyboard] seven oh eight ... OK it's going to take just a minute for that to go through
> Provider: alright
> [printer sounds]
> Provider: OK it declined on that
> Student: it declined? oh well then use this
> Provider: OK ... OK try that
> [printer sounds]
> Student: it's probably too big a withdrawal
> Provider: well yeah and uh bank cards sometimes they have a limit of like five hundred or whatever so
> Student: yeah
> [printer sounds]
> Provider: OK go ahead and sign that for me
> [printer sounds]
> there you go
> Student: thanks
> Provider: have a good day
> Student: you too

These fixed expressions should be contrasted with typical lexical bundles: Most lexical bundles are not structurally complete. Rather, they serve as discourse building blocks, providing a frame for the presentation of new information (which typically follows the lexical bundle). In contrast, these longer fixed expressions are structurally complete; in fact, they are often used as an entire turn in a service encounter. It is noteworthy that such structurally complete fixed expressions are found with high frequencies in only one register: service encounters, which is constrained by a highly restricted set of actions and topics.

## 6.4.2 Lexical bundles in non-academic written registers

Table 6.2 lists many of the most common lexical bundles in the two non-academic written registers – course management (syllabi, etc.) and institutional writing (catalogs, program brochures, etc.) – broken down by functional category. Lexical bundles in textbooks and academic prose are listed for comparison.

Figure 6.5 presents the overall distribution of bundles across functional categories, comparing the use of bundles in academic versus management/institutional registers, across speech and writing. Several interesting findings emerge from this comparison. First, lexical bundles are much more prevalent in course management and institutional writing than in the academic written registers. However, it is more surprising that course management writing uses a greater number of different bundles than any of the spoken university registers (counter to the expectations raised by all previous studies, which have shown lexical bundles to be much more common in spoken registers than in written registers).

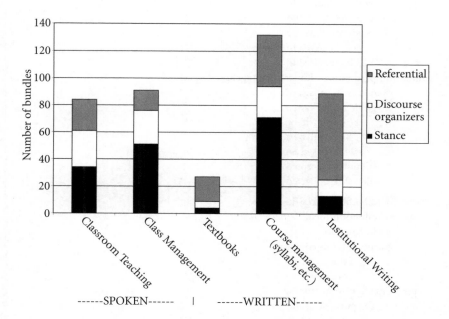

**Figure 6.5** Distribution of lexical bundles across functional categories: Comparing spoken and written academic and management registers

**Table 6.2** Functional classification and distribution of common lexical bundles across written university registers

Key to symbols:

      '\*\*'      40–99 per million words
      '\*\*\*'     over 100 per million words

| | Textbooks | Course Management | Institut. Writing | Academic Prose |
|---|---|---|---|---|
| **I.  STANCE EXPRESSIONS** | | | | |
| **Attitudinal/Modality** | | | | |
| **Obligation/directive** | | | | |
| **Personal:** | | | | |
| you are responsible for | | | \*\*\* | |
| are accountable for all | | \*\* | | |
| students are expected to | | \*\*\* | | |
| the responsibility of the | | \*\* | \*\* | |
| you are encouraged to | | \*\*\* | | |
| you are expected to | | \*\*\* | | |
| you are responsible for | | \*\*\* | | |
| **Impersonal:** | | | | |
| it is important to | \*\* | | | \* |
| must be approved by | | | \*\* | |
| must be submitted to | | | \*\* | |
| will be required to | | | \*\*\* | |
| are expected to attend | | \*\* | | |
| is important that you | | \*\* | | |
| will be asked to | | \*\*\* | | |
| will be required to | | \*\*\* | | |
| **Intention/prediction – Impersonal (agent not specified):** | | | | |
| exam(s) will consist of | | \*\*\* | | |
| grade will be based | | \*\* | | |
| the exam will be | | \*\* | | |
| there will be a | | \*\*\* | | |
| will be based on | | \*\*\* | | |
| will not be accepted | | \*\*\* | | |
| will not be collected | | \*\*\* | | |
| **II.  DISCOURSE ORGANIZERS** | | | | |
| **Topic introduction/focus** | | | | |
| is designed to provide | | \*\* | \*\* | |
| purpose of this course | | \*\*\* | | |
| of this course is | | \*\*\* | | |
| our goal is to | | \*\* | | |
| provides an introduction to | | \*\* | | |
| the purpose of this | | \*\*\* | | |
| this course is to | | \*\*\* | | |

**Table 6.2**  (*continued*)

|  | Textbooks | Course Management | Institut. Writing | Academic Prose |
|---|---|---|---|---|
| **Topic elaboration/clarification** | | | | |
| at the same time | ** | | ** | ** |
| on the other hand | ** | | | *** |
| as well as the | ** | ** | ** | * |
| **Identification/focus** | | | | |
| one of the most | ** | | ** | ** |
| which of the following | | *** | | |
| **Conditions** | | | | |
| if you are a | | | *** | |
| if you do not | | ** | ** | |
| if you have not | | | ** | |
| if you wish to | | | ** | |
| **III.   REFERENTIAL EXPRESSIONS** | | | | |
| **Specification of attributes** | | | | |
| **Quantity specification** | | | | |
| for a maximum of | | | *** | |
| all of the above | | ** | | |
| a wide range of | | ** | | |
| **Tangible framing attributes** | | | | |
| the dean of the | | | *** | |
| with a grade of | | | *** | |
| a description of the | | ** | | |
| the title of the | | ** | | |
| **Intangible framing attributes** | | | | |
| the nature of the | ** | ** | | ** |
| in the case of | ** | ** | | *** |
| in terms of the | ** | ** | | |
| as a result of | ** | ** | | ** |
| on the basis of | ** | ** | ** | ** |
| for the purpose of | | | ** | |
| in accordance with the | | | ** | |
| in addition to the | | | ** | |
| an introduction to the | | ** | | |
| an understanding of the | | ** | | |
| the relationship between the | | ** | | |
| **Time/place/text/other reference** | | | | |
| **Place or institution reference** | | | | |
| in/of the united states | *** | | *** | |
| in the college of | | | *** | |
| the office of student (financial) | | | *** | |
| to the office of | | | ** | |

Table 6.2   (*continued*)

|  | Textbooks | Course Management | Institut. Writing | Academic Prose |
|---|---|---|---|---|
| **Time reference** | | | | |
| at the time of | | | *** | ** |
| end of the semester | | ** | ** | |
| the first day of | | | *** | |
| beginning of each class | | ** | | |
| the end of each | | *** | | |
| **Multi-functional reference** | | | | |
| the end of the | ** | *** | *** | ** |
| the beginning of the | ** | *** | ** | |
| at the end of | *** | *** | ** | ** |
| at the beginning of | | *** | ** | |

Although both course management and institutional writing use a large number of lexical bundles, the functional distribution of bundles is strikingly different in the two registers. In written course management, over half of all bundles are stance bundles; referential bundles are also relatively common. Discourse organizers are less common than the other functional types in course management writing (although this category is still very common in comparison with other registers). In contrast, over 2/3 of all bundles in institutional writing are referential; stance bundles and discourse organizers are considerably less common in this register.

### 6.4.2.1 *Stance bundles in non-academic written registers*

Spoken classroom management and written course management are similar in that they both rely heavily on stance lexical bundles (Figure 6.5). However, as Figure 6.6 shows, these two registers tend to rely on different functional subcategories: Both registers use obligation bundles, but spoken classroom management also relies heavily on desire bundles (see discussion above), while written course management relies on intention/prediction bundles. Consideration of these bundles in context shows that most of them are used for directive purposes, regardless of their subcategory.

Table 6.2 shows that the obligation bundles in written course management are different from those usually found in spoken classroom management: They are usually clausal, with *you* as the grammatical subject, but the main verb is either passive or an adjectival predicate. These bundles function to explicitly spell out the requirements of a course:

> You are encouraged to take advantage of this service.

> In any case, you are responsible for information presented in classes you miss.

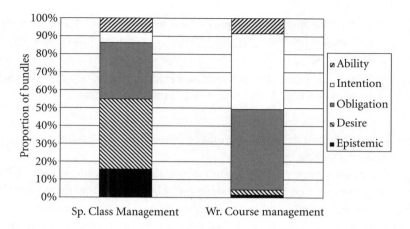

**Figure 6.6** Breakdown of stance bundles across functional categories: Spoken classroom management vs. written course management (syllabi, etc.)

Intention/prediction bundles are also common in written course management. Some of these introduce the topics and organization of a course:

> <u>We will look at</u> relevant data and file structures and incorporate database access through embedded SQL.

However, intention/prediction bundles more often have directive functions in classroom management, introducing requirements and expectations, such as:

> <u>All students will be</u> required to defend their work in oral examinations.

> <u>Homework will be assigned</u> weekly.

It is interesting that spoken classroom management and written course management use different sets of lexical bundles, having different structural characteristics, for very similar purposes (compare Tables 6.1 and 6.2). Directive functions are dominant in both registers, and they both use lexical bundles as direct expressions of obligation. Both registers also commonly use lexical bundles for indirect directives, but they prefer different bundle types: desire bundles in spoken classroom management versus intention/prediction bundles in written course management. In speech, the instructor expresses directives by telling students what he/she 'wants' or 'would like'; in writing, the instructor expresses directives by identifying events that will occur in the future, usually with a passive voice verb and no indication of the agent.

Stance bundles in institutional writing are relatively rare, but when they do occur, they are almost always obligation bundles (see Table 6.2). These bundles are usually impersonal, referring to the addressee as generic 'students' or not at all; for example:

Students participating in extra curricular or co curricular activities or receiv-
ing financial assistance <u>may be required to</u> maintain a specified minimum
academic load.

In order to compare a student's residency credit, <u>it is necessary to</u> know whether
the student is enrolled as a full time or as a part time student.

### 6.4.2.2  *Referential and discourse organizing bundles in non-academic written registers*

Referential bundles are especially common in institutional writing, and also relatively common in written course management. Figure 6.7 shows the proportional
breakdown of referential bundles across subcategories in these two registers.

Place bundles are dominant in institutional writing. This is not surprising
given the need to refer repeatedly to offices and other institutions on campus (e.g.,
*in the college of, from the office of* ). Many of these word sequences are names or titles
of an institution, rather than lexical bundles in the normal sense. For example:

at Georgia State University, Immigration and Naturalization Service,
the office of residence life

Time bundles are also relatively common in both course management and institutional writing. Many of these refer to specific times that are especially relevant to
university life, for example referring to class periods or semesters:

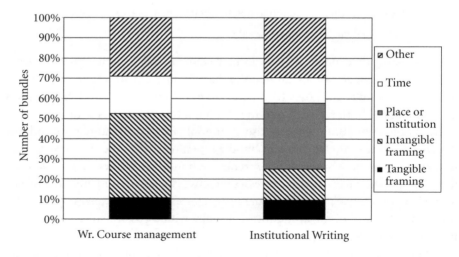

**Figure 6.7**  Breakdown of referential bundles across functional categories: Non-academic
written registers

course management:

beginning of each class, during my office hours, over the course of, the beginning of each, the end of each

institutional writing:

at the time of, fall and spring semesters, the first day of, the semester in which

Intangible framing attributes are proportionally more prevalent in syllabi and other written course management materials, being used to introduce course content and the conceptual organization of a course:

Architecture 271 is <u>an introduction to the</u> concept of fit in architecture.

An additional aim of this course is to investigate <u>the nature of the</u> ethnographic enterprise itself.

We shall analyze <u>the relationship between the</u> data they gather and the claims they make.

Finally, discourse organizing bundles are also relatively common in course management, where they indicate the overall organization and goals of a course:

Instead, <u>our goal is to</u> UNCOVER the meaning of key themes in psychology and grow in understanding and applying these themes to our world.

<u>The objective of this course</u> is to expose the student to introductory material relating to electromagnetics.

Discourse organizers are less common in institutional writing. These mostly incorporate conditional clauses: the bundle identifies a common circumstance that a student might encounter, and the following prose provides a description of the actions that the student should take under those circumstances:

<u>If you are a</u> currently enrolled student, you are eligible to obtain your health care at Fronske Health Center.

<u>If you have been</u> suspended from NAU, refer to the section titled Academic Suspension, which is in the General Academic Requirements chapter of this catalog.

## 6.5 Lexical bundles across academic disciplines

Finally, it is interesting to compare the use of lexical bundles across academic disciplines. The description here is restricted to textbooks, in an attempt to isolate the influence of academic discipline. Similar to the analyses reported in 6.4 above, the analysis of lexical bundles in textbooks was hampered by relatively small and

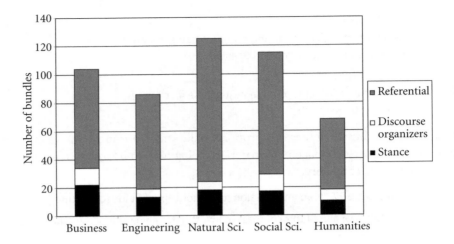

**Figure 6.8** Distribution of lexical bundles across functional categories: Academic disciplines in textbooks

uneven samples for the different disciplines.[9] As a result, the description focuses on general patterns rather than detailed discussion of specific lexical bundles.

Figure 6.8 shows surprising differences among academic disciplines in the overall use of lexical bundles. Natural science and social science show the greatest reliance on lexical bundles, while humanities is at the opposite extreme with comparatively few different lexical bundles.

These results need to be interpreted with caution, because the analysis is based on a relatively small corpus, and the samples for each discipline are not matched for size (number of texts or number of words). However, the distributional patterns seen in Figure 6.8 do not in any way correlate with sample size. In particular, the three registers with the largest samples – social science, humanities, and natural science – occupy opposite ends of the continuum in their patterns of bundle use. Thus, we can be fairly confident that these are genuine differences rather than a mere artifact of sampling differences,

Two factors are probably relevant here: technical content and stylistic preferences. Natural science textbooks convey dense technical content, and thus use specific terms and expressions to refer to that content, aiming to achieve an explicit conveyance of meaning (see Chapter 3, especially 3.3.2). It is likely that this reliance on a specific set of technical terms contributes to the dense use of lexical bundles. In contrast, humanities textbooks are more concerned with the critical discussion of ideas and interpretations. In addition, humanities authors value stylistic variation, often expressing the same idea in multiple ways for the sake of a more highly valued style. Such stylistic variation would contribute to the overall lesser reliance on lexical bundles.

Consideration of the breakdown of bundles across functional categories allows a more complete interpretation of these register differences. Table 6.3 lists common lexical bundles occurring in each of these disciplines, while Figure 6.8 shows the general distribution across functions. Both of these show that discourse organizers are the least important category in all disciplines. This finding is somewhat surprising, since it seems obvious that students would benefit from explicit signals of discourse organization to facilitate understanding. (Section 6.3 above shows that lexical bundles as discourse organizers are much more common in classroom teaching.)

Discourse organizing bundles are distributed fairly evenly across disciplines. When they do occur in textbooks, they usually function as an overt cue that further elaboration, clarification, or a point of contrast is being provided; for example:

> The lifeworlds of archaic societies are in principle accessible via their members' intuitive knowledge; **at the same time**, they stubbornly escape our comprehension [...]

> The history of sociological theory, **as well as the** current state of sociological theory, is the precipitate of dozens of such intellectual episodes.

> Some norms are proscriptive, mandating what we should not do [...] Prescriptive norms, **on the other hand**, state what we should do [...]

Figure 6.8 also shows that stance bundles are not especially common in textbooks, although they are more important than discourse organizers. Stance bundles are most common in business (where they constitute c. 20% of all bundles).

A more detailed investigation shows that stance bundles are used for different purposes in the different disciplines. Figure 6.9 displays the proportional breakdown of stance bundles across functions. Several stance functions are almost never expressed with lexical bundles in textbooks, including obligation, desire, intention/prediction, and personal expressions of stance generally. (In contrast, these personal stance functions are very common in classroom teaching and in non-academic spoken and written university registers.) Instead, in textbooks we find stance bundles being used for three main functional categories: epistemic, ability, and importance (see also Table 6.3). For example:

> Epistemic:
> Specifically, they <u>are more likely to</u> seek to become acquainted with higher-level managers.

> Ability:
> The supply system <u>can be used to</u> achieve important competitive priorities.

> Importance:
> <u>It is important to</u> emphasize the assumption that each party has complete information about the other.

**Table 6.3** Functional classification and distribution of common lexical bundles across academic disciplines in textbooks

Key to symbols:
　　'*'　　　20–39 per million words
　　'**'　　　40–99 per million words
　　'***'　　over 100 per million words

| | Business | Engineering | Natural Sci. | Social Sci. | Humanities |
|---|---|---|---|---|---|
| **I.　STANCE EXPRESSIONS** | | | | | |
| **A.　Epistemic stance – Impersonal:** | | | | | |
| are more likely to | ** | | | ** | |
| are likely to be | * | | | * | |
| the fact that the | | ** | | ** | ** |
| by the fact that | | | | ** | * |
| **B.　Attitudinal/Modality stance** | | | | | |
| **Ability/effort – Impersonal:** | | | | | |
| can be used to | ** | *** | ** | * | |
| it is difficult to | * | ** | | | |
| it is possible to | ** | ** | | | * |
| can be calculated from | | ** | | | |
| can be determined by | | ** | * | | |
| **Importance – Impersonal:** | | | | | |
| it is important to | ** | ** | * | * | * |
| an important role in | | | * | * | |
| of the most important | | | * | * | |
| **II.　DISCOURSE ORGANIZERS** | | | | | |
| on the other hand | ** | *** | *** | ** | ** |
| on the one hand | * | | | ** | ** |
| as well as the | ** | ** | ** | ** | ** |
| for the most part | * | | | | * |
| we can think of | ** | | | | |
| as long as the | | ** | * | * | |
| in this case the | | ** | | | |
| tells us that the | | | ** | | |
| at the same time | ** | ** | *** | *** | * |
| in addition to the | | | ** | * | |
| **III.　REFERENTIAL EXPRESSIONS** | | | | | |
| **Identification** | | | | | |
| is one of the | | | ** | * | |
| is referred to as | * | ** | | | |
| one of the most | | ** | *** | ** | *** |
| is known as the | | | ** | | |
| **Specification of attributes** | | | | | |
| **Quantity/mathematical expression** | | | | | |
| the rest of the | * | ** | * | ** | |
| a great deal of | ** | ** | | ** | |
| a large number of | ** | | * | | * |

**Table 6.3**  (*continued*)

|  | Business | Engineering | Natural Sci. | Social Sci. | Humanities |
|---|---|---|---|---|---|
| a wide range of | ** |  |  | ** |  |
| the sum of the | ** |  | ** |  |  |
| degrees of freedom of |  | *** |  |  |  |
| an increase in the |  | ** | * |  |  |
| of the number of |  | ** | * |  |  |
| the magnitude of the |  | *** | ** |  |  |
| the rate at which |  | *** | ** |  |  |
| the ratio of the |  | ** | ** |  |  |
| as a function of |  | *** | *** | * |  |
| **Predicative** |  |  |  |  |  |
| is equal to the | * | ** | ** |  |  |
| is given by the |  | ** | * |  |  |
| is proportional to the |  | ** | ** |  |  |
| **Tangible framing attributes** |  |  |  |  |  |
| the size of the |  |  | ** | ** |  |
| in the form of | ** | ** | ** | ** | * |
| in place of the |  | *** |  |  |  |
| the composition of the |  | *** |  |  |  |
| the length of the |  | ** |  |  |  |
| the mass of the |  |  | ** |  |  |
| **Intangible framing attributes** |  |  |  |  |  |
| the nature of the | * | ** | ** | ** | ** |
| in the case of | * | *** | ** | ** | ** |
| in terms of the | * | ** | ** | * | * |
| as a result of | ** |  | *** | ** | ** |
| in the absence of | * | ** |  | * |  |
| the context of the | ** |  |  | * |  |
| beyond the scope of |  | ** |  |  |  |
| the order in which |  | *** |  |  |  |
| the temperature of the |  | *** |  |  |  |
| the velocity of the |  | *** | ** |  |  |
| on the basis of |  | *** | ** |  | ** |
| the basis of the |  | ** | * |  |  |
| the structure of the |  | * |  |  | ** |
| in the course of |  |  |  | * | ** |
| **Time/place/text/other reference** |  |  |  |  |  |
| **Place or institution reference** |  |  |  |  |  |
| the united states and | ** |  | * | ** | * |
| in/of the united states | *** |  | *** | *** | ** |
| **General location reference or framing** |  |  |  |  |  |
| in the same direction | ** |  |  |  |  |
| at the base of |  |  | ** |  |  |
| at the bottom of |  |  | ** |  |  |
| in the vicinity of |  |  | ** |  |  |

**Table 6.3**  (*continued*)

|  | Business | Engineering | Natural Sci. | Social Sci. | Humanities |
|---|---|---|---|---|---|
| on either side of |  |  | ** |  |  |
| the position of the |  |  | *** |  |  |
| the surface of the |  |  | *** |  |  |
| the top of the |  |  | *** | * |  |
| **Text deixis** |  |  |  |  |  |
| as shown in figure/fig. |  | *** | *** | * |  |
| as we have seen |  |  |  | ** | * |
| in our discussion of | * |  | ** |  |  |
| in this chapter we | * | ** |  |  |  |
| **Multi-functional reference** |  |  |  |  |  |
| the end of the | *** |  | ** | ** | ** |
| the beginning of the | * |  | * | * | ** |
| at the end of | *** | ** | ** | ** | ** |

It is interesting to note that two of these functional categories – ability and importance – are restricted primarily to textbooks. That is, while epistemic bundles are found in most university registers, ability and importance bundles are found primarily in textbooks.

Given that textbooks have a primary purpose of conveying knowledge, it is surprising that epistemic meanings are not the main category of stance bundle in this register. It is perhaps even more surprising that epistemic bundles are least common in the natural sciences and engineering (see Figure 6.9). In contrast, epistemic stance bundles are most common in social science, and they are also relatively common in business and humanities. This pattern reflects the differing kinds of knowledge that constitute the basis of the different disciplines. Engineering and natural science are based on the 'laws' of nature, which are often treated as if they do not have exceptions, resulting in a lesser need for epistemic lexical bundles. In contrast, the social sciences are based on typical patterns of behavior; epistemic stance bundles are crucially important in telling the reader how to interpret statements about these patterns. In addition, much discussion in the social sciences and humanities compares different points of view and the likelihood that one or another is preferable. Epistemic bundles are important in such interpretive discourse, helping students to distinguish the knowledge status of different propositions (e.g., 'factual' versus 'likely' versus 'doubtful'). The following examples from social science textbooks illustrate these functions:

> These researchers conclude that, given the socioeconomic conditions of most developing societies and the inability of governments to provide substantial social service programs, there **are likely to be** increasing numbers of elderly parents with neither property, pensions, nor savings in their old age.

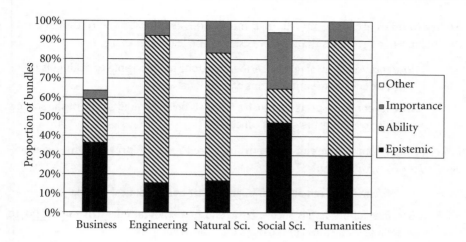

**Figure 6.9** Breakdown of stance bundles across functional categories: Academic disciplines in textbooks

> If unemployment is frequently reported higher among the urban-born than among immigrants, it is because the families of the urban-born **are more likely to be** already well established in the urban economy.

> There is always the concern that findings across cultures using these tests are confused **by the fact that the** tests may be meaningful only to American subjects.

In fact, we sometimes find multiple bundles – expressing both certainty and likelihood – in close proximity in social science textbooks. The following sentence illustrates how a 'likelihood' can be regarded as a 'fact' in this discipline:

> This racial difference may be linked **to the fact that** African Americans **are more likely to be** poor and to experience marital separation.

Ability stance bundles are generally more important than epistemic bundles in university textbooks (see Figure 6.9 and Table 6.3), but they are especially important in engineering and natural science. Most of these are passive constructions, referring to the abilities of the researcher or the student reader to carry out technical calculations or processes. For example:

> The length of the line of action **can be determined by** Equation 7.5.

> Appropriate free convection n-Pentane-copper correlations from Chapter 9 **can be used to** estimate heat transfer coefficients.

> The theorem states that **it is possible to** write any computer program by using only three basic control structures.

Ability bundles are also important in humanities textbooks, where they identify the interpretive processes that students should be learning, as in:

> To identify a fallacy of relevance, therefore, one **must be able to** distinguish genuine evidence from various forms of emotional appeal.

> Whenever one suspects that such a fallacy is being committed, he or she **should be able to** identify the correct conclusion.

Finally, stance bundles signaling importance are especially prevalent in social science textbooks; for example:

> Federalism issues remain **an important part of** our political agenda.

> Because culture fulfills such a basic and fundamental role, **it is important to** examine exactly how culture plays that role in our lives.

It is interesting that social science textbooks use the most bundles expressing both certainty and importance. These bundles provide overt signals to the (student) reader of the points that they should pay special attention to. At the other extreme, engineering textbooks use almost no lexical bundles indicating either certainty or importance.

Referential bundles are by far the most common functional category in all disciplines (see Figure 6.8 above). Referential bundles are especially important in natural science and, to a slightly lesser extent, social science. However, Figure 6.10 and Table 6.3 show that there are striking differences in the specific functions of these bundles across disciplines.

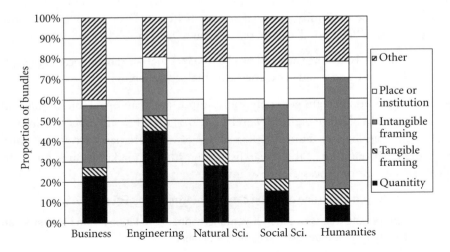

**Figure 6.10** Breakdown of referential bundles across functional categories: Academic disciplines in textbooks

One interesting pattern observed from Figure 6.10 is that quantity/mathematical bundles and intangible bundles are in complementary distribution. At one extreme, 45% of all referential bundles in engineering textbooks express quantity/mathematical meanings, while only 20% of the referential bundles in engineering express intangible meanings. At the other extreme, 55% of the referential bundles in humanities textbooks express intangible meanings (versus only 8% with quantity meanings). Natural science textbooks are relatively similar to engineering in their preference for quantity/mathematical bundles, while social science is more similar to humanities (preferring intangible bundles).

The quantity/mathematical bundles in engineering textbooks often identify the mathematical status of the following noun phrase; for example:

> and the number of, at a rate of, by a factor of, degrees of freedom of, expressed in terms of, of the number of, the magnitude of the, the rate at which, the ratio of the, the square of the, the value of the, as a function of

These bundles are used to identify the relations among the components and variables used in mathematical equations:

> The resonant frequency depends on **the ratio of the** mass to the total spring rate of the tires.

> The response properties can be presented by examining the response gain **as a function of** frequency, as shown in Figure 5.16.

> A 60 per cent aqueous sucrose solution at 20′ C flows through the bed **at a rate of** 244 lb min negative 1.

In contrast, intangible referential bundles are predominant in humanities textbooks; for example:

> the nature of the, in the case of, a part of the, in the course of, in the development of, in the process of, an analysis of the, in response to the, in the context of, in the face of, in the work of, of the relationship between, the character of the, the course of the, the notion of a, the question of whether, the use of the

These bundles provide an interpretive referential frame for the following head noun, singling out a particular abstract attribute as important:

> Second, it identifies **the nature of the** artist's special God-given talents…

> **In the process of** analyzing yourself, you should answer three questions…

> Manfredi's poems must be seen **in the context of** the burgeoning literature dedicated to defining woman and ideal femininity…

> Houclon's Cagliostro presents with exquisite acuteness **the character of the** sanctimonious fraud.

Natural science textbooks differ from the other disciplines in that they exhibit a frequent use of place/location lexical bundles, as in:

> at the bottom of, at the top of, in the direction of, in the vicinity of, on either side of, on the surface of, the base of the, the center of the, the position of the

These also have a discourse framing function, but they are much more concrete in meaning, identifying the physical location of a referent, or the physical relationship of one referent to some other referent. For example:

> The least soluble minerals are concentrated around the rim of the ancient lake and are found **at the bottom of** the evaporite sequence.
>
> Water is poured onto the tephra **in the vicinity of** the steam wells.
>
> The areas with elevated bacterial counts coincide with **the position of the** plume...

## 6.6 Postscript: The theoretical status of lexical bundles in university registers

The results presented above suggest that lexical bundles should be regarded as a basic linguistic construct with important functions for the construction of discourse in university registers. However, with respect to both structure and function, lexical bundles differ dramatically from other linguistic features (including the traditional formulaic expressions usually recognized by discourse analysts).

Given that lexical bundles are defined strictly on the basis of frequency, with no consideration of structural or functional criteria, they might be expected to be arbitrary strings of words that have no linguistic status. Instead, these frequent sequences of words turn out to be readily interpretable in both structural and functional terms. Although they are not the kinds of grammatical structures recognized by traditional linguistic theory, most lexical bundles do have well-defined structural correlates: they usually consist of the beginning of a clause or phrase plus the first word of an embedded structure (e.g., a dependent complement clause or a prepositional phrase). These sequences of words can be regarded as structural 'frames', followed by a 'slot'. The frame functions as a kind of discourse anchor for the 'new' information in the slot, telling the listener/reader how to interpret that information with respect to stance, discourse organization, or referential status.

The patterns of use for lexical bundles are strikingly different from those found for traditional lexico-grammatical features (see Chapter 4). The contrast is especially notable for classroom teaching. With respect to lexico-grammatical features, classroom teaching relies heavily on 'oral' structures, despite the need for an informational focus. Similarly, classroom teaching is similar to other spoken registers in using a restricted range of vocabulary, in contrast to the diverse range of vocabulary used in textbooks and other written university registers (see Chapter 3). These linguistic patterns indicate that the typical vocabulary and grammatical characteristics of classroom teaching are determined primarily by the 'oral' characteristics of the situation: the real-time production circumstances, and the focus on personal and interpersonal purposes.

In contrast, the analyses in the present chapter show that classroom teaching mixes 'oral' and 'literate' characteristics in the use of lexical bundles, actually going beyond the expected 'targets' in its patterns of use. That is, classroom teaching shows a more extensive use of stance lexical bundles and discourse organizing bundles than in conversation, while at the same time it shows a more extensive use of referential bundles than in academic prose.

These patterns of use indicate that lexical bundles are a fundamentally different kind of linguistic construct from productive grammatical constructions. For example, consider the use of NP/PP-based referential lexical bundles in contrast to the full range of noun-phrase and prepositional-phrase structures. Classroom teaching generally avoids the dense use of noun phrases and prepositional phrases (see Figures 4.1, 4.2, and 4.11, in Chapter 4). As a productive grammatical strategy, the dense use of complex noun phrase constructions has dramatically increased in informational written registers over the past 100 years (see Biber & Clark 2002; Biber 2003a). However, these constructions are much less common in spoken registers like conversation, presumably because they are difficult to produce and comprehend in real-time situations. In this regard, classroom teaching is typical of other 'oral' registers in avoiding the dense use of complex noun phrase structures.

Given those grammatical patterns, it is surprising that classroom teaching makes extensive use of NP/PP-based referential bundles. Although the functional need for referential expressions in classroom teaching is clear, the reliance on NP/PP-based bundles is unexpected. This pattern can be interpreted as evidence that lexical bundles are stored as unanalyzed multi-word chunks, rather than as productive grammatical constructions. The fact that referential bundles are composed of noun phrase and prepositional phrase fragments reflects their historical origins, but their frequent use in classroom teaching suggests that these sequences are now stored and used as single units, disregarding their structural correlates. As such, these bundles do not present production or comprehension difficulties for speakers and listeners in classroom teaching.

More general evidence for the importance of lexical bundles comes from their frequencies of use and obvious discourse functions. The present chapter has approached the study of lexical bundles with the general hypothesis that high frequency patterns are not accidental, but they are also not explanatory in themselves. Rather, corpus-based frequency patterns comprise descriptive facts that require explanation. In the present investigation, the facts that require explanation are the existence of common multi-word sequences which do not represent structurally complete linguistic units. Examination of these multi-word sequences in textual contexts shows that they are important building blocks of discourse, associated with basic communicative functions. In general, these lexical bundles serve as discourse framing devices: they provide a kind of frame expressing stance, discourse organization, or referential status, associated with a slot for the expression of new information relative to that frame. The functions and meanings expressed by these lexical bundles differ dramatically across registers and academic disciplines, depending on the typical purposes of each. However, the descriptions here have shown that lexical bundles are crucially important for the construction of discourse in all university registers.

## Notes

**1.** The study of lexical bundles reported in the LGSWE (Chapter 12) was based on analysis of the Longman Spoken and Written English Corpus (c. 4 million words of British English conversation; c. 3 million words of American English conversation; c. 5.3 million words of academic prose; see Biber et al. 1999:Chapter 1). The academic prose corpus comprises both academic research articles (c. 2.7 million words) and advanced academic books (c. 2.6 million words; see Biber et al. 1999:32–34). While some advanced academic books can also be used as textbooks, especially in graduate courses, the corpora of academic prose and textbooks were sampled independently: textbooks are mostly written specifically for students, while the articles and books included in the academic prose corpus are written for other professionals.

**2.** Section 6.3 of this chapter is adapted with revisions from Biber, Conrad, and Cortes (2004).

**3.** The quantitative analysis of lexical bundles was undertaken with computer programs that identified and stored every 4-word sequence in the corpus. The programs read through each text in the corpus, storing every sequence beginning with the first word of the text and advancing one word at a time. For example, the first sentence of this paragraph would have the following 4-word sequences identified:

> *the quantitative analysis of*
> *quantitative analysis of lexical*
> *analysis of lexical bundles*
> *of lexical bundles was*
> etc.

Each time a sequence was identified, it was automatically checked against the previously identified sequences, and a running frequency count showed how often each sequence was repeated. In identifying lexical bundles, we relied on orthographic word units, even though these sometimes arbitrarily combine separate words. For example, *into, cannot, self-control,* and *don't* are all regarded as single words in our analysis. Only uninterrupted sequences of words were treated as lexical bundles. Thus, lexical sequences that spanned a turn boundary or a punctuation mark were excluded.

**4.** Other sequences of words can be repeated frequently within a single text. In many cases, these sequences do not represent lexical bundles, because they are not widely distributed across multiple texts. These local repetitions reflect the immediate topical concerns of the discourse. In contrast, lexical bundles can be regarded as the more general lexical building blocks that are used frequently by many different speakers/writers within a register.

**5.** Figure 6.1 shows that textbooks uses a greater range of different lexical bundles than academic prose. Some of the bundles in academic prose occur with high frequencies, resulting in a slightly higher overall frequency of lexical bundle tokens.

**6.** In fact, some of these bundles typically have stance functions in conversation, while they usually serve discourse organizing functions in classroom teaching. The bundle *I would like to* is a good example of this type.

**7.** The distributional patterns shown in Figure 6.2 are slightly different from those presented in Biber, Conrad, and Cortes (2004), because 'identification/focus' bundles are grouped here under the 'discourse organizing' function rather than under 'referential' functions.

**8.** Some differences in the sets of lexical bundles found across registers might be due to design differences in the corpora analyzed: ranging from c. 5-million words for academic prose, to 1.2 million words for classroom teaching, and .75 million words for textbooks. However, Cortes (2002:72–75) found that analyses of smaller corpora actually yield more lexical bundles, because some bundles have artificially high frequencies in the smaller corpora that cannot be maintained in a larger collection of texts. Thus, the low number of lexical bundles found in textbooks cannot be attributed to the fact that the sub-corpus is smaller: if anything, we would expect to find an inflated number of bundles based on analysis of this smaller sub-corpus.

**9.** At one extreme, engineering textbooks are represented by only 72,000 words and 9 texts. (Education textbooks, with only 6 texts and 50,000 words, were dropped from the analysis here.) At the other extreme, social science textbooks are represented by 213,000 words and 21 texts.

The descriptions in Section 6.3 and 6.4 above show that lexical bundles are generally rare in textbooks, in comparison to other university registers. For this reason, I set a lower minimum frequency cut-off for the analyses in the present section, including all recurrent sequences occurring over 20 times per million words as a lexical bundle. In addition, the individual texts for textbooks tend to be much longer than for the other registers (usually over 5,000 words per text), resulting in relatively few textbook samples for any individual academic discipline. To adjust for this, I relaxed the requirement that a recurrent sequence must be distributed across 5 different texts to be considered a lexical bundle. Instead, the following criteria were adopted:

– any sequence occurring only 4 times must be distributed across at least 3 different texts
– any sequence occurring 5 or more times must be distributed across at least 2 different texts.

Because engineering textbooks are represented by a much smaller sample than the other disciplines, sequences that occurred only 3 times in this register actually had a normed rate of 40 per million words. I thus further adjusted the requirements to include those sequences as bundles:

– any sequence occurring only 3 times in engineering textbooks must be distributed across at least 3 different texts
– any sequence occurring 4 or more times in engineering textbooks must be distributed across at least 2 different texts.

# CHAPTER 7

# Multi-dimensional patterns of variation among university registers

## 7.1 Introduction

The preceding chapters have described the functions of individual linguistic features in university registers. These descriptions identify many important linguistic differences across registers, and they enable detailed consideration of the functions served by particular features. Taken together, these analyses suggest several general patterns of variation among university registers, including:

- spoken registers are systematically different from written registers, with respect to a wide range of vocabulary characteristics and lexico-grammatical features
- interactive registers are different from monologic registers
- academic registers are different from the behavior-management (directive) registers, whether spoken or written

The present chapter shifts to a wider perspective, using Multi-Dimensional (MD) analysis to study the overall patterns of register variation among university texts. In MD analysis, the distribution of a large set of linguistic features is analyzed in a multi-register corpus of texts. Specifically, factor analysis is used to identify the systematic co-occurrence patterns among these linguistic features – the 'dimensions' – and then texts and registers can be compared along each dimension.

Multi-Dimensional analysis provides a complementary linguistic perspective on university registers to the one developed in preceding chapters. That is, earlier chapters in this book have focused on particular linguistic levels or domains, considering linguistic features belonging to a single structural level (e.g., word choice; part-of-speech categories; dependent clause types), or considering features that all serve the same general function (e.g., expressing stance). These chapters have employed a comparative approach and quantitative analysis to determine the relative distribution of individual linguistic features. By using quantitative comparisons to the range of other university registers, the descriptions are able to determine whether a given frequency of occurrence is notably common or rare in a target register. This quantitative comparative approach treats register as a continuous construct: texts are situated within a continuous space of linguistic variation, enabling analysis of the ways in which registers are more or less different with respect to the full range of core linguistic features.

It turns out, though, that the relative distribution of common linguistic features, considered individually, cannot reliably distinguish among registers. There are simply too many different linguistic characteristics to consider, and individual features often have idiosyncratic distributions. That is, although the distributions of individual features are interpretable in functional terms, these individual patterns cannot be used to determine the extent to which any two registers are similar or different. Rather, overall register differences are describable with respect to sets of co-occurring linguistic features.

The importance of linguistic co-occurrence has been emphasized by several linguists in the past. Brown and Fraser (1979: 38–39) observe that it can be 'misleading to concentrate on specific, isolated [linguistic] markers without taking into account systematic variations which involve the co-occurrence of sets of markers'. Ervin-Tripp (1972) and Hymes (1974) identify 'speech styles' as varieties that are defined by a shared set of co-occurring linguistic features. Halliday (1988: 162) defines a register as 'a cluster of associated features having a greater-than-random ... tendency to co-occur'.

Although this general theoretical perspective has been widely accepted, linguists lacked the methodological tools required for such analyses before the availability of corpus-based techniques. The MD approach was developed to analyze the linguistic co-occurrence patterns associated with register variation in empirical/quantitative terms. Early MD studies investigated the patterns of variation among general spoken and written registers in English (Biber 1985, 1986, 1988), while subsequent studies documented the patterns of register variation in other languages (see, e.g., Biber 1995), or in more specialized discourse domains (see, e.g., Conrad & Biber 2001).

MD analysis uses the power of multivariate statistical techniques to investigate the quantitative distribution of linguistic features across texts and registers. Linguistic co-occurrence is analyzed in terms of underlying 'dimensions' of variation which are identified quantitatively, by a statistical factor analysis, rather than on an a priori functional basis. The dimensions resulting from MD analysis have both linguistic and functional content. The linguistic content of a dimension is a group of features (such as nouns, attributive adjectives, prepositional phrases) that co-occur regularly in texts. On the assumption that co-occurrence reflects shared functions, these co-occurrence patterns are interpreted to assess the situational, social, and cognitive functions most widely shared by the linguistic features.

## 7.2 Application of the 1988 MD analysis to university registers

### 7.2.1 Overview of the 1988 MD analysis

The first major MD analysis (Biber 1988; see also Biber 1985, 1986) was undertaken to investigate the relationship among general spoken and written registers in English. The corpus included 481 spoken and written texts of contemporary British English, taken from the Lancaster-Oslo-Bergen Corpus and the London-Lund Corpus. These texts were sampled from 23 major register categories, including academic prose, press reportage, fiction, letters, conversations, interviews, radio broadcasts, and public speeches.

The 1988 study used factor analysis to identify the groups of linguistic features associated with each dimension; these are the sets of linguistic features that co-occur in texts with markedly high frequencies. The factors are interpreted as functional 'dimensions' based on the assumption that linguistic features co-occur in texts because they reflect underlying shared communicative functions. 67 linguistic features were analyzed (e.g., first and second person pronouns, nominalizations, past tense verbs, *that* relative clauses, etc.), and a principal factor analysis was used with a 7-factor solution to identify the 'dimensions' of variation. (Details of the analysis are provided in Biber 1988:Chapters 4 and 5; 1995:Chapter 5.)

The first five factors from the 1988 factor analysis are readily interpretable as 'dimensions' of register variation, based on consideration of the linguistic features co-occurring on each dimension together with the similarities and differences among registers with respect to the group of features. Interpretive labels have been proposed for each dimension, reflecting the underlying functions:

1. Involved versus Informational Production
2. Narrative versus Non-narrative Concerns
3. Situation-Dependent versus Elaborated Reference
4. Overt Expression of Persuasion
5. Non-Impersonal versus Impersonal / Abstract Style

### 7.2.2 Relations among university registers with respect to the 1988 dimensions

Although these dimensions were identified from analysis of a general corpus of spoken and written texts, they can be applied to the description of more restricted discourse domains, including university spoken and written registers. Such an analysis is based on the premise that the dimensions identified in the 1988 study represent general linguistic/functional parameters of variation applicable to more specialized discourse domains. That is, because the 1988 analysis was based on a broad sample of texts and registers, and included a large sample of linguistic features from several structural and functional levels, the dimensions have been regarded as valid for the description of register variation in more specialized domains.

Biber, Conrad, Reppen, Byrd, and Helt (2002) apply the 1988 dimensions to the analysis of the university spoken and written registers in the T2K-SWAL Corpus. The results of that study show that students must negotiate registers representing a tremendous range of linguistic variation. On all dimensions except Dimension 2 (narrative discourse), university registers fell at both ends of these linguistic parameters. Students must deal not only with informationally dense prose but also with interactive and involved spoken registers. They must handle texts with elaborated reference as well as those that rely on situated reference, and texts with features of overt persuasion as well as texts that lack those features. They must understand discourse that uses an impersonal style (with many passives) as well as discourse that tends to avoid passives.

The distribution of registers along Dimension 1 – Involved versus Informational Production – is especially noteworthy. Academic registers are typically assumed to be extremely informational, but it turns out that university students also encounter academic registers that are highly interactive and involved. Even registers with a strongly informational purpose, such as classroom teaching and study groups, are marked for the features of face-to-face interaction and a focus on personal stance, rather than the features of informational production.

The 2002 MD study found that most of these dimensions show a strong polarization between spoken and written registers. The written registers – regardless of their specific purpose – are characterized by informationally dense prose (Dimension 1), a non-narrative focus (Dimension 2), elaborated reference (Dimension 3), few features of overt persuasion (Dimension 4), and an impersonal style (Dimension 5). (The only exception to this pattern is the course management register, which uses the Dimension 4 features of overt argumentation.) In contrast, the spoken registers – again regardless of purpose – are all characterized by features of involvement and interaction, situated reference, more overt persuasion, and fewer features of impersonal style. No register in the T2K-SWAL Corpus is characterized by a narrative focus (Dimension 2).

This general pattern of polarization contrasts with previous MD studies of English, which did not find spoken and written registers to be so sharply distinguished. For example, fiction writing is similar to many spoken registers (see Biber 1988: Chapter 7): fiction uses the features of both involved and informational production (Dimension 1), and it is marked strongly for the use of narrative features (Dimension 2), situation-dependent reference (Dimension 3), and non-impersonal style (Dimension 5). In contrast, no written register in the T2K-SWAL Corpus was similar to any of the spoken registers with respect to the 1988 dimensions.

The sharp divide between spoken and written university registers is especially surprising given the wide range of communicative purposes represented by the registers in the T2K-SWAL Corpus. The spoken registers, for example, range from interpersonal interactions with both social and informational purposes (e.g., service encounters and study groups), to monologic discourse with a primary informational focus (e.g., classroom teaching). However, despite these differences, all spoken university registers are sharply distinguished from written university registers with respect to the 1988 dimensions of variation.

These research findings raise the question of whether other dimensions of variation might reflect differences in purpose or task, and so distinguish among academic versus non-academic registers within the spoken and written modes. That is, the description of university register variation in Biber et al. (2002) is based on the dimensions identified previously in the 1988 MD study; those dimensions were derived from analysis of a general corpus of spoken and written registers (e.g., conversation, interviews, newspaper reportage, editorials, fiction, and academic prose). It might be the case, however, that additional dimensions of variation are important for distinguishing among university spoken and written registers. To investigate this possibility, a new factor analysis was carried out to identify the dimensions of variation that actually occur in the T2K-SWAL corpus.

## 7.3  Motivating a 'new' MD analysis of university registers[1]

The application of the 1988 dimensions to new discourse domains has been highly productive, enabling descriptions of the similarities and differences among specialized registers within that multi-dimensional linguistic space. This approach has been used in several previous studies of specialized registers (see Conrad & Biber 2001, and the survey of studies in Biber to appear); these include direct mail letters (Connor & Upton 2003), non-profit grant proposals (Connor & Upton 2004), author styles (Connor-Linton 1988, 2001; Biber & Finegan 1994b), conversational registers (Helt 2001; Quaglio 2004), and the speech of women and men in dramatic dialogue (Rey 2001; Biber & Burges 2000). As summarized in the preceding section, this same approach has also been used to investigate the overall patterns of variation among university registers.

However, this approach does not enable description of the dimensions that are actually most important in a particular domain of use. That is, linguistic features can co-occur in particular ways in different discourse domains, reflecting the specialized functional priorities of those domains.

An alternative approach is to carry out a completely new MD analysis: a new factor analysis to identify the co-occurrence patterns that actually occur in a corpus of texts. This approach is appropriate when analyzing a new discourse domain that includes many different text categories. Conducting a 'new' multi-dimensional analysis allows identification of the co-occurrence patterns specific to a given domain, and registers can then be compared with respect to those 'new' dimensions. The present chapter adopts this approach to identify the underlying dimensions of variation that distinguish among university registers, disciplines, and levels.[2]

The Multi-Dimensional analysis presented here is further different from the 1988 analysis in that it incorporates a much larger set of linguistic features, building on the detailed descriptions of linguistic features presented in Chapters 4–6. The study began with 129 linguistic features (see Appendix A), although these were subsequently reduced to 90 features that were conceptually distinct and functioned in statistically meaningful co-occurrence patterns. The following section (7.4) presents the statistical factor analysis used for this description, and then in Section 7.5, I interpret these dimensions to describe the patterns of variation among university registers.

## 7.4  Factor analysis of linguistic features in the T2K-SWAL corpus

The factor analysis of the T2K-SWAL Corpus was based on the full set of linguistic features introduced in Chapter 2 and Appendix A. Methodologically, the procedure follows the steps outlined in previous studies (Biber 1988: Chapters 5–6; Biber 1995: Chapter 5; Conrad & Biber 2001: Chapter 2). As described above, this analysis differs from most MD studies in that it is based on a separate factor analysis for this corpus of texts, rather than applying the 1988 general model of variation.

Only 90 of the original 129 linguistic features were retained in the factor analysis. Some features were dropped because they overlapped to a large extent with other features. For example, the original 129 features included counts for 'high frequency verbs', 'high frequency nouns', and 'high frequency adjectives'; and they also included counts for semantic classes of nouns, verbs, and adjectives (e.g., 'mental verbs' or 'communication verbs'). However, it turned out that the specific words included in the high frequency classes overlapped extensively with the words included in the semantic categories. For example, verbs like *think* and *know* are among the most important high frequency verbs and also important members of the 'mental verb' category. Thus, to a large extent, the high frequency categories were measuring the same constructs as the semantic category distinctions, and they were therefore dropped from the factor analysis.

In other cases, features were dropped because they were extremely rare. For example, the original set of features included separate counts for each semantic subclass of phrasal verb (such as 'intransitive activity phrasal verb' and 'transitive communication phrasal verb'). These subclasses were generally rare, and so they were all combined into a single feature: 'phrasal verbs'.

Finally, some features were dropped because they shared little variance with the overall factorial structure. ('Communality estimates' produced by the statistical analysis indicate the extent to which a given feature participates in the overall pool of shared variance accounted for by the factor analysis. In general, features with communalities below .15 do not have meaningful factor loadings on any factor.)

The solution for four factors was selected as optimal, and the factors were rotated using a Promax rotation. Solutions with fewer factors resulted in a collapsing of linguistic features onto single factors, making the interpretation of those factors difficult. Solutions with additional factors accounted for little additional variance and those factors were represented by only a few features. Biber (2003b: Appendix I) presents the full factorial structure of this analysis; the discussion here focuses on the interpretation of these dimensions.

Table 7.1 summarizes the important linguistic features defining each dimension, including only features with factor loadings larger than + or − .3. Consideration of these features provides the basis for the factor interpretations as 'dimensions' of variation, identifying the shared communicative functions underlying each set of co-occurring features.

These dimensions can be used to analyze the linguistic characteristics of texts by computing 'dimension scores' (or 'factor scores') for each text: a summation of the standardized frequencies for the features with salient loadings on a dimension. Only features with loadings greater than |.30| on a factor are used in the computation of dimension scores. For example, the Dimension 1 score for each text is computed by adding together the frequencies of contractions, demonstrative pronouns, pronoun *it*, first person pronouns, present tense verbs, etc. – the features with positive loadings on Factor 1 (from Table 7.1) – and then subtracting the frequencies of nominalizations, word length, moderately common nouns, prepositions, etc. – the features with negative loadings.

Before dimension scores are computed, the individual feature scores are standardized to a mean of 0.0 and a standard deviation of 1.0 (based on the overall mean and standard deviation of each feature in the T2K-SWAL Corpus). This process translates the scores for all features to scales representing standard deviation units. Thus, regardless of whether a feature is extremely rare or extremely common in absolute terms, a standard score of +1 represents one standard deviation unit above the mean score for the feature in question. That is, standardized scores measure whether a feature is common or rare in a text relative to the overall average occurrence of that feature. The raw frequencies are transformed to standard scores so that all features on a factor will have equivalent weights in the computation of dimension scores. If this process were not followed, extremely common features

**Table 7.1** Summary of the factorial structure of the T2K-SWAL MD analysis (factor loadings are in parentheses)

---

### Dimension 1: Oral vs. literate discourse

**Features with positive loadings:**
contractions (.91), pronouns: demonstrative (.91), pronouns: *it* (.87),
pronouns: 1st person (.81), verbs: present tense (.81), adverbials: time (.80),
adverbs: common (.80), pronouns: indefinite (.79), *that*-omission (.75),
discourse particles (.73), common verbs: mental (.73), lexical bundles: pronoun initial (.73),
stranded prepositions (.72), WH questions (.69), clause coordination (.69),
adverbial clauses: causative (.67), adverbials: place (.67), adverbs: moderately common (.66),
verbs: progressive (.65), WH clauses (.63), common verbs: activity (.58),
*that*-clauses: controlled by likelihood verbs (.58), lexical bundles: other (.58),
adverbials: certainty (.58), lexical bundles: WH word initial (.56), pro-verb *DO* (.56),
adverbials: hedges (.55), adverbial clauses: other (.55), pronouns: 2nd person (.53),
*that*-clauses: controlled by certainty verbs (.53), lexical bundles: verb initial (.50),
verbs: past tense (.50), adverbials: likelihood (.46), verbs: phrasal (.42),
common verbs: communication (.40), pronouns: 3rd person (.39),
lexical bundles: *it* initial (.35), *that*-clauses: controlled by communication verbs (.34),
adverbial clauses: conditional (.31)

**Features with negative loadings:**
nouns: nominalizations (−.95), word length (−.93), nouns: moderately common (−.90),
prepositional phrases (−.86), common nouns: abstract (−.82), adjectives: attributive (−.78),
passives: agentless (−.75), passives: postnominal (−.75), type/token ratio (−.67),
common adjectives: relational (−.67), relative clauses: WH; prep fronting (−.55),
passives: *by*-phrase (−.54), *to*-clauses: controlled by stance nouns (−.54),
phrasal coordination (−.50), relative clauses: WH; subject gaps (−.49),
common nouns: group (−.48), common adjectives: topical (−.44),
common nouns: human (−.37), common nouns: mental (−.36),
lexical bundles: preposition initial (−.36), common verbs: causative (−.34),
*to*-clauses: controlled by adjectives (−.33), adjectives: moderately common (−.30)

### Dimension 2: Procedural vs. content-focused discourse

**Features with positive loadings:**
modals: necessity (.53), common verbs: causative (.51), verbs: moderately common (.48),
pronouns: 2nd person (.44), modals: future (.43), nouns: moderately common (.43),
*to*-clauses: controlled by verbs of desire (.42), common nouns: group (.41),
adverbial clauses: conditional (.35), *to*-clauses: controlled by other verbs (.35),
common verbs: activity (.33)

**Features with negative loadings:**
adjectives: rare (−.70), nouns: rare (−.63), adverbs: rare (−.49),
common verbs: simple occurrence (−.47), common adjectives: size (−.42),
verbs: rare (−.36), *to*-clauses: controlled by probability verbs (−.36),
passives: *by*-phrase (−.34), verbs: past tense (−.31), adverbs: moderately common (−.30)

**Table 7.1** (*continued*)

---

**Dimension 3: Reconstructed account of events**

**Features with positive loadings:**
pronouns: 3rd person (.63), common nouns: human (.60),
*that*-clauses: controlled by communication verbs (.47), common verbs: communication (.45),
verbs: past tense (.36), *that*-omission (.36),
*that*-clauses: controlled by likelihood verbs (.36),
common verbs: mental (.34), common nouns: mental (.32),
*that*-clauses: controlled by stance nouns (.30)

**Features with negative loadings:**
common nouns: concrete (–.53), common nouns: technical+concrete (–.49),
common nouns: quantity (–.40)

**Dimension 4: Teacher-centered stance**

**Features with positive loadings:**
relative clauses: *that* (.56), lexical bundles: preposition initial (.41), adverbials: certainty (.39),
*that*-clauses: controlled by stance nouns (.36), adverbials: attitudinal (.36),
adverbials: likelihood (.35), lexical bundles: noun initial (.35),
adverbial clauses: other (.35), adverbial clauses: conditional (.30)

**Features with negative loadings:**
WH questions (–.39), stranded prepositions (–.36)

---

would have a much greater influence than rare features on the dimension scores. The methodological steps followed to standardize frequency counts and compute dimension scores are described more fully in Biber (1988: 93–97).

Once a dimension score is computed for each text, the mean dimension score for each register can be computed. Plots of these mean dimension scores allow linguistic characterization of any given register, comparison of the relations between any two registers, and a fuller functional interpretation of the underlying dimension. Considering all five dimensions together enables comprehensive descriptions of the linguistic characteristics of particular registers and the linguistic similarities and differences among registers.

Table 7.1 (above) includes functional labels for each of the four dimensions:

> **Dimension 1: Oral vs. literate discourse**
> **Dimension 2: Procedural vs. content-focused discourse**
> **Dimension 3: Reconstructed account of events**
> **Dimension 4: Teacher-centered stance**

The following section presents the details of these functional interpretations, including a discussion of the co-occurring linguistic features grouped on each dimension, the distribution of university registers along each dimension, and a detailed consideration of the co-occurring features in particular texts. Then, in the concluding section, I compare the dimensions of variation found for the university discourse domain to those found in the 1988 study for general spoken and written registers in English, discussing possible reasons for the observed similarities and differences.

## 7.5 Interpretation of the university (T2K-SWAL) dimensions of variation

### 7.5.1 Dimension 1: Oral vs. literate discourse

As in almost all previous MD analyses, the first dimension of the present analysis is associated with a fundamental oral/literate opposition. (Compare the surveys of other MD studies in Biber (1995, to appear).) Table 7.1 above shows that the positive features on Dimension 1 are associated with several major functional domains, including: interactiveness and personal involvement (e.g., 1st and 2nd person pronouns, WH questions), personal stance (e.g., mental verbs, *that*-clauses with likelihood verbs and factual verbs, factual adverbials, hedges), and structural reduction and formulaic language (e.g., contractions, *that*-omission, common vocabulary, lexical bundles). In contrast, the negative features are associated mostly with informational density and complex noun phrase structures (frequent nouns and nominalizations, prepositional phrases, adjectives, and relative clauses) together with passive constructions.

Figure 7.1 shows that all spoken registers in the T2K-SWAL Corpus have large positive scores on this dimension, while all written registers have large negative scores. At one level, this distribution is surprising given the major differences in purpose and planning across registers within each mode. That is, it might be expected that the informational-spoken registers – especially classroom teaching – might exploit the same styles of informational presentation as textbooks. However, with respect to Dimension 1 features, this is clearly not the case. Instead we see a fundamental opposition between the spoken and written modes here, regardless of purpose, interactiveness, or other pre-planning considerations. (Dimension 1 from the 1988 MD analysis is similarly associated with an absolute distinction between spoken and written university registers; see the discussion in Section 7.2.2 above.)

Service encounters, office hours, and study groups – the registers with the largest positive Dimension 1 scores – are all directly interactive; they are also the most conversational registers in the T2K-SWAL Corpus in terms of mixing involved, stance-focused personal purposes with the conveyance of topical information. Text Sample 7.1 illustrates the Dimension 1 characteristics of service encounters. Notice the dense use of 1st and 2nd person pronouns (*I, we, you*), contractions (e.g., *we're, don't, I'm, there's*), present tense verbs (e.g., *are, have,*

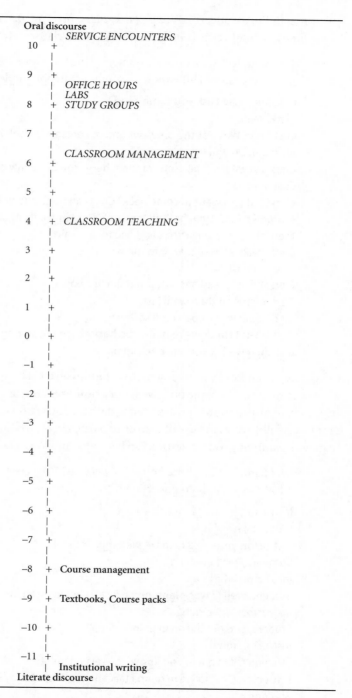

**Figure 7.1** Mean scores of university registers along Dimension 1 – 'Oral vs. literate discourse'

*get*), time and place adverbials (e.g., *back, there, here, again*), indefinite pronouns (*something*), mental verbs (*think, want*), causative clauses, etc.

> **Text Sample 7.1:**  Service encounter; at the bookstore (servenbs_n125) [selected positive Dimension 1 features are in **bold underlined**]
>
> Customer: Can **I** ask **you something**?
> Clerk: Yeah.
> Customer: **We're** at the previews and of course my book is **back there** with my husband. Do **you** have coupons?
> Clerk: No **we** don't have any of them **here**. **You** guys only get them. Yeah.
> Customer: OK.
> Clerk: Did **you want** to come **back**? **Cos I** can hold onto your stuff.
> Customer: Could **you** hold all this stuff? **Cos I know** if **I'm** getting a big sweatshirt there's one for a sweatshirt and one for a T. shirt.
> Clerk: Yeah. **I'll** just hold onto them.
> Customer: OK.
> Clerk: **I'll** go ahead and just put them in a bag.
> Customer: And **then we'll** just.
> Clerk: Yeah **we're** open until six thirty. So.
> Customer: **I think we're** gonna be **back there** registering at four or **something** and **then we'll** just come **back again**.

Office hours can be similarly interactive and involved. The following text sample illustrates many of the same positive Dimension 1 features as the service encounter (e.g., personal pronouns, present tense verbs, contractions, mental verbs). This sample also illustrates the use of discourse particles (*ok, well, oh*), progressive verbs (e.g., *was planning*), WH-questions (*what's up*), and WH-clauses (*what you did*):

> **Text Sample 7.2:**  Office hours (socpooh_n150) [selected positive Dimension 1 features are in **bold underlined**]
>
> Instructor: let **me see** [unclear]
> Student: **I need** help
> Instructor: **you need** help **OK well then** let's talk
> Student: yeah [laughing]
> Instructor: **what's up**
> Student: **well I I was planning** on just trying to do an outline of **what you did**
> Instructor: {right, right
> Student: and get the main points of realism
> Instructor: mhm
> Student: **OK I I** got it, **you know**, the several points
> Instructor: **OK** and **we're** gonna talk about it more **today** if **you've** got some
> Student: **oh**
> Instructor: still some problems

> Student: **well I I I well** maybe try to work on a thesis
> Instructor: **right OK** let's **see what you did**

At the other extreme, institutional writing has the largest negative score on Dimension 1, making it even more 'literate' than textbooks or course packs. In fact, the linguistic style found in many university catalogs and program brochures is often more reminiscent of highly technical academic prose than textbooks written for novices in an academic discipline. The following program description for an anthropology major (Text Sample 7.3) begins with a friendly, inviting sentence having an extremely simple syntactic clause structure. However, this short sentence is immediately followed by complex sentences with multiple levels of clausal and phrasal embedding. Note especially the dense use of noun phrase structures, often with adjectives and prepositional phrases as modifiers.

> **Text Sample 7.3:**  Institutional writing (Web Catalog Academic Program Descriptions: Anthropology; otcatc.ant) [nouns, adjectives, and prepositions are in **bold underlined**]
>
> PROGRAM DESCRIPTION.
>      **Anthropology** is the **study of people**. Its **perspective** is **biological**, **social** and **comparative**, encompassing all **aspects** of **human existence**, **from** the **most ancient societies to** those **of** the **present day**. **Anthropology** seeks to order and explain **similarities** and **differences between peoples of** the **world from** the **combined vantage points of culture** and **biology**.
>      **Cultural** and **Social Anthropology** deal **with** the **many aspects of** the **social lives** of **people around** the **world**, including our own **society**: their **economic systems**, **legal practices**, **kinship**, **religions**, **medical practices**, **folklore**, **arts** and **political systems**, **as well as** the **interrelationship of** these **systems in environmental adaptation** and **social change**. **Physical Anthropology** describes and compares **world human biology**. Its **focus** is **on humans** and the **primate order to** which they belong **as part of nature**, and it seeks to document and understand the **interplay of culture** and **biology in** the **course of human evolution** and **adaptation**. **Anthropological Linguistics** deals **with varied aspects of human language**, and the **characteristics of non human communication systems**, in order to achieve an **understanding of past** and **present human language systems** and their **significance in social life**.

Many of the negative features on Dimension 1 reflect the dense use of nouns and nominal modifiers in written informational texts; these features often occur together to build very complex noun phrase structures. For example, the second paragraph above begins with a very long sentence, which has only one main verb: *deal with*. Most of the sentence comprises a single noun phrase, functioning as the direct object of *deal with*. The sentence is marked up below to illustrate the extremely complex syntactic structure with multiple levels of embedding; head nouns of noun phrases are <u>underlined</u>; the main verb is in **bold**; and brackets are used to delimit postnominal modifiers.

> Cultural and Social <u>Anthropology</u> **deal with** the many <u>aspects</u> [of the social <u>lives</u> [of <u>people</u> [around the <u>world</u>]]], [including our own <u>society</u>: [their economic <u>systems</u>, legal <u>practices</u>, <u>kinship</u>, <u>religions</u>, medical <u>practices</u>, <u>folklore</u>, <u>arts</u> and political <u>systems</u>], as well as [the <u>interrelationship</u> [of these <u>systems</u> [in environmental <u>adaptation</u> and social <u>change</u>]]]].

Textbooks are similar to institutional writing in their reliance on these 'literate' Dimension 1 features, although they are usually not as densely informational as the above excerpt from a course catalog. For example, the following excerpt from an anthropology textbook (Sample 7.4) is somewhat similar in topic and purpose to Text Sample 7.3 above (from the institutional program description): both passages introduce students to anthropology. However, the linguistic features employed for this purpose are strikingly different in the two passages, with the textbook showing a much greater reliance on clause features (many more main verbs and therefore shorter clauses) and a much lesser reliance on complex noun phrase structures.

> **Text Sample 7.4:** Textbook (Anthropology; lower division; tbant1a.fpa) [nouns are in **<u>bold underlined</u>**; verbs are in *italics*]
>
> Learning About the **<u>Past</u>** – The **<u>Material Record</u>**.
>      This **<u>book</u>** *focuses* on the **<u>human past</u>**, but how do we *learn* about the **<u>past</u>**? How do we *collect* and *analyze* **<u>data</u>** about the ancient **<u>past</u>** of our **<u>species</u>**? In this **<u>book</u>** our **<u>approach</u>** to *understanding* the **<u>human past</u>** will *be* through the **<u>field</u>** of **<u>anthropology</u>**, *defined* properly as the **<u>study</u>** of **<u>humanity</u>**. If you *think* about it, though, nearly all the **<u>courses</u>** you *are* now *taking deal* in some **<u>fashion</u>** with **<u>people</u>** or their **<u>works</u>**. What *makes* **<u>anthropology</u>** different?
>
> The **<u>Anthropology</u>** of the **<u>Past</u>**: **<u>Archaeology</u>** and Physical **<u>Anthropology</u>**.
>      Many **<u>people</u>** *have* some very strange **<u>ideas</u>** about what **<u>archaeology</u>** and physical (or biological) **<u>anthropology</u>** *are* and what **<u>scientists</u>** in these **<u>fields</u>** *do*. Some **<u>people</u>** *think* **<u>archaeologists</u>** *study* **<u>dinosaurs</u>**. (They *have seen* too many **<u>episodes</u>** of "The **<u>Flintstones</u>**.") In **<u>reality</u>**, the **<u>dinosaurs</u>** *became* extinct more than 60 million **<u>years</u>** before even our earliest **<u>human ancestors</u>** *appeared* on the **<u>scene</u>**. Thanks, at least in **<u>part</u>**, to such **<u>movies</u>** as the **<u>Indiana Jones series</u>**, many *think* that **<u>archaeologists</u>** *are* tough, globetrotting **<u>vagabonds</u>** who *loot* **<u>sites</u>** for **<u>treasure</u>**. Physical **<u>anthropologists</u>** *are* often *stereotyped* as those who *identify* the skeletal **<u>remains</u>** of dead **<u>people</u>**. The most common **<u>question</u>** we *get*, even from **<u>university colleagues</u>**, *is*, "*Dig* up any interesting **<u>bones</u>** lately?" Actually, **<u>archaeology</u>** *is* simply that **<u>branch</u>** of **<u>anthropology</u>** *focusing* on the **<u>human</u>** cultural **<u>past</u>**.

Interestingly, classroom teaching is much more similar in its Dimension 1 characteristics to other spoken registers, including study groups and service encounters, than it is to written academic registers like textbooks. It is rare for an instructor in an American university to lecture for an entire class period, but there are certainly long monologic turns, as the instructor explains a concept or develops a point of view. However, even these extended turns are often highly involved, making dense use of the positive Dimension 1 features with minimal reliance on the highly informational features associated with the negative pole of Dimension 1. For example:

> **Text Sample 7.5:** Classroom teaching (Humanities; Rhetoric; graduate; humrhlegrli004) [selected positive Dimension 1 features are in **bold underlined**]
>
> Instructor: **I think** some of **us feel sort of** really caught in a bind between agency and acculturation. **sort of** um, because **you know I think** a lot of **us** do **want** to use writing, use literacy to um, say **what we want** to say and to help other people say **what they want** to say but at the same time **I think** um, **we're** caught **because we**, **I think we're** questioning **well**, **well you know**, if, if **we**, if **we** teach X-genre **are we promoting** it? if **we don't** at the same time question it and dismantle it and **kind of** take it apart and look at it, and are there, are there other ways? every established genre, every approach, every way that **everything that's** accepted for all of those things that seems like **there's**, there are things that are rejected, not done, not looked at, and as **you were** just **pointing out**, some of the ways that particular systems get promoted are not exactly ethical or correct or at the very least not **everybody** has access to being able to promote certain kinds of discourses and systems, **so I guess**, **I don't know whether** this is really a question or just a comment though **I think we're**, **think** a lot of **us feel** very **sort of** trapped between buying into this is **how** it is and **since it's** this way, **let's** do the best **we** can with it and **sort of saying**, **who's** got the agency **here**? **you know**, **how** is the system beneficial for people? **who** is it hurting?

## 7.5.2 Dimension 2: Procedural vs. content-focused discourse

In contrast to the spoken-written split identified by Dimension 1, Dimension 2 cuts directly across the spoken/written continuum. Figure 7.2 shows that the registers with large positive scores on this dimension all deal with the rules and procedures expected in university settings, whether in speech (classroom management, service encounters, and office hours) or in writing (course management and institutional writing). At the negative extreme, we find only written academic registers – course packs and textbooks – which have an almost exclusive focus on informational content. Classroom teaching and study groups have intermediate scores on this dimension.

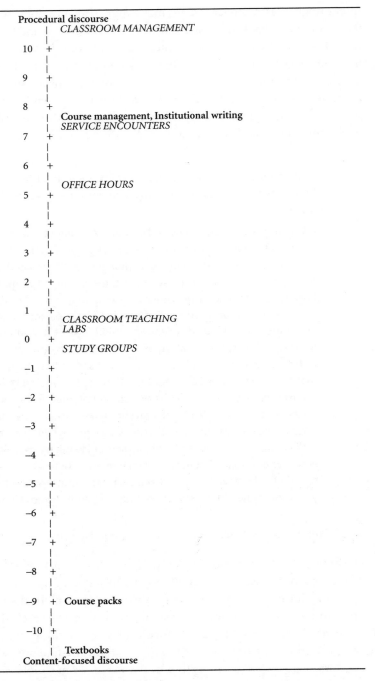

**Figure 7.2** Mean scores of registers along Dimension 2 – 'Procedural vs. content-focused discourse'

Considering both the co-occurring linguistic features, together with this distribution of registers, the interpretive label 'procedural vs. content-focused discourse' can be proposed for this dimension. Table 7.1 shows that the linguistic features associated with 'procedural discourse' include necessity and prediction modal verbs, 2nd person pronouns, causative verbs, *to*-clauses with verbs of desire (e.g., *want*), and conditional adverbial clauses. These features are most common in spoken classroom management:

> **Text Sample 7.6:** Classroom management (Humanities; History; upper division; humhicmud_n070) [Positive Dimension 2 features are in **bold underlined**]
>
> OK so, after test number one, **you** can, pretty much push everything out of **your** mind and [3 sylls] and absorb everything for that time and then start over again, OK, although certainly **if you** understand concepts from the first section it **will help you** understand concepts in the second section. These are blue book exams **you'll need to** bring a bluebook, they are mostly essay. uh, one other thing I stated last semester I'm **gonna** do again is that I'm also **gonna** give **you** a take home essay. The take home essay **will** be part of every exam, I**'ll** give **you** the question a week before the exam, **you'll have to** take it home, write it up, type it, and bring it in on the day of the test. it **will** come – it **will** amount to thirty points of **your** one-hundred point exam.
> [...]
> um, let's see, **if** a student misses more than one week of classes **you** should talk to me immediately, **if** you know **you**'re **gonna** be gone. let's say for example **you**'re **gonna** go to Montana for a couple of days this week or something like that **you** might **let** the instructor know **you**'re **gonna** be gone. uh, **if you**'re, I had a woman who was pregnant one semester and she, said well I'm **gonna** be missing part of the class and I said yeah, I think you probably **will** be. OK, but **let** me know. um, **you should let** me know **if you** miss more, **if you** miss a test, **you'd have to** bring me some type of written evidence as to why **you** were gone, just so that it's fair for everybody so that they don't **have to** deal with a whole lot of excuses.

These same features are common in written course management materials. Thus, compare the above excerpt to the following examples from course syllabi:

> At the end of each chapter, **you will** be assigned a series of problems to **help you** write a Chapter Summary. The purpose of the Chapter Summary problems is to **help you** pull together the main ideas of each chapter...
>
> **If you** miss class for two consecutive weeks, **you will** be dropped.
>
> **You will need to** access available resources to find answers to **your** questions and be willing to ask when **you** can't find them. **You will** find that many issues have answers which are complex or ambiguous.

One difference from spoken classroom management is that written course management intermixes personal directives to the individual student (*you*) with impersonal general directives to *students*; for example:

> **Students will need to** visit the bookstore …
>
> **You** should answer the questions at the end of each chapter to test **your** knowledge of the material, even though there will be few formal assignments. *Some students* will have to devote more time to their studies and attend office hours more frequently if *they* expect to perform adequately.

In large part, the negative features on Dimension 2 represent technical vocabulary, with 'rare' words from all four content classes (adjectives, nouns, adverbs, and verbs; see Table 7.1). These are all content words that occur in only one text in the T2K-SWAL Corpus. Other negative Dimension 2 features include simple occurrence verbs (e.g., *become, happen, change, decrease, occur*), probability verb + *to*-clause (e.g., *seem / appear to*…), and size adjectives (e.g., *high, large*). The dense use of these co-occurring features is restricted to the written academic registers in the T2K-SWAL Corpus. Text Sample 7.7 illustrates these features in a graduate-level chemistry textbook:

> **Text Sample 7.7:** Textbook (Natural science; chemistry; graduate; TBCHM3.gns)
>
> CHAPTER 11: THE PROTON MAGNETIC RESONANCE SPECTRA OF ORGANIC MOLECULES
>
> Up to now we have been concerned with the magnetic resonance of a single nucleus and with explaining the physical basis of an nmr experiment. We will now turn our attention to the nuclear magnetic resonance spectra of organic molecules and in so doing will encounter two new phenomena: the chemical shift of the resonance frequency and the spin-spin coupling. These two phenomena form the foundation for the application of nuclear magnetic resonance spectroscopy in chemistry and related disciplines.
>
> 1. THE CHEMICAL SHIFT.
>
> The hypothetical spectrum of dimethyltrifluoroacetamide presented at the end of Chapter 1 may have suggested that nmr spectroscopy is employed for the detection of magnetically different nuclei in a compound. For at least two reasons this is not the case. Firstly, experimental considerations make such an application difficult, if not impossible, since conditions and techniques must be modified to measure the resonance frequencies of different nuclei. Secondly, the elemental composition of organic compounds can be determined far more easily and accurately by other techniques such as elemental analysis or mass spectrometry.
>
> …

The following general statements can be made. For aliphatic C-H bonds the shielding decreases in the series CH3 > CH2 > CH. While the protons of methyl groups at saturated centres absorb at 6 0.9, the resonance for the protons of cyclohexane occurs at 6 1.4. An exception is observed in the case of cyclopropane, the protons of which absorb at 6 0.22. For olefinic protons, the resonances lie in the region from 6 4.0 to 6.5, and only in special instances, such as with compound like acrolein (CH2=CHCHO), below 6 6.5. The resonance signals of protons in aromatic molecules occur in a characteristic region between 67.0 and 8.0. Although Sp2-hybridized bonds are present, as in the olefins, an additional deshielding obviously exists here.

Classroom teaching has an intermediate score on this dimension. In part, this distribution reflects the real time production circumstances of classroom teaching, making it difficult for instructors to use technical/rare vocabulary to the same extent as textbook writers (see the discussion in Chapter 3). In addition, this distribution probably reflects the fact that management talk and content-focused academic talk are less sharply distinguished in classroom teaching than in textbooks.

### 7.5.3 Dimension 3: Reconstructed account of events

Dimension 3 is in part associated with a narrative orientation, reflected by features like 3rd person pronouns, human nouns, communication verb + *that*-clauses, and past tense (see Table 7.1). However, these features co-occur with a number of other features that express epistemic stance, including likelihood verb + *that*-clause (usually verbs expressing uncertainty, such as *assume, believe, doubt, gather, guess, imagine, seem, suppose, think*); mental verbs (e.g., *think, remember, understand*); mental nouns (e.g., *assumption, attitude, feeling, idea, opinion*); and epistemic stance noun + *that*-clause (e.g., *conclusion, fact, assumption, claim, feeling, idea, impression, opinion, possibility, suggestion, suspicion*). *That*-omission also co-occurs with these features, suggesting that they are usually used in colloquial rather than formal registers.

Figure 7.3 shows that the distribution of registers along Dimension 3 is strongly associated with the spoken versus written modes (similar to Dimension 1): spoken university registers are consistently more 'narrative' than related written registers. Interestingly, the management registers are the least 'narrative' within each mode. Study groups and office hours are especially marked for the use of positive Dimension 3 features.

Consideration of texts from these registers shows that Dimension 3 features are often used to recall what the course instructor said in class. Examples like the

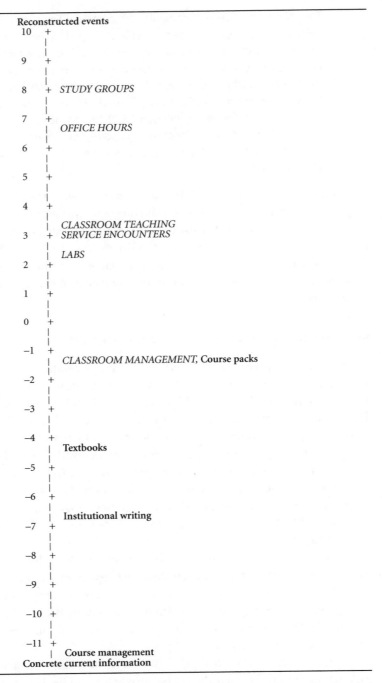

**Figure 7.3** Mean scores of registers along Dimension 3 – 'Reconstructed account of events'

following occur frequently in study groups (selected Dimension 3 features are **bold
underlined**):

> I **thought he said** it wasn't supposed to change unless you changed it.

> Like .. **she said** like the only thing we **went** over in quantum mechanics is Heisen-
> burgs theory and Schroedener's equation. Those er- Schroedener's equation
> those are the only two things that we **covered** in quantum mechanics. That's
> all **she said** we need to **know** out of it. She said the rest of it is covered like
> in organics.

Similarly, in office hours instructors recall what they said in class:

> so I **mean** here's here's what I what I **did** is I just set up the simplex method and I
> **said** well you **know** the simplex method would normally have you go uh –
> Instructor: mhm, uh the key word here was uh uh drilling. so you'd still have to
> drill to put in a 'pazometer' (sp?).
> Student: right, but I didn't **know** 'pazometer' was considered a well because it,
> you never **said** there was a pump in it. you just **said** it was like a soda straw. and
> it was only open at the bottom.
> Instructor: yeah again, the key word there was drilling.

In study groups, it is also common to find students negotiating with one another,
trying to reconstruct course content without direct reference to a specific class
or what the instructor specifically said. Stereotypical narrative features are used
to report past events and situations, while epistemic stance features are used by
students to indicate varying degrees of (un)certainty about their knowledge. The
following example illustrates a discussion of this type:

> **Text Sample 7.8:** Study group (socposgudpn173) [positive Dimension 3 fea-
> tures are marked in **bold underline**]
> 1: Uh in fact as far as, the three major religions, Muslim, Christian and Jew? The
>    Islam are the most –
> 2: Tolerant.
> 1: Tolerant of all the three. So there **was** probably quite a few, in uh, in all the
>    middle eastern countries for that matter. Because –
> 2: All for, the whole two thousand years?
> 1: Yeah because um, **they were**n't **they were**n't as discriminated against as
>    **they were** in Europe and other countries so **they** –
> 2: OK.
> 1: All **they**, **everybody had** to pay tithes. See that's the other myth about Islam
>    is **they** say, well it's the theocracy and **they** make you pay ten percent of
>    your money.

2:    Oh I **remember** – **they, they created** a um, what **did**-what **were they** called those uh, villages those districts with Jews and Christians? In the time of Mohammed? All the way through I can't **remember** what **they**'re called.

1:    Mhm. But the point is **they, they** um, **did**n't tax. So, in this country if you come and you make money, you pay twenty percent tax.

2:    Something like that.

1:    In the middle east, in Islam countries you go and you make money and you pay a ten percent tithe, and that's wrong. But it's OK to pay a twenty percent tax. See what I **mean**?

2:    Oh yeah I **remember** that.

1:    It's like um.

2:    I **forgot** about that . . well I **was thinking** also um, that there might have been more Jews uh, during British occupation because they might have immigrated from uh, Great Britain?

1:    Mhm I **suppose** it, you **know**, I don't **know**

. . .

2:    Well that's the **impression** I got, that that, the Israelis –

1:    **They were** the, **they were** the legal nation state, and pretty much, with the backing of the U.S. government, in the, and the British **went** in there and **took** it away from them and, **put** Is-the Jews in there.

1:    And **started** Israel.

2:    Right. Well my **understanding** is that the Israelis are pretty much the primary aggressors. And they uh, well of course they **took** Jerusalem, I can't remember **was** it sixty seven? Something like that?

1:    Sixty seven **was** like, one of the major wars.

2:    Yeah that **was** something else though. I'm trying to **remember**.

1:    The six day war **was** in like seventy three or something.

2:    Yeah.

The negative pole of Dimension 3 includes only three linguistic features: common nouns with concrete/tangible reference (inanimate objects that can be touched, such as *phone, picture, truck, newspaper, handout, syllabus, modem, book, handbook, paper, computer, textbook*); common nouns with concrete but technical reference (tangible objects that are not normally perceived and/or cannot normally be touched, such as *bacteria, electron, sample, schedule, software, solution, margin, virus, mark, internet, message, paragraph, sentence, poem, chapter, equation, exam, statement, diagram*); and common quantity nouns, which relate to quantities, amounts, or durations (e.g., *frequency, future, semester, number, amount, week, month*).

Written course management (syllabi, assignments, and exams) has by far the largest negative score on Dimension 3 (see Figure 7.3). This extreme score reflects a dense use of these negative features coupled with the near total absence of positive

Dimension 3 features. Text Sample 7.9 illustrates these features in an engineering course assignment:

> **Text Sample 7.9:** Written course management (course assignment; engineering; lower division; CMENG1.ASN) [negative Dimension 3 features are marked in **bold underline**]
>
> Overview: There are two **parts** to this **project**. The first **part** is the practice work in **Chapter** A and **Chapter** B where you created the **pages** nomad.htm nomad2.htm and nomad3.htm. The second **part** consists of four steps, where you create a **web page** called project3.htm.
>
> The work that you do as you are reading through the **chapters** in the HTML **text** is practice. Therefore, it will be graded for being attempted, not for being 100% accurate. The **files** you created as you worked through **Chapter** A (nomad.htm) and **Chapter** B (nomad2.htm and nomad3.htm), must be uploaded to your **web directory** on your H drive. Do not put an index.htm **file** in this **directory**.

### 7.5.4 Dimension 4: Teacher-centered stance

Finally, Dimension 4 seems to be associated with academic styles of stance. The linguistic features defining this dimension include the range of stance adverbials (certainty, likelihood, and attitudinal) and *that*-clauses controlled by stance nouns (e.g., *the fact that…*). *That*-relative clauses and lexical bundles with 'referential' functions (preposition-initial and noun-initial) co-occur with these stance features. Figure 7.4 shows that these features are used primarily in the instructor-controlled spoken registers: classroom management, classroom teaching, and office hours. All written university registers are characterized by the relative absence of these features, as are the student-centered spoken registers (labs, study groups, and service encounters). Following are several examples of these academic stance features in classroom management:

> Instructor: **actually** while I finish the outline, let me pass out the uh **something I'd like you to uh look over** here real quick and sign for me – that you acknowledge **the fact that** you've read and understand the syllabus.
>
> Instructor: January eighteenth **of course** we don't have class. What day is that?
> Student: [unclear]
> Instructor: it's also my birthday, I **always** think that we're taking off on my birthday. uh, but if you link on the jazz home page, you can, there are, there's **actually** jazz music from the twenties
>
> Instructor: all right for the remaining writings, when you take test one – **probably** the second week after spring break on, Tuesday, not Tuesday
> Student: Thursday

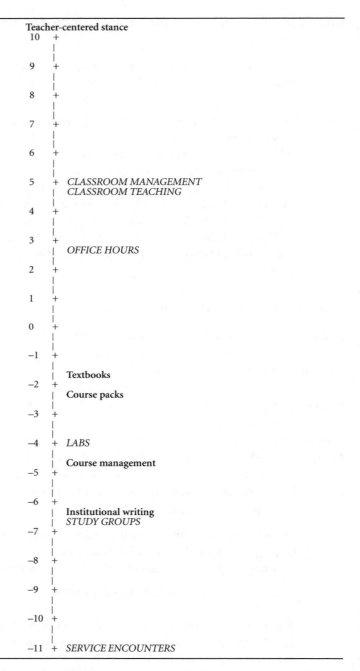

**Figure 7.4** Mean scores of Registers along Dimension 4 – 'Teacher-centered stance'

Instructor: Thursday. you're going to have I think fifteen items, comparable to fifteen of the next twenty three or twenty four [unclear]. so what you have to understand when we go over these items. know which one is correct. and why. make sure you know which one is correct and why. they won't be the exact wording of these but, **certainly** very comparable wording.

Instructor: Let's tabulate those tomorrow, too. Let's do this. Quite **possibly** none of these will be **entirely** satisfactory. [. . .] So **those of you that** have the book, you can, well I guess we've gotta wait. **Those of you that** don't have the book you can do it now.

Instructor: quickly now – the department came down and I know, Mark's been working on those so, **hopefully**, first of next week, at the latest we ought to have it up and working. **kind of**, continuing the tradition that has gone on in the past, several semesters or at least the past semester. I, am following Professor Anderson's lead on doing a number of things – **one of the things that** he did, was have, uh, Professor Brown from the English, department come over and make a presentation. uh, last year, and [er] last semester. I invited her back she **gracefully** agreed to do that and she's going to, talk to us about, can we be a good engineer if you can't communicate?

The same combination of academic stance features associated with Dimension 4 is common in classroom teaching, as in:

Instructor: uh what they have done here if you don't have this, I **really** can't write the whole thing out but uh **hopefully** by, you know, just going through your notes you'll be able to relate this to the problem. they give us a linear programming problem and then they say which of the following is the initial tableau for the whole problem. now uh I think there **probably** could be more than one way of getting there, but only one of these will be correct.

. . .

we're going to have a less than or equal to constraint for the second constraint, but the third constraint will be an equal to constraint. so **one of the things that** we can do is uh I mean **actually** this **maybe** gets us almost where we need to be.

Instructor: um well **actually** it's two questions. one how like I know **a lot of people that** are **really really** good at their job? and they're **really** not interested in telling people about it and about how to do it.

## 7.5.5 The distribution of stance features across the university dimensions

It is interesting to note that three of the four dimensions in this analysis are strongly associated with spoken/written differences, and stance features are important defining characteristics for all three dimensions. Dimension 1 is the most general spoken/written distinction, with all spoken registers having positive scores, and all written registers having negative scores. This dimension shows that all spoken university registers are characterized by a focus on personal stance, represented by:

- *that*-clauses controlled by likelihood verbs (e.g., *think*),
- *that*-clauses controlled by certainty verbs (e.g., *know*),
- *that*-clauses controlled by communication verbs (e.g., *said*),
- certainty stance adverbials (e.g., *actually*),
- hedges (e.g., *kind of, something like*),
- likelihood stance adverbials (*maybe*),
- lexical bundles consisting of clause segments, which often serve stance functions:
  pronoun-initial (*I don't know if*)
  WH-word initial (*what do you think*)
  verb initial (*want to talk about*).

These stance features on Dimension 1 occur together with features of interaction and high involvement (e.g., contractions, 1st and 2nd person pronouns, questions, etc...), reflecting the general discourse styles and priorities of spoken university registers.

Dimension 3 also includes several stance features:

- *that*-clauses controlled by communication verbs (e.g., *said*),
- *that*-clauses controlled by likelihood verbs (e.g., *think*),
- *that*-clauses controlled by stance nouns (e.g., *fact*).

These features co-occur with features reflecting a general narrative orientation, functioning as speakers' attempts to reconstruct past events. Similar to Dimension 1, Dimension 3 features are common in most spoken university registers; they are especially prevalent in 1-on-1 interactions about academic topics: study groups and office hours.

Several of the same stance features that occur on Dimensions 1 or 3 are also found co-occurring on Dimension 4:

- certainty stance adverbials (e.g., *actually*),
- attitudinal stance adverbials (e.g., *amazingly*),
- likelihood stance adverbials (e.g., *maybe*),
- *that*-clauses controlled by stance nouns (e.g., *fact*).

However, in this case these features co-occur with 'informational' features, such as *that* relative clauses and preposition-initial lexical bundles. Dimension 4 features are common in several spoken registers, while all written university registers are marked by the relative absence of these features. However, Dimension 4 also distinguishes among different kinds of spoken university registers: only the teacher-centered spoken registers – office hours, classroom teaching, and class-room management – are marked for the dense use of the academic stance features associated with Dimension 4. In contrast, student-centered registers, even when they focus on academic topics (as in study groups), are marked by the absence of these co-occurring features.

Dimension 2 is also defined in part by stance features, especially modal verbs (necessity and prediction) and verbs of desire+*to*-clause constructions expressing procedural/directive functions. Unlike the other three dimensions, the stance fea-tures grouped on Dimension 2 are associated with both speech and writing, but restricted to the 'management' registers.

Thus, although they are all associated with the expression of stance, these four dimensions reflect very different functional considerations, and as a result, they distinguish among different sets of registers:

| Dimension | 1 | 2 | 3 | 4 |
|---|---|---|---|---|
| Functional interpretation of positive features | stereotypically 'oral'; interaction and high personal involvement | procedural / directive discourse | collaborative reconstruction of past events | academic stance |
| Registers marked for these stance features | ALL spoken university registers | spoken and written management registers | 1-on-1 spoken academic registers, especially study groups and office hours | teacher-centered registers: classroom management, classroom teaching, and office hours |

## 7.5.6 Differences among academic disciplines

Two of the university dimensions are also associated with important differences across academic disciplines: Dimension 2 ('Procedural vs. content-focused dis-course'), and Dimension 3 ('Reconstructed account of events'). Figures 7.5 and 7.6 plot the dimension scores for each discipline in classroom teaching and textbooks. The distributions are highly systematic along both dimensions, with disciplines following the same pattern within both textbooks and classroom teaching.

Figure 7.5 shows that Dimension 2 ('Procedural vs. content-focused dis-course') distinguishes sharply between the two technical disciplines: Engineering is 'procedural' in orientation (in both speech and writing), while natural science is by far the most 'content-focused'. Business and education also show a strong tendency to favor procedural styles. These differences are found in both classroom teaching and in textbooks.

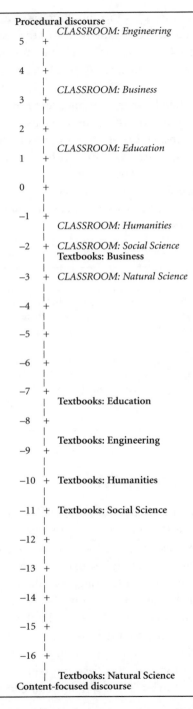

**Figure 7.5** Mean scores of disciplines along Dimension 2 – 'Procedural vs. content-focused discourse'

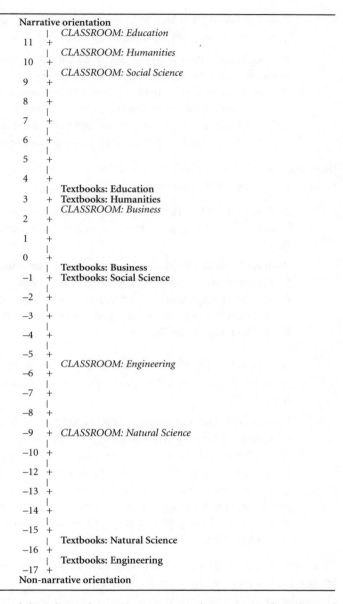

**Figure 7.6** Mean scores of disciplines along Dimension 3 – 'Reconstructed account of events'

In engineering classroom teaching, procedural discourse is part of normal class lessons, where students are asked to think through the logical steps required to solve real-world problems. For example:

Text Sample 7.10: Classroom teaching (engineering; upper division; engceleudli029) [positive Dimension 2 features are marked in **bold underline**]

And **you**, one of the things that seems to me **you'd wanna** look at very quickly is, steam is very expensive, raw material basically **you**'re **using** steam [5 sylls]. When **you**, convince the steam, to appear somewhere, uh, first of all **you**'ve **built** the energy into generating that steam and then **you**'re venting it out here and, it's not, it vents it out just not pure enough to go to the boiler feed water. **You**'ve **got**, [3 sylls], so **you** now **you have to** treat it **if you're going to** recycle it.

Business and education classroom teaching also commonly use the "procedural" features associated with Dimension 2:

Text Sample 7.11: Classroom teaching (business; upper division; busacleudms058) [positive Dimension 2 features are marked in **bold underline**]

We **have to** determine basis for gains, basis for loss, and we're **gonna put** a rate for depreciation in there as well. Now the reason I **want to let you help** me write these rules in, when **you** have a dual basis rule that is a basis for gain and a basis for loss there's only so many ways **you** can describe it. OK once **you** know what this is, this **has to** be similar to it.

Text Sample 7.12: Classroom teaching (education; upper division; edubeleudhn133) [positive Dimension 2 features are marked in **bold underline**]

I think that Alb offered some suggestions in the book that first **you need to** preview the book before you read it to the class. uh, Second, perhaps **you need to** sit down with the other teachers that you plan with on a regular basis, and see how the book really fits into your current thematic unit. [. . .] I'm, um, I'm **going to give you** some information now about selecting multi-cultural textbooks. And, **you** know I think we **need to** be sensitive to the population of students in the classroom. And, I'm **going to give you** some examples of choosing books for Native Americans.

Textbooks are generally much less marked for 'procedural' features than classroom teaching. However, we find similar differences among the disciplines. Business textbooks are the most marked for the use of procedural features; for example:

Text Sample 7.13: Textbook (business; upper division; tbmkt2.cmr) [positive Dimension 2 features are marked in **bold underline**]

After specifying the basic information that **will** be sought, the researcher **needs to** specify how it will be gathered. [. . .] **If** the researcher decides on a disguised unstructured questionnaire in which subjects **will** be **shown** a picture and asked to tell a story about it, a telephone interview **would** be out of the question [. . .]

> **If** researchers decided to **use** a lengthy attitude scale, for example, they **would** probably **have to** rule out telephone interviews. [. . .] Thus, the researcher **must** specify precisely what primary data are needed, how these data might be collected, what degree of structure and disguise **will** be **used**, and then how the questionnaire **will** be administered.

Education and engineering textbooks also use these features to a greater extent than the other disciplines:

Examples from education textbooks:

> One of the best teaching manuals says **you should** ask a question first, then name the child **you want to** have answer it.

> Do not make any rule that **you** are not willing to enforce every time it is broken. [. . .] **If** the behavior in question is not serious enough for **you** to enforce every time, the rule is not worth having. **If you fail to** enforce one of your classroom rules, **you** have just taught the entire class that your rules are hot air.

Examples from engineering textbooks:

> **If you apply** the phase rule to a multi-component gas-liquid system at equilibrium, **you will** discover that the compositions of the two phases at a given temperature and pressure are not independent.

> To design a separation process unit, **you must** know certain physical properties of the system with which **you will be working**. Before **you** can design a distillation column, for example, **you must** know how volatile each feed component is [. . .]

At the opposite extreme, natural science textbooks are characterized by a heavy reliance on technical vocabulary and 'rare' words, coupled with the absence of 'procedural' discourse features. Text Sample 7.7 (in Section 7.5.2 above) illustrates these characteristics in a chemistry textbook.

In contrast to their opposite characteristics along Dimension 2, Figure 7.6 shows that engineering and natural science are similar to each other in favoring non-narrative styles along Dimension 3, in both speech and writing. At the other extreme, education, humanities, and social science are all much more likely to incorporate reconstructed accounts of past events. These features are most prominent in classroom teaching, but textbooks from the same disciplines are also marked for the relatively frequent use of narrative features. Text Sample 7.14 illustrates these characteristics from history classroom teaching, as the instructor tries to reconstruct historical settings and events in response to a student question:

> **Text Sample 7.14:**  Classroom teaching; History (upper division; humhileudmn089) [past tense verbs and 3rd person pronouns are **bold underlined**; other positive Dimension 3 features are in ***bold italics***]

**Student:** But why would, I *mean*, why would, uh, China want to throw out Soviet technocrats [. . .]

**Instructor:** And I *think* that's, you *know*, that's like the key issue there in, is absolute [2 sylls] relationship as it develops that, that it's not one [2 sylls] process. [. . .] OK? Um, and-and-uh, so what we have here, of course one can face Mao's dissatisfaction to some extent, the very very early roots of Mao's dissatisfaction with, uh, ideological dissatisfaction, I'm not *talking* just about personal dis-dissatisfaction, but from **his** ideological point of view from the way **he interpreted** history is toward the development, social development and the revolution particularly. From that view point, **his** earliest dissatisfactions with the, uh, leadership of the Soviet Union, with Stalin's leadership of the Soviet Union, will go all the way back to the nineteen thirties. I *mean* **he**, **believed**, even then, that there **was** not a clear understanding of China's situation, China's revolutionary situation, on the part of Stalin and the Soviet nation. Whereas Mao **was**, even back in the nineteen thirties **he was** already formulating that [2 sylls] strategy. Formulating that strategy which **was called**, you *know*, countryside surrounding the cities. That's a way to conduct revolution . At that same time, **he was** already mindful of the *fact that* the Soviet leadership **was** of a different kind. Standing from the *fact that* the Soviet experience itself **was** by and large an urban revolution, experience. The workers in Moscow, you *know*, in the Soviet Union the peasants **had** consistently had very little, a small role in the revolution. More of an exploited role than an active role . And Mao **had** already kind of seen that distinction in the ideological between **himself** and the Soviet leadership in terms of ideology of revolution.

In education classroom teaching, positive Dimension 2 features often convey personal narratives coupled with personal commentary, rather than being used to reconstruct past historical events. For example:

Text Sample 7.15: Classroom teaching; Education (graduate; edubelegrhn161) [past tense verbs and 3rd person pronouns are **bold underlined**; other positive Dimension 3 features are in *bold italics*]

**Instructor:** [. . .] I'm sorry I **interrupted** someone here. Um. Jenny?
**Student:** [unclear]
**Instructor:** No go ahead. Go ahead Jenny.
**Student:** Um, [8 sylls] I **came** here when I was thirteen and I **went** to public school in California, and I **went** [3 sylls] to school, my, teacher **did**n't, as you *know* [4 sylls] care when I, I, **did**n't [3 sylls] pronunciation [6 sylls] thirty to thirty five kids in a class. And then, I **went** to college and then, after college I **was** *thinking* oh my God my mom, [3 sylls] for ten years, and, I **did**n't get anywhere. [6 sylls], Mom [1 syll], and always [8 sylls] on southeast, Asian countries that, [4 sylls], they **came** here and [10 sylls] my sister **went** to college, she has to pay like thousand dollar per, um, quarter, for her tuition. And I **was** *thinking*, how am I even going,

I don't have any [5 sylls] um, um, education. I *feel* I cannot, I should *say* this, [7 sylls], for selfish. I *mean*. Where's my mom [3 sylls] where's my chance [3 sylls]. And I can *understand* [8 sylls] opinion and I can *understand* those people I *think* because, **they** paying the tax, but **they didn**'t get anything from, their money. I don't *know*.

**Instructor:** OK so we *see* a real decline in public support for education that's reflected in, in the tax rates in California. And also just reflected in general opinions of, of California's schools. I **went** through school in California, um, a long time ago. Um, and when I **went** through the University of California system it only cost ninety nine dollars a quarter. Um, in my high school we **had** sixteen national merit finalists and it **was** a public high school. Everyone **did** well, uh, **went** on to college and **did**n't have to pay much for college. But in, in the generation that **ensued** we've *seen*, a real change in expectations, in attitudes, and just in support for public education. And this is a real crisis that goes beyond um, a simple um, discussion of language in a classroom, or how we're going to, um, work with new immigrants to the California community. And, and I *think* these are serious issues that we *need* to *talk* about, and, and solve.

Textbooks from disciplines with a focus on the past (e.g., history) rely more heavily on narrative discourse, including long narrative sections written entirely in the past. Many lower division history textbooks are written primarily in the past tense, since they simply narrate past events and circumstances. These books sometimes also document the beliefs, expectations, and other attitudes of historical characters (using verb+*that*-clause constructions), but the majority of the text is given to simple narration; for example:

**Text Sample 7.16:** Textbook; Humanities (history, lower division; tbhis1.bap) [past tense verbs and 3rd person pronouns are **bold underlined**; other positive Dimension 3 features are in ***bold italics***]

Much of the early history of the United States **was** written by New Englanders, who **were** not disposed to emphasize the larger exodus of Puritans to the southerly islands. When the mainland colonists **declared** independence in 1776, they ***hoped that*** these island outposts would join them, but the existence of the British navy **had** a chilling effect.

These common convictions deeply **shaped** the infant colony's life. Soon after arrival the franchise **was** extended to all "freemen" [. . .]

As mentioned above, engineering and natural science texts – from both classroom teaching and textbooks – have large negative scores on Dimension 3. These scores result from the absence of positive Dimension 3 features, coupled with frequent use of the negative features: especially quantity nouns (e.g., *length, amount*) and concrete nouns (including nouns referring to a specific entity but having technical meaning, like *electron*). These negative Dimension 3 scores reflect an interesting

mixture of topics and referring expressions in these disciplines, with highly technical discourse that discusses complex mathematical relationships among everyday
concrete entities.

**Text Sample 7.17:** Classroom teaching; Engineering (Electrical engineering;
lower division; engeeleldli015.txt) [concrete nouns and quantity/mathematical
nouns are **bold underlined**]

let's continue to look at this problem and then we want to move on. the author
says that given these .. the structure he's going to do a field **map**. now this **book**
for, unfortunately this **book** doesn't have the method to do **field** mapping so unless [unclear words] you're responsible for doing **field** mapping, uh although it's
a fun project, but if you are given a field **map**, you should be able to figure out
the **capacity**. you're told, the author says that he's going to do each one of these
as **squares** curvilinear **squares**, and so starting out in the center, these are little
**squares**, and on each of the little **squares**, there is a equal potential **line** .. and
there are flux **tubes**. now what do we mean by flux **tubes**? … we mean that if
we take the **integral** of V dot V.S. over the **area** of the flux **tube** we get the same
answer everywhere. in that **tube**. now the **integral** of V dot V.S. here if these are
nice and square, the **integral** of V. dot V.S. on this top surface, is a flux, remember
the (E) **field** is going through here like this … mm, the flux coming down here
like that, so is a same flux running through every one of the **tubes**.

**Text Sample 7.18:** Textbooks; Engineering (Mechanical engineering; graduate; TBMCE3.GVD) [concrete nouns and quantity/mathematical nouns are
**bold underlined**]

Although many ride problems are peculiar to a specific **road**, or **road** type, the
notion of "**average**" **road** properties can often be helpful in understanding the
response of a **vehicle** to **road** roughness. The general similarity in the **spectral
content** of the **roads** seen in Figure 5.2 (that **elevation amplitude** diminishes
systematically with increasing **wavenumber**) has long been recognized as true
of most **roads**.

Consequently, **road inputs** to a **vehicle** are often modeled with an **amplitude**
that diminishes with **frequency** to the second or fourth **power** approximat-
ing the two linear segments of the **curve** shown in the figure. The **average
properties** shown in the figure are derived from recent studies of a large **number**
of **roads**.

## 7.6 Comparison of the general spoken/written dimensions (1988) and the T2K-SWAL dimensions of variation

There are several interesting points of similarity and contrast between the 1988 MD model of register variation and the MD analysis of university registers presented here. Dimension 1 is especially similar in the two analyses: in both cases, Dimension 1 represents a fundamentally important parameter of variation, composed of an extremely large set of linguistic features, and defining a basic opposition between oral and literate registers. However, two interesting points of difference emerge even for this dimension: First, Dimension 1 in the T2K-SWAL analysis actually collapses three major oral/literate dimensions from the 1988 analysis (Dimensions 1, 3, and 5). Second, the mode differences were not as sharply distinguished in the 1988 analysis. That is, while Dimensions 1, 3, and 5 in the 1988 analysis all distinguished between stereotypical speech and writing (e.g., conversation and academic prose), they also showed overlap among other spoken and written registers (such as fiction and personal letters). In contrast, Dimension 1 in the T2K-SWAL analysis shows an absolute difference between spoken and written registers in the university context.

In some respects, Dimension 3 in the T2K-SWAL analysis ('Reconstructed account of events') resembles Dimension 2 in the 1988 analysis ('Narrative discourse'). However, Dimension 2 in the 1988 analysis had an even stronger association with stereotypically narrative styles (e.g., features like 3rd person pronouns, past tense verbs, perfect aspect, and communication verbs), which are especially common in written fiction. As noted in 7.2.2 above, the Biber et al. (2002) study showed that the 1988 Dimension 2 does not discriminate among university registers. That is, no university register is marked for the dense use of the stereotypical narrative features that define the 1988 Dimension 2. In contrast, the T2K-SWAL Dimension 3 incorporates both narrative features and stance features, functioning together in collaborative reconstructions of past events (rather than stereotypical fictional narrative). This dimension is associated with important differences among university registers (including a general distinction between spoken and written university registers), plus important differences among academic disciplines.

The other two dimensions in the T2K-SWAL analysis do not have close counterparts in the 1988 MD analysis. Dimension 4 ('Academic stance') is in some ways similar to Dimension 4 in the 1988 analysis ('Overt persuasion'), but the T2K-SWAL dimension plays a much more important role in distinguishing among university registers. Dimension 2 in the T2K-SWAL analysis ('Procedural vs. content-focused') has no counterpart in the 1988 analysis, indicating a parameter of variation that is distinctively important in the university setting.

Another important difference between the two analyses is the ubiquitous distribution of stance features across all four T2K-SWAL dimensions. In the 1988 MD analysis, stance features are restricted primarily to Dimension 1 ('Involved vs informational production') and Dimension 4 ('Overt argumentation or persuasion'). In contrast, stance features are prominent on all four T2K-SWAL dimensions. In part, this difference is due to the inclusion of additional stance features in the factor analysis for the T2K-SWAL study. However, the difference in the analyses also reflects the variety in the kinds of stance expressed in university registers, as well as a greater reliance on stance features overall. I return to the general importance of stance in university registers in Chapter 8.

Finally, the T2K-SWAL dimensions correspond to important differences among academic disciplines, while there are no important differences between disciplines identified with respect to the 1988 dimensions (see Biber et al. 2002). In particular, important differences were found here with respect to both T2K-SWAL Dimension 2 (engineering, business, education versus natural science) and T2K-SWAL Dimension 3 (education, humanities, social science versus engineering and natural science). Methodologically, these patterns illustrate the utility of carrying out a new factor analysis for a specific discourse domain. That is, the T2K-SWAL factor analysis identified important patterns of linguistic variation among academic disciplines, realized by specific configurations of linguistic features that were not captured in the general 1988 factor analysis. By basing the T2K-SWAL factor analysis on a corpus that represented both register differences and disciplinary differences, the study was able to capture dimensions that reflected the patterns of co-occurrence and alternation across the full range of university varieties.

## Notes

1. See Biber (2003b) for a preliminary report on this analysis.

2. The only previous MD analysis of school registers based on a new factor analysis has been Reppen (2001). That study analyzed a corpus of elementary students' spoken and written texts (including both textbooks and essays written by the students). The resulting factor analysis had five primary dimensions. Some of these are similar to dimensions in the general adult (1988) model; for example, Dimension 1 in the student model, which was interpreted as 'Edited informational vs. on-line informational discourse', is similar to Dimension 1 in the 1988 model. However, other dimensions are unique to the student model; for example, Dimension 4 was interpreted as 'Projected scenario', and Dimension 5 was interpreted as 'Other-directed idea justification' (see Reppen 2001: 191–194).

# CHAPTER 8

# Synthesis and future directions

The preceding chapters have documented many important linguistic characteristics of university language. These descriptions have shown that there are highly systematic patterns of use across university registers and academic disciplines. At the same time, these patterns of linguistic variation are complex, with each linguistic feature being distributed in particular ways in accordance with its associated communicative functions. Table 8.1 summarizes the major patterns of variation, identifying the features that are especially prevalent in particular registers.

There are several surprising findings that emerge from these linguistic descriptions. Six of these patterns are especially noteworthy:

1. The fundamental importance of the distinction between speech and writing;
2. The relative importance of advising/management as a communicative purpose that cuts across speech and writing;
3. The relative <u>un</u>importance of academic instruction as a communicative purpose that cuts across speech and writing;
4. The relative unimportance of differences in audience and interactivity as parameters that distinguish among the spoken registers;
5. The central importance of linguistic features used for the expression of stance;
6. The complex patterns of use across academic disciplines.

In the following sections, I discuss each of these major patterns in turn.

## 8.1 Speech versus writing in the university

Probably the most surprising finding of the study is the fundamental importance of the spoken versus written mode. The study was designed to include a wide range of the registers found in American universities, sampled across many different situational parameters: different purposes and communicative goals, different settings, individual addressees versus large audiences, status differences among participants, degrees of interactivity, etc. These are all potentially relevant influences on the choice of linguistic style. However, it turns out that the distinction between speech and writing is by far the most important factor in determining the overall patterns of linguistic variation across university registers.

Table 8.1 shows that clausal features are common in all spoken university registers and relatively rare in all written registers. These features include the various verb categories, adverbs, active voice, progressive aspect, and many dependent clause types (*that*-clauses, *WH*-clauses, and adverbial clauses). In contrast, complex noun phrase features are common in all written university registers and relatively rare in all spoken registers. These features include nouns, adjectives, prepositional phrases, relative clauses, etc.

The results of the Multi-Dimensional analysis, reported in Chapter 8, similarly highlight the importance of the spoken/written distinction. Although each dimension is associated with particular functions (such as a focus on 'reconstructed events' versus 'concrete, current information'), it turns out that three of the four dimensions are also strongly associated with speech versus writing:

– Dimension 1 defines an absolute difference between the spoken registers ('oral') and written registers ('literate');
– Dimension 3 defines a near absolute difference between the spoken registers ('reconstructed events') and written registers ('concrete, current information');
– Dimension 4 distinguishes between the spoken teacher-centered registers ('teacher-centered stance') and all other registers.

Dimension 2 ('procedural versus content-focused discourse') has a strong association with advising/management communicative purposes, but even this dimension distinguishes between spoken classroom management at one extreme, versus textbooks and course packs at the other extreme. The register patterns identified in Biber et al. (2002), based on the 1988 dimensions of variation, similarly showed that spoken and written university registers were polarized opposites on most dimensions.

This split between speech and writing is especially surprising given the numerous communicative purposes and other situational factors represented in the T2K-SWAL Corpus. The spoken registers, for example, range from interpersonal interactions with both social and informational purposes (e.g., service encounters and study groups), to monologic discourse with a primary informational focus (e.g., some types of classroom teaching). However, the analyses here show that physical mode – the distinction between speech and writing – is by far the most powerful determinant of linguistic variation.

The sharp linguistic distinction between speech and writing in university language has several functional sources. Most importantly, this difference is related to the production circumstances of speech and writing: speech produced in 'real-time' versus writing which has been carefully planned, revised, and edited. None of the spoken university registers in the T2K-SWAL corpus are scripted, and only one register – classroom teaching – is typically planned ahead of time. The speak-

**Table 8.1**  Distinctive linguistic characteristics of university registers

*** = extremely common; much more frequent than in other registers

* = very common; generally more frequent than in other registers

| Linguistic Feature | Spoken registers | | | Interactive | | Written registers | | |
|---|---|---|---|---|---|---|---|---|
| | Academic Classroom Teaching | Management/Advising Classroom Management | Office Hours | Study Groups | Service Encounters | Academic Textbooks | Management/Advising Course Management | Institutional Writing |
| verbs | * | * | * | * | * | | | |
| mental verbs | * | * | * | * | * | | | |
| activity verbs | * | *** | * | * | *** | | | |
| adverbs | * | * | * | * | * | | | |
| stance adverbs | * | * | * | * | * | | | |
|   certainty adverbs | *** | * | *** | * | * | | | |
|   likelihood adverbs | * | * | *** | * | * | | | |
|   style adverbs | | | | | | * | | |
| 1st person pronouns | * | * | * | * | * | | | |
| 2nd person pronouns | * | * | * | * | * | | | |
| 3rd person pronouns | * | * | * | *** | *** | | * | |
| modal verbs | * | *** | * | * | * | | | |
|   possibility modals | * | * | * | * | *** | * | | * |
|   obligation modals | * | * | * | * | * | | * | * |
|   prediction modals | * | *** | * | * | *** | | *** | |
| active voice | * | * | * | * | * | | | |
| progressive aspect | * | * | * | * | | | | |
| discourse markers | * | *** | *** | *** | * | | | |
| adverbial clauses: | | | | | | | | |
|   conditional clauses | * | *** | *** | * | * | | * | * |
|   causative clauses | * | * | *** | *** | * | | | |

Table 8.1 (continued)

| Linguistic Feature | Spoken registers | | | | | Written registers | | |
|---|---|---|---|---|---|---|---|---|
| | Academic | Management/Advising | | | Interactive | Academic | Management/Advising | |
| | Classroom Teaching | Classroom Management | Office Hours | Study Groups | Service Encounters | Textbooks | Course Management | Institutional Writing |
| *that*-clauses | | | | | | | | |
| verb + *that*-clause | * | * | *** | *** | * | | | |
| certainty verb + *that*-clause | *** | * | *** | * | *** | | | |
| likelihood verb + *that*-clause | * | * | *** | *** | * | | | |
| attitude verb + *that*-clause | * | | | | | | * | |
| communication V + *that*-cls | * | | * | *** | | | | |
| noun + *that*-clause | | | | | | * | | |
| WH-clauses | * | * | *** | *** | * | | | |
| *to*-clauses | | | | | | | | |
| verb + *to*-clause | * | *** | * | | * | | * | * |
| desire verb + *to*-clause | * | *** | *** | * | *** | | | * |
| effort verb + *to*-clause | * | *** | * | | * | | * | *** |
| mental verb + *to*-clause | | | | | | * | *** | * |
| probability verb + *to*-clause | * | | | | | * | | |
| adjective + *to*-clause | | | | | | * | * | |
| noun + *to*-clause | | | | | | | * | |
| diversified vocabulary | | | | | | * | | |
| nouns | | | | | | *** | *** | **** |
| rare nouns | | | | | | * | * | * |
| abstract/process nouns | | | | | | * | * | * |
| adjectives | | | | | | * | * | |
| linking adverbials | | | | | | *** | * | * |
| passive voice | | | | | | * | * | * |

Table 8.1 (*continued*)

| | Spoken registers | | | | | Written registers | | |
| | Academic | Management/Advising | | Interactive | | Academic | Management/Advising | |
| Linguistic Feature | Classroom Teaching | Classroom Management | Office Hours | Study Groups | Service Encounters | Textbooks | Course Management | Institutional Writing |
|---|---|---|---|---|---|---|---|---|
| relative clauses | * | | | | | * | * | * |
| prepositional phrases | *** | | | | | *** | *** | *** |
| Lexical bundles: | | | | | | | | |
| stance bundles | * | *** | * | * | * | | *** | |
| epistemic bundles | * | * | | *** | | | *** | |
| desire bundles | | *** | | * | * | | | |
| obligation bundles | * | * | * | * | * | | *** | |
| intention bundles | * | | | | | | *** | |
| discourse organizers | *** | *** | * | * | | * | *** | *** |
| referential bundles | * | * | | | | | | |
| formulaic expressions | | | | | *** | | | |
| Dimensions: | | | | | | | | |
| Dim 1: 'oral' | * | * | *** | *** | *** | | * | *** |
| Dim 3: 'reconstructed events' | * | * | *** | *** | * | | | |
| Dim 4: 'teacher stance' | *** | *** | * | | | | *** | * |
| Dim 1: 'literate' | | | | | | *** | * | *** |
| Dim 2: 'content-focused' | | | | | | ** | *** | |
| Dim 3: 'concrete, current info' | | | | | | * | *** | * |
| Dim 2: 'procedural' | *** | *** | * | | *** | | *** | *** |

ers in all these spoken registers produce language at the same time that they think about what to say next. Once an utterance has been spoken, it 'exists'. The speaker can produce a new utterance, to say what they really meant, but the original utterance cannot be retracted or revised. In contrast, all written university registers in the T2K-SWAL corpus have been carefully pre-planned and revised. Authors can take as long as they want to produce language in the first place, and then they are free to revise and edit the final text that becomes publicly available.

The evidence from language use suggests that some kinds of linguistic structures are relatively easy to produce in 'real-time' circumstances, while others are restricted to circumstances that allow time for careful production. In particular, clause structures generally seem to pose no difficulty for speakers. Even some kinds of dependent clauses – especially *that*-complement clauses and adverbial clauses – are extremely frequent in all spoken registers, indicating that they are easy to produce in 'real-time'. In contrast, complex phrasal structures are generally rare in speech but common in writing. That is, the typical syntactic structure found in academic writing is a simple main clause with relatively few dependent clauses, but numerous complex noun phrases and prepositional phrases. These structures are rare in speech, apparently because they are difficult to produce under 'real-time' circumstances. Vocabulary choice is another factor that can be tied directly to production circumstances: most speakers rely on a relatively small set of words, because it is difficult to access rare specialized words in real-time circumstances; in contrast, authors use a much larger set of words, including relatively rare or specialized words, because they have the time to reflect and choose the exact term that they want.

At the same time, it is important to recognize that physical mode entails other associated factors in the university context. For example, speakers in all these spoken university registers interact with their addressees, and they have a high level of personal involvement, revealing their own attitudes, feelings, and 'stance' (see 8.5 below). In contrast, authors are less likely to refer directly to themselves or their readers, because they are separated in space and time, and cannot directly interact. These factors (discussed further in 8.3 below) also result in general spoken/written linguistic differences, even though they are not directly associated with the physical production characteristics of the two modes.

## 8.2  Linguistic correlates of advising/management

A second noteworthy finding is the importance of student advising/management as a general communicative purpose in the university context. Table 8.2 isolates the effect of communicative purpose in university registers. The table compares the spoken versus written realizations of two specific communicative purposes:

academic instruction: classroom teaching and textbooks;
student advising/management: spoken classroom management and written
course management

Linguistic features associated with communicative purpose will be shared across
the spoken and written registers serving the same purpose; these features are
highlighted with an underscore in Table 8.2.

Student advising/management is one of the few situational characteristics that
has strong linguistic correlates across the spoken and written modes in the university context. That is, student management registers share a reliance on several
of the same linguistic characteristics, regardless of whether they are realized in
speech or writing. (Academic discipline is another important situational characteristic; see 8.6 below. In contrast, academic instruction is not an important factor
for determining language use across spoken and written registers; see 8.3 below.)

The comparison of spoken classroom management and written course management in Table 8.2 shows that several linguistic features are common in both
registers, including: obligation modals, prediction modals, conditional clauses,
verb + to-clause, and lexical bundles (stance, discourse, and referential). Many of
these features are also common in the other management/advising registers (office
hours and institutional writing). In the Multi-Dimensional analysis, Dimension 2
('Procedural versus content-focused-discourse') was associated primarily with the
distinction between management registers and all other registers.

However, there are more subtle differences for these shared linguistic characteristics, showing that the opposition between speech and writing is important
even here. For example, verb + to-clause is common in both classroom and course
management, but the two registers rely on different classes of controlling verb:
desire verb + to-clause is especially common in classroom management, while
mental verb + to-clause is especially common in written course management. Effort verbs + to-clause are used in both registers, although they are much more
common in spoken classroom management. Similarly, stance lexical bundles are
common in both registers, but again they rely on different sub-types: epistemic
bundles and desire bundles are common in spoken classroom management, while
intention bundles are common in written course management. Obligation bundles are used in both registers, although they are much more common in written
course management. The discussions in Chapters 4–6 have described the specific
communicative functions associated with these features in each register.

Overall, we see a complex pattern of use here: Spoken and written manage-
ment/advising registers use many of the same general linguistic features, because
they have similar directive communicative purposes, telling students what they
need to do in order to succeed in the university. At the same time, these registers differ in their contexts of use: face-to-face and interactive, with the speaker

**Table 8.2** Comparison of instructional and management registers across speech and writing

*** = extremely common; spoken registers
* = very common; spoken registers
+++ = extremely common; written registers
+ = very common; written registers

| Linguistic Feature | Instructional registers | | Management registers | |
|---|---|---|---|---|
| | Classroom Teaching | Textbooks | Classroom Management | Course Management |
| verbs | * | | * | |
| mental verbs | * | | * | |
| activity verbs | * | | *** | |
| adverbs | * | | * | |
| stance adverbs | * | | * | |
|    certainty adverbs | *** | | * | |
|    likelihood adverbs | * | | * | |
|    style adverbs | | + | | |
| 1st person pronouns | | | * | |
| 2nd person pronouns | | | * | |
| 3rd person pronouns | * | | * | |
| modal verbs | * | | *** | + |
|    possibility modals | * | + | * | |
|    obligation modals | | | * | + |
|    prediction modals | * | | *** | +++ |
| active voice | * | | * | |
| progressive aspect | * | | * | |
| discourse markers | * | | *** | |
| adverbial clauses | | | | |
|    conditional clauses | * | | *** | + |
|    causative clauses | * | | * | |
| complement clauses | | | | |
| *that*-clauses | | | | |
|    verb + *that*-clause | * | | * | |
|    certainty verb + *that*-clause | *** | | * | |
|    likelihood verb + *that*-clause | * | | * | |
|    attitude verb + *that*-clause | | | | + |
|    communication V + *that*-cls | * | | | |
|    noun + *that*-clause | | + | | |
| WH-clauses | * | | * | |
| *to*-clauses | | | | |
|    verb + *to*-clause | * | | *** | + |
|    desire verb + *to*-clause | * | | *** | |
|    effort verb + *to*-clause | * | | *** | + |
|    mental verb + *to*-clause | | + | | +++ |
|    probability verb + *to*-clause | * | + | | |
|    adjective + *to*-clause | | + | | + |

Table 8.2  (*continued*)

| Linguistic Feature | Instructional registers | | Management registers | |
|---|---|---|---|---|
| | Classroom Teaching | Textbooks | Classroom Management | Course Management |
| diversified vocabulary | | + | | |
| nouns | | +++ | | +++ |
| rare nouns | | + | | |
| abstract/process nouns | | + | | + |
| adjectives | | + | | + |
| linking adverbials | | +++ | | + |
| passive voice | | + | | + |
| relative clauses | | + | | + |
| prepositional phrases | | +++ | | +++ |
| Lexical bundles: | | | | |
| stance bundles | * | | *** | +++ |
|   epistemic bundles | * | | * | |
|   desire bundles | | | *** | |
|   obligation bundles | * | | * | +++ |
|   intention bundles | * | | | +++ |
| discourse organizers | *** | | *** | + |
| referential bundles | * | + | * | +++ |
| Dimensions: | | | | |
| Dim 1: 'oral' | * | | * | |
| Dim 3: 'reconstructed events' | * | | | |
| Dim 4: 'teacher stance' | *** | | *** | |
| Dim 1: 'literate' | | + | | + |
| Dim 2: 'content-focused' | | +++ | | |
| Dim 3: 'concrete, current info' | | + | | +++ |
| Dim 2: 'procedural' | | | *** | +++ |

revealing personal feelings and attitudes, versus distanced and impersonal, with the writer addressing a more general audience of readers. These situational differences, associated with the general distinction between speaking and writing, are fundamentally important in determining the specific linguistic characteristics of these two registers, even for those linguistic features associated specifically with a student management communicative purpose.

## 8.3 The relative <u>unimportance</u> of academic instruction as a communicative purpose that cuts across speech and writing

Table 8.2 also isolates the comparison between spoken and written academic instruction: classroom teaching versus textbooks. However, in this case, there are very few shared linguistic characteristics associated with this communicative purpose. No dimension in the MD analysis identified linguistic similarities between classroom teaching and textbooks; in fact, these two registers were polar opposites on three of the four dimensions (1, 3, and 4). Similarly, only a few of the individual linguistic features investigated in the study are common in both registers (e.g., possibility modals, probability verb + *to*-clause). Referential lexical bundles are moderately common in both registers, but there are actually different sub-classes of bundles used in each one (imprecision bundles and quantity specification in classroom teaching, versus framing attributes in textbooks).

The general picture that emerges from this comparison is one of difference rather than similarity. This finding is especially surprising given the perception that academic instruction – and specifically the conveyance of informational content – is the primary purpose of a university education (for both spoken and written instructional registers). To the extent that this perception reflects actual practice, the linguistic analyses here show that informational communication is accomplished through very different linguistic means in speech and writing. That is, the different production circumstances of the two modes, coupled with the different situational contexts (e.g., face-to-face with a small audience versus distanced with a relatively unspecified audience), results in fundamentally different styles of linguistic expression in classroom teaching versus textbooks.

However, the analyses here have additionally shown that the perception itself is not entirely accurate. In particular, instructors in classroom teaching incorporate a range of communicative purposes beyond the conveyance of informational content. These additional functions include the expression of personal attitudes and evaluations, an overt signaling of discourse organization, and direct interaction with students. Apparently the face-to-face context of classroom teaching prompts instructors to reveal their own personal experiences and attitudes, in an attempt to make course content more immediate and relevant to students. In contrast, textbooks are focused to a much greater extent on the conveyance of informational content. Authors are less likely to refer directly to themselves or their readers, because they are separated in space and time, and cannot directly interact. Apparently for the same reasons, authors are less likely to reveal their own personal feelings in written university registers.

These differences in interactivity and personal involvement represent present-day language use in American universities. It is certainly possible to imagine a style of university classroom teaching that focuses exclusively on the presentation of course content, with no interaction between instructor and students, and no personal information about the instructor being revealed. In fact, this is the stereotype of university lectures from earlier times. However, that stereotype bears little resemblance to current classroom teaching practices in American universities. And as a result, all spoken university registers, regardless of purpose, are sharply distinguished from written university registers in most of their typical linguistic characteristics.

## 8.4 The relative unimportance of differences in audience and interactivity as parameters that distinguish among the spoken registers

As noted in 8.1 above, one of the most striking general patterns in Table 8.1 is the extent to which linguistic characteristics are shared across <u>all</u> spoken registers, regardless of differences in audience, interactivity, or communicative purpose. At one extreme, service encounters are direct interactions between two individuals, often relying on formulaic exchanges, focused on the immediate task of providing a service. At the other extreme, classroom teaching is mostly teacher-centered, with an instructor addressing a relatively large audience, focused on the tasks of communicating informational content and expressing personal evaluations and stance. Registers like office hours and study groups are intermediate between these two extremes in their situational and communicative characteristics. However, to a large extent, <u>all</u> spoken registers are similar in their typical linguistic characteristics.

In the MD analysis, all spoken registers are 'oral' (Dimension 1) and rely on 'reconstructed events' (Dimension 3). The spoken 'teacher-centered' registers (classroom teaching, classroom management, and office hours) all make extensive use of the stance features associated with Dimension 4. Table 8.1 shows that these shared patterns of use are even stronger for the individual linguistic features: most 'spoken' features are commonly used across the full set of spoken university registers, regardless of differences in audience or interactivity.

These patterns of use reinforce the fundamental importance of the speaking/writing distinction in the university context. Speaking encompasses a number of different situational influences, including real-time production circumstances, the immediate presence of addressees, the possibility of direct interaction, shared time and place, and an inclination on the part of the speaker to reveal their own personal stance. These characteristics are shared, to greater or lesser extents, across all spoken university registers. The surprising finding here is that the situational differences among spoken registers do not have many noteworthy linguistic consequences. Rather, all spoken registers, whether they are casual dialogues or more informational monologues, are highly similar in their typical linguistic characteristics when they are contrasted to written university registers.

## 8.5  The central importance of stance

It has long been recognized that we use language for a number of basic com-municative functions, including: 'ideational', 'textual', 'contextual', 'personal', and 'interpersonal' functions (see Hymes 1974; Halliday 1978; Biber 1988: 35). The preceding chapters have shown that these are all relevant considerations in inter-preting the patterns of linguistic variation among university registers. For example, 'ideational' functions (using language to convey propositional information) are important for explaining the dense use of nouns, adjectives, prepositional phrases, and complex noun phrases in the written university registers. Features such as discourse markers, linking adverbials, and discourse organizing lexical bundles are strongly associated with 'textual' functions; while features like 3rd person pronouns and the noun *thing* are used for 'contextual' functions in the spoken university registers.

It is not surprising that language use in university registers would be influ-enced by all these basic functions. What is surprising, though, is the pervasive importance of the 'personal' and 'interpersonal' functions. These functions have been discussed in the present book under the rubric of 'stance', including the per-sonal expression of attitudes, intentions, and evaluations of certainty, and also the interpersonal expression of directive language. In many cases, these two general functions work together, as with the use of a desire verb + *to*-clause to express both personal feelings and an interpersonal directive (e.g., *I would like you to...*).

One of the most interesting aspects of stance functions in the present analy-sis is how it is spread across all structural categories, and found in different ways and to different extents in all university registers. For example, in the MD analysis, stance features were found on all four dimensions. The stance features grouped on Dimension 2 ('Procedural' versus 'content focused') were associated primar-ily with directive (interpersonal) functions, while the stance features grouped on the other three dimensions were associated with epistemic and attitudinal (per-sonal) functions. Only one of these other dimensions was interpreted as relating primarily to stance: Dimension 4 ('teacher-centered stance'), defined mostly by the co-occurrence of adverbial stance constructions. The other two dimensions (1 and 3) were interpreted in relation to other underlying functions (general 'oral' versus 'literate' for Dimension 1; 'reconstructed accounts of past events' for Dimension 3), but both of these included major stance features among the co-occurring features that define the dimension. Thus, although the MD analysis was interpreted by reference to many different communicative functions, stance func-tions are especially noteworthy because they are pervasive throughout the entire multi-dimensional structure.

Similarly, the analyses in Chapters 4, 5, and 6 showed how stance functions are important for the interpretation of many different linguistic structures. These include modal verbs, adverbial phrases and clauses, and complement clause constructions (*that*-clauses, *WH*-clauses, *to*-clauses).

The analysis of lexical bundles in Chapter 6 showed that stance bundles were the most common functional category in all spoken university registers. These bundles were used for both personal functions (e.g., epistemic bundles and intention bundles) and interpersonal bundles (e.g., obligation bundles). Desire bundles were especially common in classroom management, serving both personal and directive/interpersonal functions. One of the most surprising results coming out of the lexical bundle analysis is the fact that stance bundles are even more common in written course management than in any of the spoken registers. In this register, stance bundles are used mostly for directive/interpersonal functions, rather than expressions of personal attitudes. In contrast, the instructional/academic written registers (textbooks and course packs) show the least reliance on stance features, although even here we find the use of specialized stance features like stance noun + *that*-clause, or probability verb + *to*-clause. Overall, the patterns of register variation show that linguistic features are used to express a wide range of stance meanings, and that these stance features are frequent and pervasive in the university context.

## 8.6 The complex patterns of use across academic disciplines

Differences among academic disciplines were also investigated for some linguistic features. Table 8.3 shows that the disciplines form a kind of cline, with social science and humanities often patterning together at one extreme, and business and engineering often patterning together at the other extreme. Natural science texts are interesting in that they are similar to social science/humanities in some respects, but similar to engineering in other respects.

Two dimensions from the MD analysis were strongly associated with systematic disciplinary differences in both classroom teaching and textbooks: On Dimension 2, business and engineering texts were marked as being 'procedural', while natural science, social science, and humanities were similar to one another in being 'content-focused'. On Dimension 3, social science and humanities were similar to each other in their focus on 'reconstructed accounts of events'. In contrast, natural science and engineering were similar in having a strong non-narrative orientation. Business texts were intermediate along this dimension.

As noted above, social science and humanities are similar to each other in their reliance on many individual linguistic features as well. Social science and humanities are similar to natural science in their reliance on a large and diversified vocabulary, including many specialized terms. In contrast, business and engineering rely on a smaller set of words with fewer rare or specialized terms, although

**Table 8.3**  Distinctive linguistic characteristics of academic disciplines

*** = extremely common; much more frequent than in other disciplines
* = very common; generally more frequent than in other disciplines

| Linguistic Feature | Business | Engineering | Natural Science | Social Science | Humanities |
|---|---|---|---|---|---|
| In textbooks: | | | | | |
| diversified vocabulary | | | * | *** | *** |
| specialized vocabulary | | | * | *** | *** |
| abstract/process nouns | *** | *** | | * | |
| concrete (technical) nouns | | * | * | | |
| passive voice | | * | * | | |
| Lexical bundles: | | | | | |
| referential lexical bundles | * | * | *** | *** | * |
| intangible framing bundles | * | | | * | *** |
| place referential bundles | | | *** | * | |
| quantity referential bundles | * | *** | * | | |
| epistemic stance bundles | * | | | * | |
| ability stance bundles | | * | * | | * |
| importance stance bundles | | | | * | |
| Dimensions (classroom teaching and textbooks): | | | | | |
| Dim 2: 'procedural' | * | * | | | |
| Dim 2: 'content-focused' | | | *** | * | * |
| Dim 3: 'narrative' | | | | * | * |
| Dim 3: 'non-narrative' | | * | * | | |

many 'common' words are used with technical meanings in these disciplines. These patterns are most pronounced in textbooks, although the same trends exist for classroom teaching (see Figures 3.6 and 3.7 in Chapter 3). In other respects, natural science is more similar to the other 'technical' disciplines, for example, in its frequent use of passive constructions, quantity referential bundles, and ability stance bundles.

Two general patterns emerge from these comparisons: First, there are systematic linguistic differences associated with the distinction between the 'professional' disciplines (business and engineering) and the more traditionally 'academic' disciplines (humanities and social sciences). The 'professional' disciplines emphasize the mastery of technical methods and procedures, while the 'academic' disciplines emphasize the discovery of new knowledge, the critical evaluation of information, and discussions of alternative perspectives. These differences in emphasis have strong linguistic correlates, for both vocabulary and grammatical features.

The natural sciences are intermediate in their typical linguistic characteristics because they combine both emphases. In this respect, the natural sciences are illustrative of the second general pattern: that each discipline has it's own characteristic linguistic features, which reflect the particular communicative priorities of that area of study. Social science and humanities are the two most similar disciplines included in the present study, but even these differ in some respects: for example, humanities has a greater reliance on intangible framing lexical bundles, while social science has a greater reliance on place referential bundles and importance stance bundles. Business and engineering are also different from one another; for example, business has a greater reliance on intangible framing lexical bundles and epistemic stance bundles, while engineering has a greater reliance on passive voice verbs and ability stance bundles.

The analysis here has been structured around five high-level academic disciplines, showing systematic linguistic differences across those distinctions. However, previous research has shown that similar linguistic differences exist at much more specified levels of analysis, considering particular research genres in specific academic disciplines (see, for example, the survey of research on PhD dissertations from different disciplines in Swales 2004: Chapter 4). In future research, the analytical approach developed in the present book could fruitfully be extended to consideration of the patterns of linguistic variation across specific academic disciplines.

## 8.7  Future directions

The research project undertaken for the present study can be extended in several ways. First of all, it would be useful to study particular university registers at a much more specified level. For example, classroom teaching is a general register in the present study, including different situations that vary according to class size, preference for lecture or discussion formats, and level of instruction. It is reasonable to expect that there are systematic linguistic differences associated with these more specific situational differences. Similarly, office hours include detailed explanations of academic topics, mentoring of student research, and student advising. Such sub-registers are associated with their own systematic patterns of linguistic variation and could usefully be investigated within all of the general register categories included in the present study.

An even more important extension to the present study is to investigate the linguistic characteristics of student language in the university. There have been many studies of student writing over the years, but fewer studies of student speaking in the university, and I know of no comprehensive study of linguistic variation for the full set of spoken and written registers produced by students in the university context. However, such a study would provide crucially important information for a full understanding of the linguistic demands placed on students in the university.

Taken together, these studies would provide the background descriptions required to fully address the four traditional skills of ESL/EFL instruction: listening, reading, speaking, and writing. The present study has shown that the opposition between listening and reading in university contexts is a fundamentally important one. Spoken university registers are strikingly different in their typical linguistic characteristics from written university registers. The findings presented here show that ESL/EFL instruction in listening and reading needs to emphasize more than the differing comprehension strategies required by the two modes. Rather, students need to be able to process fundamentally different sets of words and linguistic structures, used for different communicative purposes, in the two modes. For example, listening tasks in the university require the ability to process complex clausal structures, and to distinguish among a large set of words and structural devices used to express a wide range of stance meanings. In contrast, reading tasks in the university require the ability to process complex phrasal structures (especially noun phrase and prepositional phrase structures), used to express informational meanings as well as directive meanings in registers like course syllabi and department web sites.

A future comprehensive study of student language in the university would complete this picture, providing linguistic descriptions of the full range of speaking/writing tasks required of students in the university. Taken together, such descriptions would provide the basis for more principled approaches to ESL/EFL teaching methods, both in general and for EAP approaches. By synthesizing the results of the present study on university registers with future research on student registers, it should be possible to achieve a comprehensive description of language use in the university. Such a description would provide a framework for studies of language development, and for complementary perspectives on the approaches that might prove effective in university composition and public speaking courses. The present study, by focusing on the spoken and written registers that students encounter in the university, has provided a first step towards this eventual goal.

# References

Adolphs, S. & N. Schmitt (2003). Lexical coverage of spoken discourse. *Applied Linguistics, 24*, 425–438.

Altenberg, B. (1998). On the phraseology of spoken English: The evidence of recurrent word-combinations. In A. Cowie (Ed.), *Phraseology: Theory, Analysis and Applications* (pp. 101–122). Oxford: Oxford University Press.

Altenberg, B. & M. Eeg-Olofsson (1990). Phraseology in spoken English. In J. Aarts & W. Meijs (Eds.), *Theory and Practice in Corpus Linguistics* (pp. 1–26). Amsterdam: Rodopi.

Atkinson, D. (1992). The evolution of medical research writing from 1735 to 1985: The case of the *Edinburgh Medical Journal*. *Applied Linguistics, 13*, 337–374.

Atkinson, D. (1996). *The Philosophical Transactions of the Royal Society of London*, 1675–1975: A sociohistorical discourse analysis. *Language in Society, 25*, 333–371.

Atkinson, D. (1999). *Scientific Discourse in Sociohistorical Context: The Philosophical Transactions of the Royal Society of London*, 1675–1975. Maywah, NJ: Lawrence Erlbaum.

Atkinson, D. (2001). Scientific discourse across history: A combined multi-dimensional/rhetorical analysis of the *Philosophical Transactions of the Royal Society of London*. In Conrad & Biber (Eds.), pp. 45–65.

Barton, E. (1993). Evidentials, argumentation, and epistemological stance. *College English, 55*, 745–769.

Basturkmen, H. (2003). So what happens when the tutor walks in? Some observations on interaction in a university discussion group with and without the tutor. *Journal of English for Academic Purposes, 2*, 21–33.

Bazerman, C. (1988). *Shaping Written Knowledge: The Genre and Activity of the Experimental Article in Science*. Madison, WI: University of Wisconsin Press.

Bazerman, C. (1997). The life of genre, the life in the classroom. In W. Bishop & H. Ostrum (Eds.), *Genre and Writing* (pp. 19–26). Portsmouth, NH: Boynton/Cook.

Beach, R. & C. M. Anson (1992). Stance and intertextuality in written discourse. *Linguistics and Education, 4*, 335–357.

Bejar, I., D. Douglas, J. Jamieson, S. Nissan, & J. Turner (2000). *TOEFL 2000 Listening Framework: A Working Paper*. (ETS TOEFL Monograph Series, MS-19). Princeton, NJ: Educational Testing Service.

Belcher, D. & A. Hirvela (Eds.). (2001). *Linking Literacies: Perspectives on L2 Reading/Writing Connections*. Ann Arbor, MI: University of Michigan Press.

Benson, M. J. (1994). Lecture listening in an ethnographic perspective. In Flowerdew (Ed.), pp. 181–198.

Berkenkotter, C. & T. Huckin (1995). *Genre Knowledge in Disciplinary Communication*. Hillsdale, NJ: Lawrence Erlbaum.

Bhatia, V. J. (2002). A generic view of academic discourse. In J. Flowerdew (Ed.), pp. 21–39.

Biber, D. (1985). Investigating macroscopic textual variation through multi-feature / multi-dimensional analyses. *Linguistics, 23,* 337–360.

Biber, D. (1986). Spoken and written textual dimensions in English: Resolving the contradictory findings. *Language, 62,* 384–414.

Biber, D. (1988). *Variation across Speech and Writing.* Cambridge: Cambridge University Press.

Biber, D. (1990). Methodological issues regarding corpus-based analyses of linguistic variation. *Literary and Linguistic Computing, 5,* 257–269.

Biber, D. (1993). Representativeness in corpus design. *Literary and Linguistic Computing, 8,* 243–257.

Biber, D. (1995). *Dimensions of Register Variation: A Cross-Linguistic Comparison.* Cambridge: Cambridge University Press.

Biber, D. (2003a). Compressed noun phrase structures in newspaper discourse: The competing demands of popularization vs. economy. In J. Aitchison & D. Lewis (Eds.), *New Media Language* (pp. 169–181). London: Routledge.

Biber, D. (2003b). Variation among university spoken and written registers: A new multi-dimensional analysis. In C. Meyer & P. Leistyna (Eds.), *Corpus Analysis: Language Structure and Language Use* (pp. 47–70). Amsterdam: Rodopi.

Biber, D. (2004a). Historical patterns for the grammatical marking of stance: A cross-register comparison. *Journal of Historical Pragmatics, 5,* 107–135.

Biber, D. (2004b). Modal use across registers and time. In A. Curzan & K. Emmons (Eds.), *Studies in the History of the English Language II: Unfolding Conversations* (pp. 189–216). Berlin: Mouton de Gruyter.

Biber, D. (to appear). Multidimensional approaches. In A. Lüdeling & M. Kytö (Eds.), *Corpus Linguistics: An International Handbook.* Berlin: Mouton de Gruyter.

Biber, D. & J. Burges (2000). Historical change in the language use of women and men: Gender differences in dramatic dialogue. *Journal of English Linguistics, 28,* 21–37.

Biber, D. & V. Clark (2002). Historical shifts in modification patterns with complex noun phrase structures: How long can you go without a verb? In T. Fanego, M. J. Lopez-Couso, & J. Perez-Guerra (Eds.), *English Historical Syntax and Morphology* (pp. 43–66). Amsterdam: John Benjamins.

Biber, D. & S. Conrad (1999). Lexical bundles in conversation and academic prose. In H. Hasselgard & S. Oksefjell (Eds.), *Out of Corpora: Studies in Honor of Stig Johansson* (pp. 181–189). Amsterdam: Rodopi.

Biber, D., S. Conrad, & V. Cortes (2003). Lexical bundles in speech and writing: An initial taxonomy. In A. Wilson, P. Rayson, & T. McEnery (Eds.), *Corpus Linguistics by the Lune: A Festschrift for Geoffrey Leech* (pp. 71–92). Frankfurt/Main: Peter Lang.

Biber, D., S. Conrad, & V. Cortes (2004). *If you look at. . .:* Lexical bundles in university teaching and textbooks. *Applied Linguistics, 25,* 371–405.

Biber, D., S. Conrad, & R. Reppen (1998). *Corpus Linguistics: Investigating Language Structure and Use.* Cambridge: Cambridge University Press.

Biber, D., S. Conrad, R. Reppen, P. Byrd, & M. Helt (2002). Speaking and writing in the university: A multi-dimensional comparison. *TESOL Quarterly, 36,* 9–48.

Biber, D., S. Conrad, R. Reppen, P. Byrd, & M. Helt (2003). Strengths and goals of multi-dimensional analysis: A response to Ghadessy. *TESOL Quarterly, 37,* 151–155.

Biber, D., S. Conrad, R. Reppen, P. Byrd, M. Helt, V. Clark, V. Cortes, E. Csomay, & A. Urzua (2004). *Representing Language Use in the University: Analysis of the TOEFL 2000 Spoken and Written Academic Language Corpus.* (ETS TOEFL Monograph Series, MS-25). Princeton, NJ: Educational Testing Service.

Biber, D. & E. Finegan (1988). Adverbial stance types in English. *Discourse Processes, 11*, 1–34.

Biber, D. & E. Finegan (1989). Styles of stance in English: Lexical and grammatical marking of evidentiality and affect. *Text, 9*, 93–124.

Biber, D. & E. Finegan (Eds.). (1994a). *Sociolinguistic Perspectives on Register*. New York: Oxford University Press.

Biber, D. & E. Finegan (1994b). Multi-dimensional analyses of authors' styles: Some case studies from the eigtheenth century. In D. Ross & D. Brink (Eds.), *Research in Humanities Computing 3* (pp. 3–17). Oxford: Oxford University Press.

Biber, D. & E. Finegan (1994c). Intra-textual variation within medical research articles. In N. Oostdijk & P. de Haan (Eds.), *Corpus-based Research into Language* (pp. 201–222). Amsterdam: Rodopi. (Reprinted in Conrad & Biber (2001), pp. 108–123.)

Biber, D., S. Johansson, G. Leech, S. Conrad, & E. Finegan (1999). *The Longman Grammar of Spoken and Written English*. London: Longman.

Braine, G. (2002). Academic literacy and the nonnative speaker graduate student. *Journal of English for Academic Purposes, 1*, 59–68.

Brown, P. & C. Fraser (1979). Speech as a marker of situation. In K. R. Scherer & H. Giles (Eds.), *Social Markers in Speech* (pp. 33–62). Cambridge: Cambridge University Press.

Bruthiaux, P. (1994). Me Tarzan, you Jane: Linguistic simplification in "personal ads" register. In Biber & Finegan (1994a, Eds.), pp. 136–154.

Bruthiaux, P. (1996). *The Discourse of Classified Advertising: Exploring the Nature of Linguistic Simplicity*. New York: Oxford University Press.

Bunton, D. (2002). Generic moves in PhD thesis Introductions. In J. Flowerdew (Ed.), pp. 57–75.

Butler, C. S. (1997). Repeated word combinations in spoken and written text: Some implications for Functional Grammar. In C. S. Butler, J. H. Connolly, R. A. Gatward, & R. M. Vismans (Eds.), *A Fund of Ideas: Recent Developments in Functional Grammar* (pp. 60–77). Amsterdam: IFOTT, University of Amsterdam.

Bybee, J. & S. Fleischman (Eds.). (1995). *Modality in Grammar and Discourse*. Amsterdam: John Benjamins.

Byrd, P. (1997). Naming practices in academic writing: Another thought. *English for Specific Purposes, 16*, 339–343.

Camiciottoli, B. C. (2004). Interactive discourse structuring in L2 guest lectures: Some insights from a comparative corpus-based study. *Journal of English for Academic Purposes, 3*, 39–54.

Carkin, S. (2001). *Pedagogic Language in Introductory Classes: A Multi-Dimensional Analysis of Textbooks and Lectures in Biology and Macroeconomics*. PhD Dissertation. Northern Arizona University.

Carrell, P. L., P. A. Dunkel, & P. Mollaun (2002). *The Effects of Notetaking, Lecture Length and Topic on the Listening Component of the TOEFL 2000*. (TOEFL Monograph Series #MS-23). Princeton, NJ: Educational Testing Service.

Carson, J. (2001). A task analysis of reading and writing in academic contexts. In D. Belcher & A. Hirvela (Eds.), *Linking Literacies: Perspectives on L2 Reading/Writing Connections* (pp. 48–83). Ann Arbor, MI: University of Michigan Press.

Carson, J., N. Chase, & S. Gibson (1993). *Academic Demands of the Undergraduate Curriculum: What Students Need*. Atlanta: Center for the Study of Adult Literacy, Georgia State University.

Carson, J., N. Chase, S. Gibson, & M. Hargrove (1992). Literacy demands of the undergraduate curriculum. *Reading Research and Instruction, 31*, 25–50.

Chafe, W. L. (1986). Evidentiality in English conversation and academic writing. In Chafe & Nichols (Eds.), pp. 261–272.

Chafe, W. L. & J. Nichols (Eds.). (1986). *Evidentiality: The Linguistic Coding of Epistemology*. Norwood, NJ: Ablex.

Charles, M. (2003). 'This mystery...': A corpus-based study of the use of nouns to construct stance in theses from two contrasting disciplines. *Journal of English for Academic Purposes, 2*, 313–326.

Chaudron, C. & J. Richards (1986). The effect of discourse markers on the comprehension of lectures. *Applied Linguistics, 7*, 113–127.

Chih-Hua, K. (1999). The use of personal pronouns: Role relationships in scientific journal articles. *English for Specific Purposes, 18*, 121–138.

Connor, U. & T. Upton (2003). Linguistic dimensions of direct mail letters. In C. Meyer & P. Leistyna (Eds.), *Corpus Analysis: Language Structure and Language Use* (pp. 71–86). Amsterdam: Rodopi.

Connor, U. & T. Upton (2004). The genre of grant proposals: A corpus linguistic analysis. In U. Connor & T. Upton (Eds.), *Discourse in the Professions* (pp. 235–56). Amsterdam: John Benjamins.

Connor-Linton, J. (1988). Authors style and world-view in nuclear discourse: A quantitative analysis. *Multilingua, 7*, 95–132.

Connor-Linton, J. (2001), Authors style and world-view: A comparison of texts about nuclear arms policy. In Conrad & Biber (Eds.), pp. 84–93.

Conrad, S. (2001). Variation among disciplinary texts: A comparison of textbooks and journal articles in biology and history. In Conrad & Biber (Eds.), pp. 94–107.

Conrad, S. (1996). Investigating academic texts with corpus-based techniques: An example from biology. *Linguistics and Education, 8*, 299–326.

Conrad, S. & D. Biber (2000). Adverbial marking of stance in speech and writing. In Hunston & Thompson (Eds.), pp. 56–73.

Conrad, S. & D. Biber (Eds.). (2001). *Variation in English: Multi-Dimensional Studies*. London: Longman (Pearson Education).

Cortes, V. (2002). *Lexical Bundles in Academic Writing in History and Biology*. Doctoral dissertation. Northern Arizona University.

Cortes, V. (2004). Lexical bundles in published and student disciplinary writing: Examples from history and biology. *English for Specific Purposes, 23*, 397–423.

Couture, B. (1986). Effective ideation in written text: A functional approach to clarity and exigence. In B. Couture (Ed.), *Functional Approaches to Writing: Research Perspectives* (pp. 69–91). Norwood, NJ: Ablex.

Coxhead, A. (2000). A new academic word list. *TESOL Quarterly, 34*, 213–238.

Crompton, P. (1997). Hedging in academic writing: Some theoretical problems. *English for Specific Purposes, 16*, 271–287.

Crookes, G. & S. Gass (Eds.). (1993). *Tasks and Language Learning: Integrating Theory and Practice*. Clevedon, Avon: Multilingual Matters.

Csomay, E. (2000). Academic lectures: An interface of an oral and literate continuum. *novELTy, 7*, 30–46.

Cutting, J. (1999). The grammar of the In-group code. *Applied Linguistics, 20*, 179–202.

DeCarrico, J. & J. R. Nattinger (1988). Lexical phrases for the comprehension of academic lectures. *English for Specific Purposes, 7*, 91–102.

DeCock, S. (1998). A recurrent word combination approach to the study of formulae in the speech of native and non-native speakers of English. *International Journal of Corpus Linguistics, 3*, 59–80.

Edwards, J. A. & M. D. Lampert (Eds.). (1993). *Talking Data: Transcription and Coding in Discourse Research*. Hillsdale: Lawrence Erlbaum.

Ellis, N. (1996). Sequencing in SLA: Phonological memory, chunking, and points of order. *Studies in Second Language Acquisition, 19*, 91–126.

Enright, M. K., W. Grabe, K. Koda, P. Mosenthal, P. Mulcahy-Ernt, & M. Schedl (2000). *TOEFL 2000 Reading Framework: A Working Paper*. (ETS TOEFL Monograph Series, MS-17). Princeton, NJ: Educational Testing Service.

Ervin-Tripp, S. (1972). On sociolinguistic rules: Alternation and co-occurrence. In J. J. Gumperz & D. Hymes (Eds.), *Directions in Sociolinguistics* (pp. 213–250). New York: Holt.

Farr, F. (2003). Engaged listenership in spoken academic discourse: The case of student-tutor meetings. *Journal of English for Academic Purposes, 2*, 67–85.

Ferguson, C. A. (1983). Sports announcer talk: Syntactic aspects of register variation. *Language in Society, 12*, 153–172.

Ferguson, C. A. (1994). Dialect, register, and genre: Working assumptions about conventionalization. In Biber & Finegan (Eds.), pp. 15–30.

Ferguson, G. (2001). If you pop over there: A corpus-based study of conditionals in medical discourse. *English for Specific Purposes, 20*, 61–82.

Fitzmaurice, S. (2002). Politeness and modal meaning in the construction of humiliative discourse in an early eighteenth-century network of patron-client relationships. *English Language and Linguistics, 6*, 239–266.

Fitzmaurice, S. (2003). The grammar of stance in early eighteenth-century English epistolary language. In C. Meyer & P. Leistyna (Eds.), *Corpus Analysis: Language Structure and Language Use* (pp. 107–132). Amsterdam: Rodopi.

Flowerdew, J. (1992). Defintions in science lectures. *Applied Linguistics, 13*, 202–221.

Flowerdew, J. (Ed.). (1994). *Academic Listening: Research Perspectives*. New York: Cambridge University Press.

Flowerdew, J. (Ed.). (2002). *Academic Discourse*. New York: Longman.

Flowerdew, J. & S. Tauroza (1995). The effect of discourse markers of second language lecture comprehension. *Studies in Second Language Acquisition, 17*, 435–458.

Flowerdew, L. (2002). Corpus-based analyses in EAP. In J. Flowerdew (Ed.), pp. 95–115.

Fortanet, I. (2004). The use of 'we' in university lectures: Reference and function. *English for Specific Purposes, 23*, 45–66.

Garside, R., G. Leech, & G. Sampson (Eds.). (1987). *The Computational Analysis of English: A Corpus-Based Approach*. London: Longman.

Gilbert, G. & M. Mulkay (1984). *Opening Pandora's Box: A Sociological Analysis of Scientific Discourse*. Cambridge: Cambridge University Press.

Gledhill, C. (2000). The discourse function of collocation in research article introductions. *English for Specific Purposes, 19*, 115–135.

Goulden, R., P. Nation, & J. Read (1990). How large can a receptive vocabulary be? *Applied Linguistics, 11*, 341–363.

Grabe, W. (1987). Contrastive rhetoric and text-type research. In U. Connor & R. B. Kaplan (Eds.), *Writing across Languages: Analysis of L2 Text* (pp. 115–137). Reading, MA: Addison-Wesley.

Grabe, W. & R. B. Kaplan (1996). *Theory and Practice of Writing*. London: Longman.

Grabe, W. & R. B. Kaplan (1997). On the writing of science and the science of writing: Hedging in science text and elsewhere. In R. Markkanen & H. Schroder (Eds.), *Hedging and Discourse: Approaches to the Analysis of a Pragmatic Phenomenon in Academic Texts* (pp. 151–167). Berlin: Walter de Gruyter & Co.

Granger, S. (Ed.). (1998a). *Learner English on Computer*. London: Longman.

Granger, S. (1998b). Prefabricated patterns in advanced EFL writing: Collocations and formulae. In A. Cowie (Ed.), *Phraseology* (pp. 145–160). Oxford: Oxford University Press.

Hale, G., C. Taylor, B. Bridgeman, J. Carson, B. Kroll, & R. Kantor (1996). *A Study of Writing Tasks Assigned in Academic Degree Programs*. (TOEFL Research Report, 54). Princeton, NJ: Educational Testing Service.

Halliday, M. A. K. (1978). *Language as Social Semiotic: The Social Interpretation of Language and Meaning*. London: Edward Arnold.

Halliday, M. A. K. (1988). On the language of physical science. In M. Ghadessy (Ed.), *Registers of Written English* (pp. 162–78). London: Pinter.

Halliday, M. A. K. & J. R. Martin (1993). *Writing Science: Literacy and Discursive Power*. Pittsburgh: University of Pittsburgh Press.

Heath, S. B. & J. Langman (1994). Shared thinking and the register of coaching. In Biber & Finegan (Eds.), pp. 82–105.

Helt, M. (2001). A multi-dimensional comparison of British and American spoken English. In Conrad & Biber (Eds.), pp. 171–184.

Herdan, G. (1960). *Type-Token Mathematics: A Textbook of Mathematical Linguistics*. The Hague: Mouton.

Hewings, M. (Ed.). (2001). *Academic Writing in Context: Implications and Applications*, Birmingham: The University of Birmingham Press.

Hewings, A. & M. Hewings (2001). Anticipatory "it" in academic writing: An indicator of disciplinary difference and developing disciplinary knowledge. In Hewings (Eds.), pp. 199–214.

Hirsh, D. & P. Nation (1992). What vocabulary size is needed to read unsimplified texts for pleasure? *Reading in a Foreign Language, 8*, 689–696.

Holmes, J. (1986). Doubt and certainty in ESL textbooks. *Applied Linguistics, 9*, 21–43.

Honoré, A. (1979). Some simple measures of richness of vocabulary. *Association for Literary and Linguistic Computing Bulletin*, 172–177.

Howarth, P. (1996). *Phraseology in English Academic Writing*. Tübingen: Max Niemeyer Verlag.

Huckin, T., M. Haynes, & J. Coady (Eds.). (1995). *Second Language Reading and Vocabulary Learning*. Norwood, NJ: Ablex Publishing Corporation.

Huckin, T. & L. H. Pesante (1988). Existential *there*. *Written Communication, 5*, 368–391.

Hunston, S. (1994). Evaluation and organization in a sample of written academic discourse. In M. Coulthard (Ed.), *Advances in Written Text Analysis* (pp. 191–218). London: Routledge.

Hunston, S. (1995). A corpus study of some English verbs of attribution. *Functions of Language, 2*, 133–158.

Hunston, S. & G. Thompson (Eds.). (2000). *Evaluation in Text: Authorial Stance and the Construction of Discourse*. New York: Oxford University Press.

Hyland, K. (1994). Hedging in academic writing and EAP textbooks. *English for Specific Purposes, 13*, 239–256.

Hyland, K. (1996a). Talking to the academy: Forms of hedging in science research articles. *Written Communication, 13*, 251–281.

Hyland, K. (1996b). Writing without conviction? Hedging in science research articles. *Applied Linguistics, 17*, 433–454.

Hyland, K. (1998). *Hedging in Scientific Research Articles*. Philadelphia: John Benjamins.

Hyland, K. (1999). Talking to students: Metadiscourse in introductory coursebooks. *English for Specific Purposes, 18*, 3–26.

Hyland, K. (2001). Bringing in the reader: Addressee features in academic articles. *Written Communication, 18*, 549–574.

Hyland, K. (2002a). Authority and invisibility: Authorial identity in academic writing. *Journal of Pragmatics, 34*, 1091–1112.

Hyland, K. (2002b). Activity and evaluation: Reporting practices in academic writing. In J. Flowerdew (Ed.), pp. 115–130.

Hyland, K. (2002c). Directives: Argument and engagement in academic writing. *Applied Linguistics, 23*, 215–239.

Hymes, D. (1974). *Foundations in Sociolinguistics*. Philadelphia: University of Pennsylvania Press.

Hymes, D. (1984). Sociolinguistics: Stability and consolidation. *International Journal of the Sociology of Language, 45*, 39–45.

Jamieson, J., S. Jones, I. Kirsch, P. Mosenthal, & C. Taylor (2000). *TOEFL 2000 Framework: A Working Paper*. (ETS TOEFL Monograph Series, MS-16). Princeton, NJ: Educational Testing Service.

Johns, A. (1997). *Text, Role, and Context: Developing Academic Literacies*. Cambridge: Cambridge University Press.

Keck, C. M. & D. Biber (2004). Modal use in spoken and written university registers: A corpus-based study. In R. Facchinetti & F. Palmer (Eds.), *English Modality in Perspective: Genre Analysis and Contrastive Studies* (pp. 3–25). Frankfurt am Main: Peter Lang Verlag.

Khuwaileh, A. A. (1999). The role of chunks, phrases and body language in understanding co-ordinated academic lectures. *System, 27*, 249–260.

Klare, G. R. (1974). Assessing readability. *Reading Research Quarterly, 10*, 62–102.

Krug, M. G. (2000). *Emerging English Modals: A Corpus-Based Study of Grammaticalization*. Berlin: Mouton de Gruyter.

Kytö, M. (1991). *Variation and Diachrony, with Early American English in Focus*. Frankfurt am Main: Peter Lang.

Labov, W. (1984). Intensity. In D. Schiffrin (Ed.), *Meaning, Form, and Use in Context: Linguistic Applications* (pp. 43–70). Washington, DC: Georgetown University Press.

Lee, D. (2001). Genres, registers, text types, domains, and styles: Clarifying the concepts and navigating a path through the BNC jungle. *Language Learning and Technology, 5*, 37–72.

Leech, G. (2003). Modality on the move: The English modal auxiliaries 1961–1992. In R. Facchinetti, M. Krug, & F. Palmer (Eds.), *Modality in Contemporary English*. Berlin/New York: Mouton de Gruyter.

Leki, I. & J. Carson (1997). "Completely different worlds": EAP and the writing experiences of ESL students in university courses. *TESOL Quarterly, 31*, 39–69.

Lindemann, S. & A. Mauranen (2001). "It's just real messy": The occurrence and function of *just* in a corpus of academic speech. *English for Specific Purposes, 20*, 459–475.

Long, M. & G. Crookes (1992). Three approaches to task-bsed syllabus design. *TESOL Quarterly, 26*, 27–56.

Love, A. (1993). Lexico-grammatical features of geology textbooks: Process and product revisited. *English for Specific Purposes, 12*, 197–218.

Love, A. (2001). Introductory textbooks and disciplinary acculturation: A case study from social anthropology. In M. Hewings (Ed.), *Academic Writing in Context: Implications and Applications* (pp. 122–139). Birmingham: The University of Birmingham Press.

Love, A. (2002). Introductory concepts and 'cutting edge' theories: Can the genre of the textbook accommodate both? In Flowerdew (Ed.), pp. 76–92.

Madden, C. & C. Myers (1994). *Discourse and Performance of International Teachings Assistants.* Alexandria, VA: TESOL.

Marco, M. J. L. (1999). Procedural vocabulary: Lexical signaling of conceptual relations in discourse. *Applied Linguistics, 20,* 1–21.

Marco, M. J. L. (2000). Collocational frameworks in medical research papers: A genre-based study. *English for Specific Purposes, 19,* 63–86.

Markkanen, R. & H. Schroder (Eds.). (1997). *Hedging and Discourse: Approaches to the Analysis of a Pragmatic Phenomenon in Academic Texts.* Berlin: Walter de Gruyter & Co.

Martin, J. R. (1985). Process and text: Two aspects of human semiosis. In J. D. Benson & W. S. Greaves (Eds.), *Systemic Perspectives on Discourse* (Vol. 1) (pp. 248–74). Norwood, NJ: Ablex.

Master, P. (2001). Active verbs with inanimate subjects in scientific research articles. In Hewings (Ed.), pp. 169–181.

Mauranen, A. (2001). Reflexive academic talk: Observations from MICASE. In R. C. Simpson & J. M. Swales (Eds.), *Corpus Linguistics in North America: Selections from the 1999 Symposium* (pp. 165–178). Ann Arbor: The University of Michigan Press.

Mauranen, A. (2003a). "But here's a flawed argument": Socialisation into and through metadiscourse. In P. Leistyna & C. F. Meyer (Eds.), *Corpus Analysis: Language Structure and Language Use* (pp. 19–34). New York: Rodopi.

Mauranen, A. (2003b). "A good question." Expressing evaluation in academic speech. In G. Cortese & P. Riley (Eds.), *Domain-Specific English: Textual Practices across Communities and Classrooms* (pp. 115–140). New York: Peter Lang.

Mauranen, A. (2004). "They're a little bit different": Variation in hedging in academic speech. In K. Aijmer & A.-B. Stenström (Eds.), *Discourse Patterns in Spoken and Written Corpora* (pp. 173–197). Amsterdam: John Benjamins.

Mauranen, A. & M. Bondi (2003). Evaluative language use in academic discourse. *Journal of English for Academic Purposes, 2,* 269–271.

McCarthy, M. & R. Carter (1997). Written and spoken vocabulary. In N. Schmitt & M. McCarthy (Eds.), *Vocabulary: Description, Acquisition and Pedagogy.* Cambridge: Cambridge University Press.

Meyer, P. G. (1997). Hedging strategies in written academic discourse: Strengthening the argument by weakening the claim. In R. Markkanen & H. Schroder (Eds.), *Hedging and Discourse: Approaches to the Analysis of a Pragmatic Phenomenon in Academic Texts* (pp. 21–41). Berlin: Walter de Gruyter & Co.

Myers, G. (1989). The pragmatics of politeness in scientific articles. *Applied Linguistics, 10,* 1–35.

Myers, G. (1990). *Writing biology: Texts in the Social Construction of Scientific Knowledge.* Madison, WI: University of Wisconsin Press.

Myhill, J. (1995). Change and continuity in the functions of the American English modals. *Linguistics, 33,* 157–211.

Myhill, J. (1997). *Should* and *ought*: The rise of individually oriented modality in American English. *English Language and Linguistics, 1,* 3–23.

Nation, I. S. P. (1990). *Teaching and Learning Vocabulary.* New York: Newbury House.

Nation, I. S. P. (2001). *Learning Vocabulary in Another Language.* Cambridge: Cambridge University Press.

Nation, I. S. P. & J. Coady (1988). Vocabulary and reading. In R. Carter & M. McCarthy (Eds.), *Vocabulary and Language Teaching.* London: Longman.

Nation, P. & R. Waring (1997). Vocabulary size, text coverage and word lists. In N. Schmitt & M. McCarthy (Eds.), *Vocabulary: Description, Acquisition and Pedagogy*. Cambridge: Cambridge University Press.

Nattinger, J. R. & J. S. DeCarrico (1992). *Lexical Phrases and Language Teaching*. Oxford: Oxford University Press.

Oakey, D. (2002). Formulaic language in English academic writing: A corpus-based study of the formal and functional variation of a lexical phrase in different academic disciplines. In R. Reppen, S. Fitzmaurice, & D. Biber (Eds.), *Using Corpora to Explore Linguistic Variation* (pp. 111–129). Philadelphia: John Benjamins.

Ochs, E. (Ed.). (1989). *The Pragmatics of Affect*. Special issue of *Text*, Vol. 9.

Palmer, F. R. (1986). *Mood and Modality*. Cambridge: Cambridge University Press.

Parkinson, J. (2000). Acquiring scientific literacy through content and genre: A theme-based language course for science students. *English for Specific Purposes, 19*, 369–387.

Partington, A. & J. Morley (2004). From frequency to ideology: investigating word and cluster/bundle frequency in political debate. In B. Lewandowska-Tomaszczyk (Ed.), *Practical Applications in Language and Computers – PALC 2003* (pp. 179–192). Frankfurt a. Main: Peter Lang.

Poos, D. & R. Simpson (2002). Cross-disciplinary comparisons of hedging: Some findings from the Michigan Corpus of Academic Spoken English. In R. Reppen, S. Fitzmaurice, & D. Biber (Eds.), *Using Corpora to Explore Linguistic Variation* (pp. 3–21). Philadelphia: John Benjamins.

Powell, C. & R. Simpson (2001). Collaboration between corpus linguists and digital librarians for the MICASE web interface. In R. Simpson & J. Swales (Eds.), *Corpus Linguistics in North America* (pp. 32–47). Ann Arbor: University of Michigan.

Precht, K. (2000). *Patterns of Stance in English*. PhD dissertation, Northern Arizona University.

Precht, K. (2003). *Great* versus *lovely*: Stance differences in American and British English. In C. Meyer & P. Leistyna (Eds.), *Corpus Analysis: Language Structure and Language Use* (pp. 133–152). Amsterdam: Rodopi.

Quaglio, P. M. (2004). *The Language of NBCs Friends: A Comparison with Face-to-Face Conversation*. NAU PhD Dissertation.

Reppen, R. (2001). Register variation in student and adult speech and writing. In Conrad & Biber (Eds.), pp. 187–199.

Rey, Jennifer M. (2001). Historical shifts in the language of women and men: Gender differences in dramatic dialogue. In Conrad & Biber (Eds.), pp. 138–156.

Salager-Meyer, F. (1994). Hedges and textual communicative function in medical English written discourse. *English for Specific Purposes, 13*, 149–170.

Salager-Meyer, F. (1999). Referential behavior in scientific writing: A diachronic study (1810–1995). *English for Specific Purposes, 18*, 279–305.

Salem, A. (1987). *Pratique des Segments Répétés*. Paris: Institut National de la Langue Française.

Samraj, B. (2002). Disciplinary variation in abstracts: The case of *Wildlife Behaviour* and *Conservation Biology*. In Flowerdew (Ed.), pp. 40–56.

Schmitt, N. (2000). *Vocabulary in Language Teaching*. Cambridge: Cambridge University Press.

Schmitt, N. (Ed.). (2004). *Formulaic Sequences*. Amsterdam: John Benjamins.

Schmitt, N., Grandage, S., & S. Adolphs (2004). Are corpus-derived recurrent clusters psycholinguistically valid? In Schmitt (Ed.), pp. 127–152.

Schmitt, N. & M. McCarthy (Eds.). (1997). *Vocabulary: Description, Acquisition and Pedagogy*. Cambridge: Cambridge University Press.

Silva, T. & P. Matsuda (Eds.). (2001). *On Second Language Writing.* Mahwah, NJ: Lawrence Earlbaum.

Silver, M. (2003). The stance of stance: A critical look at ways stance is expressed and modeled in academic discourse. *Journal of English for Academic Purposes, 2,* 359–374.

Simpson, R. & D. Mendis (2003). A corpus-based study of idioms in academic speech. *TESOL Quarterly, 37,* 419–441.

Simpson, R. (2004). Stylistic features of spoken academic discourse: The role of formulaic expressions. In U. Connor & T. Upton (Eds.), *Discourse in the Professions: Perspectives from Corpus Linguistics* (pp. 37–64). Amsterdam: John Benjamins.

Spolsky, B. (1995). *Measured Words.* Oxford: Oxford University Press.

Strodt-Lopez, B. (1991). Tying it all in: Asides in university lectures. *Applied Linguistics, 12,* 117–140.

Swales, J. M. (1990). *Genre Analysis: English in Academic and Research Settings.* Cambridge: Cambridge University Press.

Swales, J. M. (2001). Metatalk in American academic talk. *Journal of English Linguistics, 29,* 34–54.

Swales, J. M. (2004). *Research Genres: Exploration and Applications.* Cambridge: Cambridge University Press.

Swales, J., U. K. Ahmad, Y. Chang, D. Chavez, D. F. Dressen, & R. Seymour (1998). Consider this: The role of imperatives in scholarly writing. *Applied Linguistics, 19,* 97–121.

Swales, J. M. & A. Burke (2003). "It's really fascinating work": Differences in evaluative adjectives across academic registers. In P. Leistyna & C. F. Meyer (Eds.), *Corpus Analysis: Language Structure and Language Use* (pp. 1–18). New York: Rodopi.

Swales, J. M. & B. Malczewski (2001). Discourse management and new-episode flags in MICASE. In R. C. Simpson & J. M. Swales (Eds.), *Corpus Linguistics in North America: Selections from the 1999 Symposium* (pp. 145–164). Ann Arbor: The University of Michigan Press.

Thompson, G. & Y. Ye (1991). Evaluation in the reporting verbs used in academic papers. *Applied Linguistics, 12,* 365–382.

Thompson, S. E. (2003). Text-structuring metadiscourse, intonation and the signaling or organization in academic lectures. *Journal of English for Academic Purposes, 2,* 5–20.

Ure, J. (1982). Introduction: Approaches to the study of register range. *International Journal of the Sociology of Language, 35,* 5–23.

Valle, E. (1999). *A Collective Intelligence: The Life Sciences in the Royal Society as a Scientific Discourse Community, 1665–1965.* PhD dissertation: University of Turku.

Varantola, K. (1984). *On Noun Phrase Structures in Engineering English.* PhD dissertation: University of Turku.

Varttala, T. (2003). Hedging in scientific research articles: A cross-disciplinary study. In G. Cortese & P. Riley (Eds.), *Domain-Specific English: Textual Practices across Communities and Classrooms* (pp. 141–174). New York: Peter Lang.

Ventola, E. (1984). Orientation to social semiotics in foreign language teaching. *Applied Linguistics, 5,* 275–286.

Weinert, R. (1995). The role of formulaic language in second language acquisition: A review. *Applied Linguistics, 16,* 180–205.

West, M. (1953). *A General Service List of English Words.* London: Longman, Green and Co.

Williams, G. C. (1998). Collocational networks: interlocking patterns of lexis in a corpus of plant biology research articles. *International Journal of Corpus Linguistics, 3,* 151–171.

Williams, I. (1996). A contextual study of lexical verbs in two types of medical research report: Clinical and experimental. *English for Specific Purposes, 15,* 175–197.

Wimmer, G. & G. Altmann (1999). Review article: On vocabulary richness. *Journal of Quantitative Linguistics, 6*, 1–9.

Wray, A. (2002). *Formulaic Language and the Lexicon*. Cambridge: Cambridge University Press.

Wray, A. & M. Perkins (2000). The functions of formulaic language: An integrated model. *Language and Communication, 20*, 1–28.

Xue, G. & P. Nation (1984). A university word list. *Language Learning and Communication, 3*, 215–229.

# Analytical procedures for the linguistic analyses

## 1. Overview of linguistic analyses

The descriptions throughout this book incorporate linguistic features from eight major categories:

1. vocabulary distributions (e.g., the number of different words in classroom teaching versus textbooks), including the distributional classifications of words from the four content word classes (e.g., common vs. rare nouns, common vs. rare verbs);
2. grammatical part-of-speech classes (e.g., nouns, verbs, first and second person pronouns, prepositions);
3. semantic categories for the major word classes (e.g., activity verbs, mental verbs, existence verbs);
4. grammatical characteristics (e.g., nominalizations, past tense verbs, passive voice verbs);
5. syntactic structures (e.g., *that* relative clauses, *to* complement clauses);
6. lexico-grammatical associations (e.g., *that*-complement clauses and *to*-complement clauses controlled by communication verbs vs. mental verbs);
7. lexical bundles – i.e. recurrent sequences of words.

The study considered the distribution of many specific linguistic features, representing a wide range of grammatical categories, semantic classes, syntactic constructions, and lexico-grammatical associations. Appendix D in Biber et al. (2004) provides a detailed breakdown of mean scores for 131 specific linguistic features across text categories (e.g., comparing the mean scores for first person pronouns across registers, academic disciplines, and levels of instruction). That appendix is available on-line at www.ets.org/ell/research/toeflmonograph.html.

Most of the features described here were analyzed using the standard procedures of corpus linguistics based on a tagged corpus. However, the analyses of vocabulary features and semantic classes require further explanation.

## 2.   Vocabulary distributions

Chapter 3 compares the words that speakers and writers use in university registers. Table A.1 lists the seven kinds of vocabulary analyses undertaken in the study.

One key research issue for vocabulary analyses is to decide what to count as a word. In the present case, the analyses were based on 'lemmas': the base form for each word, disregarding inflectional morphemes. For example, *eat, eats, ate, eating,* and *eaten* are all realizations of a single lemma: *EAT*.

An alternative approach, developed by Nation and his colleagues, is to use 'word families' as the basis for vocabulary analysis (see, e.g., Nation 2001; Nation & Waring 1997; Coxhead 2000). Word families include 'closely related derived forms' in addition to all inflected variants for a word (Nation 2001:8), based on the assumption that the meaning of some derived forms is transparently related to the core meaning of the word root.

One methodological problem for this approach is deciding which derivational variants to include as members of a word family. Nation (2001:266) gives two examples:

| Word Family: | THINK | SURE |
|---|---|---|
| Inflected forms: | *thinks, thought* | *surer, surest* |
| Transparent derivatives: | *thinker, unthinking* | *surely, ensure* |
| (included in the same word family) | | |
| Less transparent derivatives: | *unthinkable* | *surety, assure* |
| (NOT included in the same word family) | | |

The major difficulty in practice is deciding which derivatives are 'transparent' and should therefore be included in the same word family, and which ones are different enough in meaning that they should be classified as belonging to different word families. Nation and his research team at the University of Wellington have made these decisions for a large set of the most common words (see Xue & Nation 1984; Coxhead 2000; and http://www.vuw.ac.nz/lals/). However, the present study analyzes the use of all words in the T2K-SWAL Corpus (c. 45,000 words), and we found it extremely difficult to reliably group the remaining words into word fam-

Table A.1   Quantitative measures of vocabulary size and diversity

1. Type/token ratio
2. Mean word length
3. Distribution of word types by part-of-speech
4. Distribution of word types across registers
5. Distribution of word types across academic disciplines
6. Breakdown of word types by frequency level
7. Interactions of part of speech / frequency level / register distribution

ilies. As a result, the construct of lemma rather than word family was used as the basic unit of analysis here. Biber et al. (2004: 37–42) provides a detailed description of the lemmatization process.

Separate vocabulary analyses were carried out for each part-of-speech (POS; noun, verb, adjective, adverb), using the grammatical codes in the tagged version of the T2K-SWAL Corpus (see Section 2.3). Words occurring with a different POS were treated as separate lemmas. For example, *work* as a noun and *work* *as* a verb were listed as two separate lemmas. In many cases, different POS realizations of the same word form can have quite different meanings. For example, the noun and verb uses of the word forms *object, type,* and *iron* are quite distinct in meaning. The present study is one of the first large-scale vocabulary investigations to incorporate part-of-speech distinctions, allowing a more detailed description of vocabulary patterns interacting with POS distributions.

The next step in the analysis was to compute frequency measures reflecting the distribution of each lemma:

- How often the lemma occurred in each mode (spoken vs written)
- How often the lemma occurred in each register
- How often the lemma occurred in each academic discipline (only for classroom teaching and textbooks)
- How often the lemma occurred in each level of instruction (only for classroom teaching and textbooks)

These raw frequency counts were normalized to their rate of occurrence per 1 million words. For example, *work* as a noun occurs 1095 times in the spoken texts of the T2K-SWAL corpus, and the total word count for the spoken part of the corpus is c. 1,665,000 words. Thus, the normed rate of occurrence for *work/N* in the spoken mode is:

$$1{,}095 \ / \ 1{,}665{,}000 * 1{,}000{,}000 = 657.15 \text{ times per million words}$$

We grouped words into four frequency categories:

words that occur more than 1000 times per million words of text
words that occur 201–1000 times per million words;
words that occur 20–200 times per million words of text
words occurring less than 20 times per million words of text.

In Chapter 3, these categories are used to document vocabulary distributions in each register, and to make comparisons across academic disciplines.

In sum, the vocabulary analyses in the following chapters are innovative in three major ways:

- They describe the distribution of all words in the T2K-SWAL Corpus, c. 28,000 different lemmas;
- Because the analyses are based on a tagged corpus, each part-of-speech form can be treated as a separate lemma;
- They describe word use patterns across different registers and academic disciplines.

One important caveat for the vocabulary analyses is that the T2K-SWAL corpus is relatively small for lexicographic work (and the sub-corpora are considerably smaller, and not matched for size). Appendix B addresses these issues and presents a series of methodological experiments that illustrate the problems that can arise when vocabulary studies are based on corpora of different sizes. These experiments are used to develop a methodology for normalizing vocabulary counts across corpora, and the results presented in Chapter 3 are based on those methods. The results of these experiments show that vocabulary comparisons across corpora should be interpreted cautiously, because the quantitative patterns can be strongly influenced by differences in topic and corpus size.[1]

## 3. Semantic categories of the major word classes

In addition to grammatical characteristics, the descriptions here explore major content differences across registers and disciplines. As a result, they incorporate semantic as well as structural linguistic characteristics in the analyses.

The semantic analyses are based on a detailed classification of the most common words from the four content word classes (nouns, verbs, adjectives, and adverbs). Table A.2 lists the major semantic classes distinguished for each part of speech.

**Table A.2** Overview of semantic categories

**Semantic categories of nouns**
animate noun (e.g., *teacher, child, person*)
cognitive noun (e.g., *fact, knowledge, understanding*)
concrete noun (e.g., *rain, sediment, modem*)
technical/concrete noun (e.g., *cell, wave, electron*)
quantity noun (e.g., *date, energy, minute*)
place noun (e.g., *habitat, room, ocean*)
group/institution noun (e.g., *committee, bank, congress*)
abstract/process nouns (e.g., *application, meeting, balance*)

**Semantic categories of verbs**
*be* as main verb
activity verb (e.g., *smile, bring, open*)

**Table A.2** (*continued*)

communication verb (e.g., *suggest, declare, tell*)
mental verb (e.g., *know, think, believe*)
causative verb (e.g., *let, assist, permit*)
occurrence verb (e.g., *increase, grow, become*)
existence verb (e.g., *possess, reveal, include*)
aspectual verb (e.g., *keep, begin, continue*)

**Semantic categories of modal verbs**
possibility/permission/ability modals (*can, may, might, could*)
necessity/obligation modals (*ought, must, should*)
predictive/volition modals (*will, would, shall*)

**Semantic categories of phrasal verbs**
intransitive activity phrasal verb (e.g., *come on, sit down*)
transitive activity phrasal verb (e.g., *carry out, set up*)
transitive mental phrasal verb (e.g., *find out, give up*)
transitive communication phrasal verb (e.g., *point out*)
intransitive occurrence phrasal verb (e.g., *come off, run out*)
copular phrasal verb (e.g., *turn out*)
aspectual phrasal verb (e.g., *go on*)

**Semantic categories of adjectives**
size attributive adjectives (e.g., *big, high, long*)
time attributive adjectives (e.g., *new, young, old*)
color attributive adjectives (e.g., *white, red, dark*)
evaluative attributive adjectives (e.g., *important, best, simple*)
relational attributive adjectives (e.g., *general, total, various*)
topical attributive adjectives (e.g., *political, economic, physical*)

**Semantic and functional categories of adverbs and adverbials**
place adverbials (e.g., *above, beside, upstairs*)
time adverbials (e.g., *again, early, later, now*)
downtoners (e.g., *barely, nearly, slightly*)
hedges (e.g., *at about, something like, almost*)
amplifiers (e.g., *absolutely, extremely, perfectly*)
emphatics (e.g., *a lot, for sure, really*)
discourse particles (e.g., sentence initial *well, now, anyway*)
linking adverbials (e.g., *consequently, furthermore, however*)
stance adverbials:
certainty adverbs (e.g., *undoubtedly, obviously, certainly*)
likelihood adverbs (e.g., *evidently, predictably, roughly*)
style adverbs (e.g., *frankly, mainly, truthfully*)
attitude adverbs (e.g., *surprisingly, hopefully, wisely*)

For verbs, adjectives, and adverbs, the semantic classification was based on
the analytical distinctions and word lists from LGSWE. These lists include only
the most common words occurring in the 40-million word Longman Spoken and
Written English Corpus. For semantic categories that are represented by a large

number of words – like 'activity' verbs (see Table A.3 below) – only high frequency words are included (in this case, only verbs occurring at least 50 times per million words). However, other semantic categories were represented by fewer words – like 'occurrence' verbs in Table A.3 (below) – and so lower frequency words were included for those categories (in this case, all verbs occurring over 20 times per million words). We undertook a similar classification process of our own for nouns (see below), because the LGSWE did not include that information.

For the most part, the semantic classification of words is based on their core meanings (i.e., the meaning that speakers tend to think of first). However, it is important to recognize that many words have multiple meanings/uses from different semantic domains. This is especially true of the most common words. For example, a verb like *follow* can express either a physical activity or a mental process. A verb like *admit* can express a physical activity, a mental process, or a speech act. Most words have core meanings belonging to only one semantic domain, and so in general the semantic classification of words was not problematic. However, it is important to note that the semantic analyses presented in the following chapters are not intended as authoritative descriptions of any individual word. Rather, the goal here is to compare the overall tendencies of registers and academic disciplines. The following subsections provide more detailed descriptions of the semantic categories used for the analysis of verbs and nouns.

**Table A.3**  List of words included in the semantic classes for verbs (based on LGSWE, pp. 361–371)

1. **Activity:** 'primarily denote actions and events that could be associated with choice, and so take a subject with the semantic role of an agent' (LGSWE, pp. 361–362, 367–368, 370):
*buy, make, get, go, give, take, come, use, leave, show, try, work, move, follow, put, pay, bring, meet, play, run, hold, turn, send, sit, wait, walk, carry, lose, eat, watch, reach, add, produce, provide, pick, wear, open, win, catch, pass, shake, smile, stare, sell, spend, apply, form, obtain, arrange, beat, check, cover, divide, earn, extend, fix, hang, join, lie, obtain, pull, repeat, receive, save, share, smile, throw, visit, accompany, acquire, advance, behave, borrow, burn, clean, climb, combine, control, defend, deliver, dig, encounter, engage, exercise, expand, explore, reduce*
Phrasal activity verbs (LGSWE, pp. 409–410):
*come along, come on, come over, get out, get up, go ahead, go off, sit down, shut up, sit up, stand up, carry out, get back, get in, get off, look up, make up, pick up, put on, set up, take off, take on, take over, take up*

2. **Mental verbs:** 'denote a wide range of activities and states experienced by humans; they do not involve physical action and do not necessarily entail volition. Their subject often has a semantic role of a recipient' (LGSWE, pp. 362–363, 368–369, 370). Mental verbs include cognitive meanings (e.g., *think, know*), emotional meanings expressing various attitudes and desires (e.g., *love, want*), perception (e.g., *see, taste*), and receipt of communication (e.g., *read, hear*):
*see, know, think, find, want, mean, need, feel, like, hear, remember, believe, read, consider, suppose, listen, love, wonder, understand, expect, hope, assume, determine, agree, bear, care, choose,*

**Table A.3**  (*continued*)

---

*compare, decide, discover, doubt, enjoy, examine, face, forget, hate, identify, imagine, intend, learn, mind, miss, notice, plan, prefer, prove, realize, recall, recognize, regard, suffer, wish, worry, accept, afford, appreciate, approve, assess, blame, bother, calculate, conclude, celebrate, confirm, count, dare, deserve, detect, dismiss, distinguish, experience, fear, forgive, guess, ignore, impress, interpret, judge, justify, observe, perceive, predict, pretend, reckon, remind, satisfy, solve, study, suspect, trust*

**3. Communication verbs:** 'a special subcategory of activity verbs that involve communication activities (speaking, writing)' (LGSWE, pp. 362, 368, 370):
*say, tell, call, ask, write, talk, speak, thank, descibe, claim, offer, admit, announce, answer, argue, deny, discuss, encourage, explain, express, insist, mention, offer, propose, quote, reply, shout, sign, sing, state, teach, warn, accuse, acknowledge, address, advise, appeal, assure, challenge, complain, consult, convince, declare, demand, emphasize, excuse, inform, invite, persuade, phone, pray, promise, question, recommend, remark, respond, specify, swear, threaten, urge, welcome, whisper, suggest*

**4. Existence or relationship verbs:** These verbs 'report a state that exists between entities. Some of the most common verbs of existence or relationship are copular verbs' (e.g., *be, seem, appear*). Other verbs in this category 'report a particular state of existence (e.g., *exist, live, stay*) or a particular relationship between entities (e.g., *contain, include, involve, represent*)' (LGSWE, pp. 364, 369, 370–371):
*seem, look, stand, stay, live, appear, include, involve, contain, exist, indicate, concern, constitute, define, derive, illustrate, imply, lack, owe, own, possess, suit, vary, deserve, fit, matter, reflect, relate, remain, reveal, sound, tend, represent*

**5. Occurrence verbs:** 'report events (typically physical events) that occur apart from any volitional activity. Often their subject has the semantic affected role' (LGSWE, pp. 364, 369, 370):
*become, happen, change, die, grow, develop, arise, emerge, fall, increase, last, rise, disappear, flow, shine, sink, slip, occur*

**6. Facilitation or causation verbs:** 'indicate that some person or inanimate entity brings about a new state of affairs. These verbs often occur together with a nominalized direct object or complement clause following the verb phrase, which reports the action that was facilitated' (LGSWE, pp. 363, 369, 370):
*help, let, allow, affect, cause, enable, ensure, force, prevent, assist, guarantee, influence, permit, require*

**7. Aspectual verbs:** 'characterize the stage of progress of some other event or activity, typically reported in a complement clause following the verb phrase' (LGSWE, pp. 364, 369, 371):
*start, keep, stop, begin, complete, end, finish, cease, continue*

---

## 3.1  Semantic categories for verbs

The descriptions in Chapter 4 distinguish among seven major semantic categories of verbs: Activity, Mental, Communication, Existence/relationship, Occurrence, Facilitation/causation, Aspectual. Table A.3 lists the verbs included under each category, together with a short definition of the category.

## 3.2 Semantic categories for nouns

Unlike verbs, adjectives, and adverbs, there were no previous corpus-based seman-tic classifications for nouns that could be used for the analysis here. Therefore, we produced a list of all common nouns in the T2K-SWAL Corpus (all lemmas occurring more than 20 times per million words) and grouped those into major se-mantic classes. The classification proceeded inductively: simply grouping together the nouns that expressed similar kinds of meaning, and then afterwards assigning a semantic label to the class. The goal in doing this was not to make a strong claim about the semantic category of individual words. Rather, the primary goal was to identify major semantic classes of nouns that could be used to compare university registers and disciplines.

Table A.4 lists the semantic categories resulting from this analysis and shows the full list of nouns included in each category. Eight major semantic classes are distinguished:

> **Animate:** humans or animals
> **Cognitive:** mental/cognitive processes or perceptions
> **Concrete:** inanimate objects that can be touched
> **Technical/concrete:** tangible objects that are not normally perceived and/or cannot normally be touched
> **Place:** places, areas, or objects in a fixed location
> **Quantity:** nouns specifying a quantity, amount, or duration
> **Group/institution:** nouns that denote a group or institution
> **Abstract/process:** intangible, abstract concepts or processes

**Table A.4** List of words included in the semantic classes for nouns (based on all lemmas occurring more than 20 times per million words in the T2K-SWAL Corpus)

**1. Animate:** humans or animals.
*family, guy, individual, kid, man, manager, member, parent, teacher, child, people, person, student, woman, animal, applicant, author, baby, boy, client, consumer, critic, customer, doctor, employee, employer, father, female, friend, girl, god, historian, husband, American, Indian, instructor, king, leader, male, mother, owner, president, professor, researcher, scholar, speaker, species, supplier, undergraduate, user, wife, worker, writer, accountant, adult, adviser, agent, aide, ancestor, anthropologist, archaeologist, artist, artiste, assistant, associate, attorney, audience, auditor, bachelor, bird, boss, brother, buddha, buyer, candidate, cat, citizen, colleague, collector, competitor, counselor, daughter, deer, defendant, designer, developer, director, dog, driver, economist, engineer, executive, expert, farmer, feminist, freshman, eologist, hero, host, hunter, immigrant, infant, investor, jew, judge, lady, lawyer, learner, listener, maker, manufacturer, miller, minister, mom, monitor, monkey, neighbor, observer, officer, official, participant, partner, patient, personnel, peer, physician, plaintiff, player, poet, police, processor, professional, provider, psychologist, resident, respondent, schizophrenic, scientist, secretary, server, shareholder, sikh, sister, slave, son, spouse, supervisor, theorist, tourist, victim, faculty, dean, engineer, reader, couple, graduate*

**Table A.4** (*continued*)

**2. Cognitive:** mental/cognitive processes or perceptions.

*analysis, decision, experience, assessment, calculation, conclusion, consequence, consideration, evaluation, examination, expectation, observation, recognition, relation, understanding, hypothesis, ability, assumption, attention, attitude, belief, concentration, concern, consciousness, concept, fact, idea, knowledge, look, need, reason, sense, view, theory, desire, emotion, feeling, judgement, memory, notion, opinion, perception, perspective, possibility, probability, responsibility, thought*

**3. Concrete:** inanimate objects that can be touched.

*tank, stick, target, strata, telephone, string, telescope, sugar, ticket, syllabus, tip, salt, tissue, screen, tooth, sculpture, sphere, seawater, spot, ship, steam, silica, steel, slide, stem, snow, sodium, mud, solid, mushroom, gift, muscle, glacier, tube, gun, nail, handbook, newspaper, handout, node, instrument, notice, knot, novel, lava, page, food, transcript, leg, eye, lemon, brain, magazine, device, magnet, oak, manual, package, marker, peak, match, pen, metal, pencil, block, pie, board, pipe, heart, load, paper, transistor, modem, book, mole, case, motor, computer, mound, dollar, mouth, hand, movie, flower, object, foot, table, frame, water, vessel, arm, visa, bar, grain, bed, hair, body, head, box, ice, car, item, card, journal, chain, key, chair, window, vehicle, leaf, copy, machine, document, mail, door, map, dot, phone, drug, picture, truck, piece, tape, note, liquid, wire, equipment, wood, fiber, plant, fig, resistor, film, sand, file, score, seat, belt, sediment, boat, seed, bone, soil, bubble, bud, water, bulb, portrait, bulletin, step, shell, stone, cake, tree, camera, video, face, wall, acid, alcohol, cap, aluminium, clay, artifact, clock, rain, clothing, asteroid, club, automobile, comet, award, sheet, bag, branch, ball, copper, banana, counter, band, cover, wheel, crop, drop, crystal, basin, cylinder, bell, desk, dinner, pole, button, pot, disk, pottery, drain, radio, drink, reactor, drawing, retina, dust, ridge, edge, ring, engine, ripple, plate, game, cent, post, envelope, rock, filter, root, finger, slope, fish, space, fruit, statue, furniture, textbook, gap, tool, gate, train, gel, deposit, chart, mixture*

**4. Technical/concrete:** tangible objects that are not normally perceived and/or cannot normally be touched.

*cell, unit, gene, wave, ion, bacteria, electron, chromosome, element, cloud, sample, isotope, schedule, neuron, software, nuclei, solution, nucleus, atom, ray, margin, virus, mark, hydrogen, mineral, internet, molecule, mineral, organism, message, oxygen, paragraph, particle, sentence, play, star, poem, thesis, proton, unit, web, layer, center, matter, chapter, square, data, circle, equation, compound, exam, letter, bill, page, component, statement, diagram, word, dna, angle, fire, carbon, formula, graph, iron, lead, jury, light, list*

**5. Place:** places, areas, or objects in a fixed location.

*apartment, interior, bathroom, moon, bay, museum, bench, neighborhood, bookstore, opposite, border, orbit, cave, orbital, continent, outside, delta, parallel, desert, passage, estuary, pool, factory, prison, farm, restaurant, forest, sector, habitat, shaft, hell, shop, hemisphere, southwest, hill, station, hole, territory, horizon, road, bottom, store, boundary, stream, building, top, campus, valley, canyon, village, coast, city, county, country, court, earth, front, environment, district, field, floor, market, lake, office, land, organization, lecture, place, left, room, library, area, location, class, middle, classroom, mountain, ground, north, hall, ocean, park, planet, property, region, residence, river*

**6. Quantity:** nouns specifying a quantity, amount, or duration.

*cycle, rate, date, second, frequency, section, future, semester, half, temperature, height, today, number, amount, week, age, day, century, part, energy, lot, heat, term, hour, time, month, mile,*

### Table A.4  (*continued*)

*period, moment, morning, volume, per, weekend, percentage, weight, portion, minute, quantity, percent, quarter, length, ratio, measure, summer, meter, volt, voltage*

**7. Group/institution:** nouns that denote a group or institution.

*airline, institute, colony, bank, flight, church, hotel, firm, hospital, household, college, institution, house, lab, laboratory, community, company, government, university, school, home, congress, committee*

**8. Abstract/process:** intangible, abstract concepts or processes.

*action, activity, application, argument, development, education, effect, function, method, research, result, process, accounting, achievement, addition, administration, approach, arrangement, assignment, competition, construction, consumption, contribution, counseling, criticism, definition, discrimination, description, discussion, distribution, division, eruption, evolution, exchange, exercise, experiment, explanation, expression, formation, generation, graduation, management, marketing, marriage, mechanism, meeting, operation, orientation, performance, practice, presentation, procedure, production, progress, reaction, registration, regulation, revolution, selection, session, strategy, teaching, technique, tradition, training, transition, treatment, trial, act, agreement, attempt, attendance, birth, break, claim, comment, comparison, conflict, deal, death, debate, demand, answer, control, flow, service, work, test, use, war, change, question, study, talk, task, trade, transfer, admission, design, detail, dimension, direction, disorder, diversity, economy, emergency, emphasis, employment, equilibrium, equity, error, expense, facility, failure, fallacy, feature, format, freedom, fun, gender, goal, grammar, health, heat, help, identity, image, impact, importance, influence, input, labor, leadership, link, manner, math, matrix, meaning, music, network, objective, opportunity, option, origin, output, past, pattern, phase, philosophy, plan, potential, prerequisite, presence, principle, success, profile, profit, proposal, psychology, quality, quiz, race, reality, religion, resource, respect, rest, return, risk, substance, scene, security, series, set, setting, sex, shape, share, show, sign, signal, sort, sound, spring, stage, standard, start, stimulus, strength, stress, style, support, survey, symbol, topic, track, trait, trouble, truth, variation, variety, velocity, version, whole, action, account, condition, culture, end, factor, grade, interest, issue, job, kind, language, law, level, life, model, name, nature, order, policy, position, power, pressure, relationship, requirement, role, rule, science, side, situation, skill, source, structure, subject, type, information, right, state, system, value, way, address, absence, advantage, aid, alternative, aspect, authority, axis, background, balance, base, beginning, benefit, bias, bond, capital, care, career, cause, characteristic, charge, check, choice, circuit, circumstance, climate, code, color, column, combination, complex, connection, constant, constraint, contact, content, contract, context, contrast, crime, criteria, cross, current, curriculum, curve, debt, density*

## Notes

**1.** Type/token ratio is not a linear variable. Words tend to be repeated in a text: the larger a text is, the more repeated words there are, and therefore, proportionally, the fewer word types. To control for this, type/token ratio in the multi-dimensional analysis is computed based on only the first 400 words in a text.

**2.** Chapter 4 presents the major distributional patterns for words but no word lists. Readers are referred to Biber et al. (2004, Appendix B) for the complete word lists from the T2K-SWAL Corpus. These lists are organized by frequency level and distribution across varieties (e.g., words occurring over 70% of the time in speech; over 70% of the time in writing; and words occurring in both modes).

# Methodological issues in quantitative vocabulary analyses

Two major methodological issues must be addressed for quantitative analyses of vocabulary: (1) the representativeness of the corpus, and (2) difficulties in comparing vocabulary distributions across corpora of different size (because the quantitative measures are not linear).

## 1.  Representativeness of the corpus

The representativeness of the corpus is a fundamentally important consideration for any corpus-based linguistic study (see, e.g., Biber 1990, 1993). Two major factors must be considered: size and composition.

A corpus must be large enough to adequately represent the occurrence of the features being studied. In grammatical studies, this is generally not a problem for common features, like the overall frequencies of nouns and verbs. Because these features occur frequently and regularly, they can be studied in a small corpus. However, a much larger corpus is required to study less common features, like extraposed clauses or cleft constructions. A small corpus may contain an accidental sample of rare features, leading to incorrect conclusions about frequency. For example, consider the frequency of extraposed *to*-clauses (such as *it is important to stay cool*). Analysis of a large (c. 20-million words) written corpus shows that extraposed *to*-clauses are relatively uncommon, occurring around 500 times per million words (see LGSWE, p. 723). However, it would be easy to reach incorrect conclusions based on analysis of a small corpus. For example, a 10,000-word corpus might not have any extraposed clauses, in which case we might conclude that this construction is extremely rare. In contrast, if a 10,000 word corpus happened to have 50 extraposed clauses, we would conclude that this is an extremely frequent feature (5000 occurrences per million words).

For vocabulary studies, corpus size is an even more important consideration. Most individual words tend to occur much less frequently than grammatical constructions. In fact, most words occur fewer than 10 times per million words in a general corpus of English, and many words would occur only once (or not at all) in a million word corpus. Very large corpora are thus required to study the use of these less common words.

In addition to being large enough, a corpus must have samples that are diverse enough to represent the variation in the kinds of texts being studied. A corpus must be sampled deliberately from particular registers, since linguistic features vary systematically across registers. To continue the example from grammatical analysis, extraposed *to*-clauses are rare in conversation (less than 50 per million words), but they are relatively common in academic writing (around 1,500 per million words; see Figure 9.20 in LGSWE). A corpus that disregarded register would obviously produce misleading findings regarding the frequency and use of such grammatical features.

Similarly, the composition of the corpus is a crucial consideration for vocabulary studies. Register is important because many words are used primarily in a particular spoken or written register (as discussed in Chapter 3). In addition, topic is an important consideration influencing the choice of vocabulary. Unlike the use of most grammatical features, the words that we choose are very dependent on topic. As a result, corpora for vocabulary studies should be not only large, but also sampled deliberately from different registers and across a range of topics.

The design of the T2K-SWAL Corpus includes a careful representation of register differences and a wide sampling of topic differences within those registers. However, the T2K-SWAL Corpus is quite small for the purposes of vocabulary studies. The size limitations become especially obvious when we begin to investigate more specific research questions. For example, the sub-corpora for some academic disciplines are very small: 116,200 words for business textbooks and 72,000 words for engineering textbooks. Even the largest sub-corpora for academic disciplines – 248,600 words for humanities classroom teaching and 294,400 words for social science classroom teaching – are small for investigating the use of moderately common words (occurring between 5–10 times per million words). Because of the small size of the corpus, the analyses in the present book are based on the distribution of lexical categories (e.g., all words at a given frequency level) rather than individual words. Nevertheless, the quantitative findings on vocabulary use must be interpreted with caution, particularly for the vocabulary distributions across academic disciplines (reported in Section 3.2.2).

## 2.    Comparisons across corpora

The second methodological issue that needs to be addressed has to do with comparing vocabulary distributions across corpora of different sizes. In general, it is easy to compare the use of linguistic features across corpora, because linguistic counts can be 'normalized' to a rate of occurrence. For example, if a 500,000-

word corpus contained 7,000 passive verbs, this would correspond to a normalized rate of 14,000 passive verbs per million words. A 2-million-word corpus containing 28,000 passive verbs would have the same normalized rate of occurrence. It is methodologically appropriate to normalize counts of grammatical features in this way because they represent **linear** distributions. That is, common grammatical features are distributed consistently over the course of a text or a corpus of texts from a single register (see Biber 1990, 1993).

In contrast, vocabulary distributions describing the number of word 'types' (i.e., different words) are not linear. This is because words tend to be repeated in a corpus, and the larger a corpus is, the more repeated words there are. For example, we might find 500 word types in a 1,000-word text, but it is very unlikely that we would find 5,000 word types in a 10,000-word corpus, and it would be impossible to find 500,000 word types in a 1-million-word corpus (especially since there are only around 200,000 word types in the entire word stock of English). Thus, vocabulary occurs with non-linear distributions: as a corpus becomes larger, we find only proportionally small increases in the number of new word types. As a result, it is difficult to compare vocabulary distributions across sub-corpora of different sizes.

## 2.1 Experiments on the influence of corpus design on vocabulary distributions

To illustrate the effects of these methodological considerations, I carried out a series of experiments with the T2K-SWAL Corpus, studying the stability of vocabulary distributions across subsamples from the corpus. In general, these experiments indicate that a subcorpus with 1/2 the texts in the full corpus will contain approximately 70% of the different word types found in the larger corpus. For example, Table B.1 shows that there are 27,312 word types found in the complete corpus of spoken texts from the T2K-SWAL Corpus (1,66 million words).[1] In comparison, there are 19,342 different word types in a random sample of half the texts

Table B.1 Comparison of vocabulary distributions in the full corpus and a half-corpus from all spoken texts

|  | Full corpus | Half-corpus | Percentage representation |
|---|---|---|---|
| # of texts: | 291 | 146 |  |
| # of words | 1,665,624 | 806,023 |  |
| # of word types | 27,312 | 19,342 | 70.8% |
| # common word types* | 859 | 859 | 100% |

* common word types = more than 100 occurrences per 1-million words

**Table B.2** Comparison of vocabulary distributions in the full corpus and a half-corpus from all written texts

|  | Full corpus | Half-corpus | Percentage representation |
|---|---|---|---|
| # of texts: | 172 | 86 |  |
| # of words | 1,073,508 | 512,865 |  |
| # of word types | 39,053 | 27,409 | 70.2% |
| # common word types* | 1,432 | 1,430 | 99% |

* common word types = more than 100 occurrences per 1-million words

**Table B.3** Comparison of vocabulary distributions in the full corpus and a half-corpus from all written social science texts

|  | Full corpus | Half-corpus | Percentage representation |
|---|---|---|---|
| # of texts: | 35 | 18 |  |
| # of words | 262,707 | 139,230 |  |
| # of word types | 17,935 | 12,641 | 70.5% |
| common word types* | 1,449 | 1,431 | 98.8% |

* common word types = more than 100 occurrences per 1-million words

from the full spoken corpus. This comparison illustrates how vocabulary distributions are not linear: although this subcorpus is only half the size of the full corpus, it still represents 70.8% of the word types found in the larger corpus. The representation of "common" word types (occurring more than 100 times per million words) is even better: all of the common words in the full spoken corpus were also found in the half corpus.

Table B.2 shows the same comparison for written texts from the T2K-SWAL Corpus, again with c. 70% of the word types being represented in the half corpus.

Interestingly, the same kind of relationship seems to hold even for much smaller samples. For example, Tables B.3 and B.4 show the vocabulary distributions in half corpora taken from all written social science texts (Table B.3) and written natural science texts (Table B.4). In the case of natural science, the full corpus is quite small, comprising only 153,165 total words, yet we still find the half corpus containing roughly 70% of the word types in the full corpus.

Table B.5 illustrates how this same pattern is repeated as we continue to split subcorpora (based on analysis of spoken social science texts). The half corpus contains c. 70% of the word types in the full corpus, but a 1/4 corpus contains only 45.3% of the word types in the full corpus. A sub-corpus with 1/8 of the texts from the full corpus contains only 31.9% of the word types from the full corpus. However, the 70% rule still holds generally for each of these comparisons. That is, each of these subcorpora is a half-corpus of the preceding sample. For example,

**Table B.4** Comparison of vocabulary distributions in the full corpus and a half-corpus from all written natural science texts

|                    | Full corpus | Half-corpus | Percentage representation |
|--------------------|-------------|-------------|---------------------------|
| # of texts:        | 23          | 14          |                           |
| # of words         | 153,165     | 91,290      |                           |
| # of word types    | 12,982      | 9,720       | 74.9%                     |
| common word types* | 1,502       | 1,468       | 97.7%                     |

* common word types = more than 100 occurrences per 1-million words

**Table B.5** Comparison of vocabulary distributions in the full corpus and three smaller samples (50%, 25%, and 12%) from all spoken social science texts

|                          | Full corpus | Sub-corpus | Percentage representation |
|--------------------------|-------------|------------|---------------------------|
| **50% sample for subcorpus** |         |            |                           |
| # of texts:              | 53          | 27         |                           |
| # of words               | 347,917     | 173,440    |                           |
| # of word types          | 12,787      | 8,797      | 68.8%                     |
| common* word types       | 857         | 854        | 99%                       |
| **25% sample for subcorpus** |         |            |                           |
| # of texts:              | 53          | 14         |                           |
| # of words               | 347,917     | 84,694     |                           |
| # of word types          | 12,787      | 5,786      | 45.3%                     |
| common* word types       | 857         | 843        | 98%                       |
| **12% sample for subcorpus** |         |            |                           |
| # of texts:              | 53          | 7          |                           |
| # of words               | 347,917     | 41,306     |                           |
| # of word types          | 12,787      | 4,081      | 31.9%                     |
| common* word types       | 857         | 804        | 94%                       |

* common word types = more than 100 occurrences per 1-million words

the 1/4 corpus is half of the half-corpus (i.e. 84,694 words of text sampled from 173,440 words of text). There are 8,797 word types in the half-corpus, and 5,786 word types in the 1/4 corpus, making for a 65.8% representation. Similarly, the 1/8 corpus represents 70.5% of the word types in the 1/4 corpus (4,081/5,786). Thus, a general rule of thumb is that a half corpus will contain c. 70% of the word types in the full comparison corpus. While this rule is only a general approximation and may vary for extremely small or large corpora, it can be used as a good estimation for comparisons across corpora of moderately large sizes.

Appendix A describes how the variables for grammatical features are 'normalized' to allow comparisons across corpora of different sizes. This norming computes a rate of occurrence, so that we can project what the number of occurrences would be in a corpus of a given size. Grammatical features have a linear distribution, so the formula for norming grammatical feature counts to a rate per 1-million words is very simple:

normed feature count = (observed feature count / corpus size) × 1,000,000

For example, if a 500,000-word corpus contained 7,000 passive verbs, this would correspond to a normalized rate of 14,000 passive verbs per million words:

(7,000 / 500,000) × 1,000,000 = 14,000 per million words

Note that in a linear relationship, a half corpus contains 50% as many occurrences of the linguistic feature as in a full corpus.

In contrast, as shown above, word type distributions have non-linear relationships, which can be approximated by the generalization that a half corpus contains roughly 70% of the word types observed in the corresponding full corpus. Many formulas have been proposed to normalize the number of word types, adjusting for the fact that this measure increases as a non-linear function of corpus size (see, e.g., Herdan 1960; Honoré 1979; Wimmer & Altmann 1999). Most of the more sophisticated formulas incorporate logarithms, exponential components, and/or factors that adjust for relatively rare word types. However, for our purposes here, we use a formula that simply adjusts the number of word types to the square root of the corpus size:

adjusted # of word types = # of word types / Square root of corpus size

Note that the 70% rule found in the experiments reported above (see Tables B.1–B.5) is captured by this formula, because the square root of ½ is 0.707. Thus, the formula states that the adjusted number of word types in a half-corpus should be 0.707 times the number of word types in the full corpus. For comparisons between moderately large subcorpora, this formula works well.

In order to compute a normalized rate of occurrence – the number of word types per million words – we need to multiply the adjusted number of word types by the square root of 1,000,000; i.e. 1,000:

normed # of word types = (# of word types / Square root of corpus size) × 1,000

If we apply this formula to the data derived from the above experiments, we find that the normalized number of word types in a half corpus is roughly the same as for the full corpus. This is the intended result, since samples from a single corpus should all have the same rate of occurrence of word types.

For example, the normed number of word types for the full spoken corpus (corresponding to Table B.1 above) is:

$(27,312 / \mathrm{SqrRoot}(1,665,624)) \times 1,000 = 21,155$ word types per million words

This is roughly the same rate that occurs in the half spoken corpus (from Table B.1 above):

$(19,342 / \mathrm{SqrRoot}(806,023)) \times 1,000 = 21,539$ word types per million words

Thus, by using the above formula, we can compute a rough estimate of what the number of word types would be in a 1-million word corpus.

As a further test, consider corpora from different registers which are likely to have different densities of word types. In general, we would expect a written corpus to have a wider range of vocabulary than in a spoken corpus, reflecting the writer's opportunity for careful planning and revision during production. The normed number of word types for the full written corpus (corresponding to Table B.2 above) supports this expectation:

$(39,053 / \mathrm{SqrRoot}(1,073,508)) \times 1,000 = 37,692$ word types per million words

This again is roughly the same rate that occurs in the half written corpus (from Table B.2 above):

$(27,409 / \mathrm{SqrRoot}(512,865)) \times 1,000 = 38,273$ word types per million words

In Chapter 3, this procedure is used to compare the normed number of word types between classroom teaching and textbooks (Figure 3.1) and across academic disciplines (Figure 3.6).

## Note

1. The experiments reported in the appendix are based on unedited lemma databases. As a result, the vocabulary counts reported here are inflated, because they include some mis-spelled words and mis-tagged words that had not been removed from the databases. In contrast, the findings in Section 3.3 are based on an edited version of a complete database for the entire corpus.

# Index

In the series *Studies in Corpus Linguistics (SCL)* the following titles have been published thus far or are scheduled for publication: